D1795495

Winning That Job

A kill or be-killed guide to job search and interview preparation for students and graduates

By

Jon Gregory

COPYRIGHT

Copyright © Jon Gregory 2014

All rights reserved

Produced in the United Kingdom

10 9 8 7 6 5 4 3 2 1

Gregory, Jon

Winning that job: A kill or be-killed guide to job search and interview preparation for students and graduates.

ISBN : 978 0 9575769 1 9

Published in the United Kingdom by:

Firewalk Technology Ltd.

Barcombe Mills

Lewes

East Sussex BN8 5BP

United Kingdom

books@letsfirewalk.com

First Published September 2013 as an e-book

No part of this publication may be reproduced, stored in or introduced into a retrieval system, or transmitted, in any form or by any means, (electronic, mechanical, photocopying, recording, or otherwise) without the prior permission of the publisher. Requests for permission should be directed to permissions@letsfirewalk.com

The right of Jon Gregory to be identified as the author of this work has been asserted by him in accordance with the Copyright, Designs and Patents act, 1988.

The web and email addresses and data referenced in this book were correct at the time of going to press but may be subject to change.

Limit of Liability/Disclaimer of Warranty: the author and the publisher have used their best efforts in preparing this book. They make no representations or warranties with respect to the accuracy or completeness of the contents and specifically disclaim any implied warranties or merchantability of fitness for a particular purpose. The advice, strategies and suggested actions contained herein are generic or general and may not be suitable in every case and all situations. Neither the publisher nor the author shall be liable for any loss of profit or other personal or commercial damages, including but not limited to special, incidental, consequential or other damages.

Preface

Winning that job

This book uses the analogy that winning a job is, figuratively, a fight to the death in the Darwinistic jungle-like world of job hunting. When you follow a search, application and selection process, you either get the job, or you're dead. It's a brutal world with absolutely no second prizes.

If you're after a job and you're determined to get it, this book is written for you. I've been right through the mill, winning a succession of jobs as I went. I did so by learning how to show that I was the best person for the job at each selection stage.

If you want to win that job, you need to select the best 'weapons', train hard and use them more effectively than the other applicants. I can help you to be the one left holding the offer letter when the battle is over.

It's a shame about the others but hey, it's them or you.

If you're not comfortable with that, this book is not for you. If you accept that winning a job is a kill or be-killed situation, then whether you step confidently into enemy territory as a dressed-to-kill smooth operator, or whether you prefer to run at the machine guns banzai-style, it doesn't matter provided that you're willing to fight. Male or female, extrovert or introvert, sportsperson or slob, if you learn to fight, you can win that job.

The world is the way it is. Whatever form it takes, combat is a fact of life. Recognise reality and learn to deal with it. If you want something, a job for example, no one is just going to hand it to you. You have to fight for it, within the currently prevailing rules imposed by our society.

That doesn't mean that you have to become immoral, behave like an animal, or betray everyone you know and meet. Far from it. You definitely do not need to become the look-out-for-number-one, self-serving monster commonly portrayed in dramas, sit-coms and reality TV shows.

On the contrary, I would strongly argue that the more integrity you possess, the more likely you are to win, over the long haul. If you have a set of positive values by which you want to live your life, keep them and apply them.

Regardless, you will need to fight, so I set out to help you get to grips with the challenge of today's ultra-competitive world of employment by deliberately choosing a kill or be-killed analogy. I've lightened the tone with a twist of 'commando humour' and a sprinkling of colourful language. If it's good enough for the Royal Marines …

Whilst the analogy in this book does get a tad graphic on occasions, in the real world I obviously do not advocate murder, running amok with guns, slitting people's throats or literally fighting to the death with your bare hands. Especially not in interviews.

Similarly, I do not actually advocate cannibalism or the abuse of alcohol, tobacco, drugs, substances or animals and I am definitely not trying to suggest that suicide really is an appropriate course of action in certain career circumstances. I certainly don't advocate the infringement of anyone's human, legal, physical or sexual rights.

I did not set out to offend anyone along the way but if you do object to anything I've said or proposed, please let me know.

Evolution in action

Arguably, the world of employment, or certainly a very large part of it, is shifting back to the way it used to be before the industrial revolution.

Until recently, it was common for degree-educated people to undergo a full selection process a very limited number of times during their careers. Indeed, some people would do so only once, joining a large, job-for-life employer.

Our life-expectancy, job-wise, is now shortening and there are consequences.

- We're having to change employers regularly, even re-train;
- More of us than ever will sell our skills as contractors and never know what a 'permanent' employer is;
- We often need a regular part-time job to fund education costs;
- If we want to work when we qualify, we need work experience first.

You can be pretty sure that, if you learn a good set of search, application and interview skills now, you're going to have lots and lots of opportunity to re-use them during the course of your working life.

This book will teach you the rules of the job hunting game and show you how to play to win. All of the techniques have been successfully used by myself or by people I've trained or mentored. They worked for me as I hurled myself out of university and they've worked for many years since. They will also work for you, if you apply yourself.

Do please remember that the suggestions in this book are generic and may not all apply to you in every single circumstance. Think about whether you should adapt certain actions according to the specific situations that you face.

The journey to winning that job can be a tough old road but I strongly advocate persistence, an optimistic approach and keeping a sense of humour.

I'm not going to lie, some of the knock-backs you'll experience along the way will be very hard to take. It may be some time before you really appreciate that those experiences will make you stronger if you refuse to lie down. The harder you struggle, the further you'll eventually get, if you persist.

If you remember nothing else from this book, when times are tough remember the following – tomorrow is another day. Rise from the dead, pick yourself up, dust yourself down and get ready to give it hell.

I wish you every success, I'm with you all the way. Let me know how it goes.

> With all best wishes,
>
> Jon Gregory
>
> @letsfirewalk
>
> jon.gregory@win-that-job.com

Contents

Chapter 1 – Welcome to the jungle …

"The Romans conquered the world. Not because they organised better committees but because they killed the opposition." Bill Sweetenham, British Olympic Rowing Coach

Looking for a job? Please read this book, it might just save your life.

Doubtful?

If you sit very still and look toward your planning horizon, you will notice something a tad disturbing - they're coming for you.

Once you've shaken your head in disbelief, rubbed your eyes and refocused, you'll realise something even more disturbing – they will get you. They can see the red mist and they'll use every weapon they've got to hunt you down, cut you to pieces and bury your remains in a quiet place, where even you will hope that no one ever finds them.

Trust me, I know because it's happened to me.

They don't know who you are. They don't know where you are. They don't know one damn thing about you. It's nothing personal, you're just in the way and they want you gone.

That's the bad news. The good news is: you can do something about it. For a start, you can arm yourself. But you can not only defend, you can attack. You can hunt them down in return, one by one, until there's no-one left but you.

Don't like the sound of that? I'm really sorry but it's kill or be-killed. At every battle, the pile of dead may be more than a hundred strong but you can stand victorious on top of the heap or you can lay down under it. It's your choice.

Hold on a minute though. Amidst the stress, anxiety and sweat, I can hear the cogs clanking as your brain conjures up 'The Third Option'. You know: the one the liberal, pink-and-fluffy-bunny brigade usually come up with.

> "Hey, let's not take part. Screw 'em, let's walk a different road. Life doesn't have to be like that. It doesn't have to be a competition for life or death. We can all just give each other a bit of elbow room and rub along quite nicely together, can't we? … Can't we?"

As one of my old bosses used to say, "For God's sake, get a grip."

At this stage, I'm really hoping that you didn't go to one of those cloud cuckoo-land schools where everyone loves each other, the whole world is equal, competition is bad and sports day only ever happens on condition that no one actually loses and everyone gets at least one prize. If you did, then the road for you is tougher than for the rest of us. But if you did, I'm here for you, even if they brain-washed you to the point where you can't pass a tree without feeling that little tug at your heart strings and the need for a hug.

So what's the problem with this Third Option?

You'll starve to death.

Sure, if you decide not to take part, you might avoid being one piece of debris in a large-scale massacre, but you certainly won't get enough to eat. Over time your interests will have to forcibly narrow. The heart of your social circle will rot. Your prospects of successful procreation will shrink. Death will be slow but inevitable. From behind the veil, a thousand generations of your dead ancestors will scream in anguish as your bloodline threatens to slip from the gene pool.

So, no pressure there then.

It is still your choice but, speaking personally, I really do recommend that, for a short while at least, you lay down the caring part of your being and get ready for some action. Load up your weapons, train hard, learn how to kill and then howl defiantly at the moon, whilst beating your chest.

It really isn't so bad. People will congratulate you. Admire you, even. If you do well enough, prime ministers will invite you to Chequers. If it's morally bothersome, you might be able to rationalise things out to yourself by declaring that you really don't have a choice. Tell yourself it's just the next stage in your life. The stage that your parents, teachers and lecturers neglected to mention and now look guiltily away whenever you try to speak to them about it.

Prefer a life helping others? No worries, but do learn to kill first.

Want to do some real good in the world? Highly commendable, but learn to kill first.

Think you'd like a crack at curing cancer? Fantastic, but know how to slit throats before that.

Fancy a stab at solving world hunger? You'll make a better job of it if you learn how best to ruthlessly slaughter everyone standing in your way.

So who's coming for you? It sounds like a zombie horde. Perhaps you imagine you can become a Simon Pegg and lead a small band to victory? Unfortunately, whilst they may in fact be a form of zombie, the situation is much more terrifying than that. Think 'Invasion of the Body-Snatchers'.

The people coming for you are just like you. Literally. If you look at yourself in the mirror, you can't tell the difference between them and you. They're your age, with your background and they have your qualifications. They see the same things you do, they think the same way, they watch the same TV programmes, they play the same sports and they want exactly what you want.

That's why they're hunting you down. They want what you want.

And do you know what they want? They want that job that you want.

Simple as that. It's a fight to the death for it, figuratively speaking. There might be one hundred people all getting stuck into a mass ruck and more often than not, only one of them can win the only place on offer.

Will it be you?

Welcome to the world of serious competition. Even Olympians, trained to the hilt and truly admirable though they are, don't have it as tough as you. They still have the slightly pink and fluffy liberal option of a silver or a bronze. They can follow the advertising and sponsorship trail for many years, even without a gold to their name.

You either win that job, or you get nothing and find it hard to eat.

Like Olympians, you've trained for years too. Now it's your time to enter the arena.

Bear in mind that although you've perhaps been in education and training for seventeen years or more, you've been developing a range of specialised skills focused on enabling you to do a job or follow a career direction. If you're like most people, you've had no training or experience at all in the task of actually winning it.

Imagine if the athletes arrived at registration for a track event, only to be asked to justify why they should be allowed to race.

> "Thanks for coming along but what have you got to offer the Trottville Athletics Track in the longer term? What are your personal ambitions? Would you mind making a short presentation on the subject to a panel of assessors? Oh, we've got this personality profile test for you to sit as well, if that's okay? Don't worry, we just want to know how well you'll fit in."

It sounds mad, doesn't it? Yet that sort of unexpected shock is exactly what most of us get when we roll up for our first major interview after little or no relevant preparation.

Is it really a surprise that we initially perform badly and take time to learn the ropes? Sometimes, a long time? Is it a surprise that those first knock-backs can be very damaging to our confidence, if we've never been shown the wider picture?

So, if you want to win a particular job, you need to know what you're in for during the assessment process. You've got to learn how to fight for it. You've got to develop the extra skills that will enable you to slay the opposition. You've got to really want it and be willing to do whatever it takes to get it.

You're in a battle to the death but survival is not enough: you have to win.

There will only ever be one survivor. Will it be you?

You want a job that will, at the very least, head-off a slow lingering death. Better, you want a job that will get you the experience and salary that you really need. It might, if it's a good one, set you surfing on the crest of a wave for many years to come, as your career goes global.

Have no illusions, the day the process of targeting a job starts, you're stepping out into the jungle with a knife clamped between your teeth and your senses heightened for action. Or not.

If you hear a 'BANG' and it goes dark, I'm afraid it's game over. But if you've got your wits about you and you're one of the final few left standing in the selection process, you'll face 'The Ultimate Test' and be into close-quarters, hand-to-hand combat to see who wins that one place on offer.

Who's prepared the best? Who's the most determined? Who's got the best killer move, hidden from view?

That can be you.

Male or female, rich or poor, blindingly intelligent or most definitely from the shallow end of the gene pool, you can learn to kill in order to win that job.

In this jungle-world of job-hunting, there is absolutely no reward for second place. (Unless you happen to like the sour taste of bile, that is.) This is Darwinism in its rawest form. It seems God loves the strong, ironically.

Wow, there's a challenge then. I'll bet you're really glad you've read this far. But before depression sinks its needle-like teeth into you, and you start a hasty search for a suitably tall building with easy access, take stock and look toward the light.

So, in the aftermath of a selection process, we're all staring across a vast no-mans-land of blood-drenched desolation that makes the Somme look like a whist drive in a sanatorium. It's not all bad though. You have one big advantage when the lights do go out and you have that lingering memory of a loud 'BANG'. You can open your eyes, gaze at the clear blue sky and, just like a zombie, you can rise again. You can choose your next battle and get stuck right in.

But even better – you're stronger. Fitter. More experienced. Better prepared. Much more focused. And by God, you're ruthless now. Screw the pink fluffy bunnies and the bleeding heart liberals, where did you put that knife?

Okay, so now you're living on a diet of red meat and pink rabbit. You've sharpened your knife to the point where it'll slice concrete and you're the most feared thing in the jungle. What next?

I still remember the first ever 'real' job interview I attended. By that, I mean the first job I tried for, that was a crucial step along the road toward a career. It was for a six month work placement, part way through my four year thin-sandwich degree.

I still cringe with deep embarrassment every time I think about that interview. I tried my very best but every second was excruciating. I staggered blindly forward through the unexpected questions. I blundered from appalling answer to embarrassing mistake and back to appalling answer. Figuratively speaking, they tore up the furniture and beat me senseless with it. I was reamed, steamed and dry-cleaned. Needless to say, I didn't get the job.

What made it all considerably worse was that I was the only candidate. I had no competition. All I had to do was turn up and it should have been job done. Instead I was left thinking my career was over and wondering where the nearest A&E department was so that I could get treatment for my wounds.

It wasn't that I was stupid or had inappropriate skills for the job. It was simply that I had absolutely no idea what I was walking into. It was the first properly structured interview I had ever attended. No-one had prepared me for what to expect (why should they?) and so consequently, I'd made no preparations.

"Go and have a chat with these people," my tutor said. "They're quite nice."

Were they hell. They were monsters.

I was slaughtered. I was cut to ribbons, one piece at a time. Dr Mengele, eat your heart out. By the end of the interview, you could have redecorated the inside of the Titanic with the amount of blood up the walls. It was the longest hour of my life and, just like the Titanic, I sank without trace. I distinctly remember wondering at one stage if I should just run for the door.

I finally staggered away, not at all sure I wasn't going to throw up in the street. I somehow made it back to my flat and I confess, dear reader – I took to the bottle, like a man with a one way ticket to oblivion.

Through the haze of Guinness and Southern Comfort supplied by The General Wolfe, and with a complete lack of support from all of my friends who took the piss mercilessly, I swore that never again would I ever attend an interview, or even a meeting for that matter, without preparing myself totally beforehand.

I would research and I would plan and I would rehearse and I would do that until the bone showed through my fingertips and the smoke curled from my burned-out eye sockets. I would then be certain there was no question on earth that I could not slay.

It really cut that deep.

Looking back, it was probably the most valuable hour of my life. I just wish I could have watched some other poor wretch live through it instead of me.

Eventually, I rose from the dead – reborn into a different world. A world where I would be victorious. I pushed aside the empty cans and bottles and began the slow process of coughing up the thousand ciggies I'd just smoked. I finally plucked up the courage to face my tutor.

"I gather it didn't go that well," he said.

No shit, I thought, still nursing the cuts and bruises.

"Nah. Their interview technique was really poor. They jumped all over the place and never gave me a chance to show my best. I just couldn't get a grip on it. Have you got another?"

And that was it. I dusted myself down, picked up a knife and slipped back into the jungle. The people I was up against next never knew what hit them and I landed a great job for my six months of work experience. Much better than the other one would have been, in fact, proving Nietzsche right in his assertion that what doesn't kill you will make you stronger.

So what next for you? Well, if I can do it, you can do it. In fact, you can probably do it better than me. You're younger, you're fitter, you're undoubtedly more together than I ever was and I'm just an old fart now. But don't get in my way because, on the other hand, I am an old fart who does know how to kill people very efficiently.

Whether you've got a first or a fail, you can do it. If all you've got is one GCSE in Home Ec and even that's only an 'E', it doesn't matter, you can do it. Whether you're black, white, brown, yellow or ginger it makes no difference, you can still do it. Born with three nipples, a third eye or the mark of the beast – it makes absolutely no difference, you can still do it.

Do what? Well, learn to kill, of course. Silently, ruthlessly, remorselessly, until you win that job.

I should add a couple of notes here about expectations and practicality.

If you're walking out of Uni with the DTs, a dose of the clap and only a third to your name, it really is mindless to expect that you'll be a brain surgeon this time next year.

Wherever you're planning to go, it's a road and you've got to be able to walk down it. If you choose the long road with a shiny wet brain to play with at the end of it, just be aware that you're going to have to take all of the steps in the journey, if you really want to get there. You can't just jump right to the end point and expect to be straight in there, gaily doing frontal lobotomies.

It's like another form of gravity: that's just how it is. As Newton almost said, "The Earth sucks, deal with it." Pretending you've got an anti-gravity machine in your pocket isn't going to save you when you're lured over a chasm by someone you don't know, who's high on blood-lust with a job in their sights.

Okay, that person everyone hates – the stunningly good-looking, rich, highly gifted, charming, startlingly eloquent person with a triple first in medicine, psychology and computer science – is probably going to get there first. But so what? They're just further down the road than you are and you're not in competition with them. You're only in competition with the people trying to take the same next step as you.

You're in charge. If you want to be. If you don't, write to me and I'll send you a pink fluffy bunny as a souvenir and you can watch it rot. As the fur drops out you can use it to measure the slow disintegration of your life. There may not be zombies in this world but I bet your dead ancestors would like to take your bunny and shove it where the soap doesn't reach very easily.

If you do want to put yourself in charge of your own destiny, if you really do want to do something good in the world and make a difference, if you really are prepared to put yourself through the mill and step into the jungle to get it, drop me a line and I'll add you to my growing list of heroes.

Really want to be a brain surgeon? Find out what the next step is, prepare yourself and then fight to take it. Drop the other guy before he drops you. Do it now and become a hero. Fed up with people saying you can't do it? Screw 'em, give 'em a pink fluffy bunny and move on, one step at a time. Just choose your steps carefully and walk around the traps.

So, the journey you take is purely yours to choose, as it should be. But you want to be sure you're going to get there and, as we all know in today's climate, the going will be tough. There'll be lots of competition and there's no magic bullet you can load up and drill the opposition with.

It will be hand-to-hand fighting all the way so 'The Secret', if it can be called that, is to know what you're in for, to prepare thoroughly for it and to execute your planned strategy flawlessly. Plan to be the one holding the 'Welcome' letter, not the one laying under a mound of bleeding stiffs.

My job is to help you be The One holding that 'Welcome' letter.

I can give you a much greater insight into the overall recruitment process and show you how best to steer yourself to a successful result. I can help you to develop a higher level of skills, skills that will stay with you for the whole of the rest of your career. They'll keep you stepping up the ladder until you can see the clouds behind you and the stars ahead.

It won't always be straightforward and you'll get some knock-backs but you'll always know that you can rise again, stronger. If you keep going, you'll win.

How far can you ultimately get? It depends upon the journey you choose to take. I'm sure you'll continue to set new destinations for yourself, but with inside knowledge and an extra set of skills, you'll always be able to adapt to those new challenges, as they arise.

Make your journey one that's worth taking. It may be one step at a time but plan to go all the way. Back yourself with conviction. Give no quarter, win that job and then do it brilliantly. Put yourself onto the world stage and push your career to the very limit.

I envy you your opportunities and I hope you do well. Truly.

The start of your journey

So, take a deep breath. Let's begin.

You might have a particular job that you're already chasing. You might be limbering up for a systematic search for a job that fits in with your intended career direction. You might be chasing just any job, purely as a stop-gap, or to gain experience.

Whichever it is, the remaining chapters in this book will steer you down a path which gets you past the other people chasing that same job.

If you're already facing an interview in the next couple of days or so, by all means jump straight to Chapter 5 (Interviews: meeting the tiger) and use the techniques listed there to help you prepare thoroughly. After that, if you've still got time, I strongly recommend that you go back and read Chapters 2, 3 and 4. They will add perspective, help you to de-stress and enable you to gain a deeper insight into the challenge that you're facing.

At the end of each chapter, you'll find summarised information which gives you an overview of the topics and content of the chapter. That summarised information is broken down into:

- **Key learning points** (KLPs), important ideas to become familiar with;
- **Signposts,** lines to explore and routes to follow;
- **Actions,** proactive steps to take.

Through the course of this book, the chapters collectively provide you with end-to-end support throughout the whole process of job hunting: searching; applying; interviewing; negotiating and accepting that job.

An additional chapter extends that support through to when you're actually starting the job you've won. It helps you to prepare yourself now, for the interviews you'll face when you're chasing promotion.

I strongly recommend building a visual mind-map of each chapter, as you read it. This will give you an excellent overview and strongly reinforce your learning of the tools, training and techniques you need to become familiar with.

Revisiting the material, when you have another application to complete or interview to attend, will then be a breeze for you.

Chapter 2 (Preparation: improving your odds) aims to put the challenge of winning that job into perspective. On the one hand, it can seem like a daunting task, against a lot of stiff competition. On the other, despite what news reports often seem to imply, the vast majority of people do actually get jobs.

Chapter two will help you to recognise reality for what it is and show you how to take the positive actions which will move you forward into that winning position.

Chapter 3 (Searches: stalking the jungle) takes you through an in-depth look at the dozen or so paths to follow, in your search for suitable job opportunities. The main topics covered are:

- search strategies;
- types of employer;
- options to open up;
- search paths to explore and
- job-search actions to take.

Chapter 4 (Applications: killing the opposition) takes you through the steps of putting together a winning CV, application form and covering letter so that you can be the one to stand out above your peers. Vital ways to add perceived value to your application are:

- tailor your submission to show your added-value;
- match your skills, experience, attitude and potential to exactly what a potential employer is looking for;
- read between the lines of a job advert or brief to identify the additional, unstated desires of a potential employer.

Becoming one of the shortlisted few to win an interview place is much easier than you'd ever think, once you know how.

Chapter 5 (Interviews: meeting the tiger) takes you through the intensive interview preparation needed to become the one survivor left standing and holding that job offer in your blood-drenched hands. The chapter shows you how to:

- understand what you'll be facing at interview;
- calculate what will win the job for you;
- rehearse so that you're ready to deliver a perfect performance;
- manage your nerves;
- avoid the interview traps that'll be set for you and
- win that job the second that you step into the interview room.

Chapter 6 (Negotiations: winning the last battle) shows you how to balance getting the best deal (or at least a fair deal) against the risk of blowing it at the moment of victory. Why might that happen?

- You are the number one choice, but your prospective employer may still be grooming a stalking horse, in case you refuse the offer.
- There may still be dependencies to manage which you might fail, such as: reference checks; a medical or a fitness test.
- Negotiation over terms (salary, position, prospects) can see your offer withdrawn, unless you know the right way to raise such issues.

Find out how to navigate a safe course out of the jungle.

Chapter 7 (Work: your new mission …) helps you to successfully start the job you've won and helps you to build another winning edge, ready for when you're chasing promotion, or your next job.

Appendix A (Ammunition locker) helps to give you a flying start with your preparation and rehearsal by providing lots of practise questions covering:

- standard interview questions;
- competency-based questions;
- scenario type questions;
- creativity and lateral-thinking questions;
- role-play exercises;
- questions to ask at the end of the interview and
- the questions not to ask at the end of the interview.

Key point summary 1 – Starting off

This book will guide you through the search, application and interview preparation processes that you need to learn. It will show you how to stand taller than the other applicants. It will enable you to understand how best to impress a prospective employer so that you become the number one choice.

Key Learning Points

- Recognise reality. This may come as a shock, but Darwinism rules. The job market is a survival-of-the-fittest, winner-takes-all environment.
- Worse, the people chasing the same job as you are almost identical to you, in terms of knowledge, experience, and capability.
- As a consequence, you not only have to score highly on applications and at interviews, you must distinguish yourself from your peers.

Signposts

To win that job, plan to follow this simple process:

1. learn the new search, application and interview skills you'll need;
2. understand your target completely, when you aim at a particular job;
3. practise your new skills in advance and
4. resolve to be a killer.

Actions

Using this book, focus on the actions which will help you to win that job:

a) search for opportunities in a more structured way;
b) identify the real requirements of the jobs you find;
c) target your applications precisely;
d) rehearse for the interview battle;
e) win by killing the opposition. All of them. No prisoners.

When it finally comes down to it, you mustn't hesitate: go for the jugular. Be focused, be strong, be determined and be the winner.

Chapter 2 – Preparation: improving your odds

"You know where you want to get to, just keep plodding on and don't stop. That will get you there." Sir Ranulph Fiennes about conquering Everest at the age of 65.

Ready … Fire! Aim.

Bit of a cock-up, that. It's obvious that the last two should be the other way around, isn't it? Well, you'd think so but an astounding number of people and organisations run around like maniacs, with great vigour and lots of grunting, only to find they missed the target simply because they didn't know what it looked like and so shot their bolt too soon.

Organisations tend to do this by accident, when the people at the helm forget to tell the crew below decks what the real objective is. It's not uncommon to find some departments working really hard and pushing for expansion, whilst adjacent ones are locked into a relentless programme of masochistic cost-cutting. The result is always confusion, conflict and not much in the way of constructive progress.

The process of recovery often involves a relentless and costly search for someone to blame, who can be offered up as a blood sacrifice in an attempt to appease the Gods (aka stakeholders), to avoid the real instigators being held responsible for the problems.

You might be surprised to learn that individuals also do the 'Ready … Fire! Aim' thing frequently when they're job hunting.

It's sad, but if you've sent out 823 applications, achieved zero interviews and received barely enough response letters to make it worth your while hanging them on a nail in the loo, then you're doing something very wrong.

Again, the normal response is to allocate blame: the economy is a disaster; no-one is hiring; my course isn't well recognised; last year's graduates are stealing all the jobs; they're waiting for next year's graduates; I didn't go to the right school; I shouldn't have taken a gap year; I don't have enough experience; perhaps I should have taken a gap year; the boss in my project company just didn't like me; my tutor advised me badly; the careers office was useless; I was ill for my finals; I'm under-qualified; I'm over-qualified; hell, I'm both under and over qualified at the same time.

This goes on and on and on until, in the end, such people have all the proof they need that life is against them, there is no hope and, like Fraser in Dad's Army, they're doomed: after all, graduate unemployment is running at 28%, according to some press reports.

"What? 28%? We're doomed, I tell you. Doomed!"

Whilst identifying the source of a problem is good, using blame as a crutch will render you powerless.

It's essential to take personal responsibility for the situation you find yourself in, if you're going to win that job you really want.

Only you can move you forward.

Understanding your real situation

Let's step back, take a breath and start to recognise reality for what it is.

Negativity is all around us. We need to filter it and translate the content into something positive we can use to help us move forward. We definitely do not need to focus on it and thereby depress ourselves into inaction.

Firstly, we've all heard the apocryphal tales of school-leavers and graduates heading towards that magic 823 number. Sometimes they feature on the radio, the TV or in the press. Many of us know someone in this sort of situation, or at least one person who 'knows' someone who is.

Secondly, even worse, we might have some horrendous negative nag whispering in our ear, constantly bleating on about how we'll never get selected by anyone for anything. Horrifically, sometimes that nag is our own subconscious, when we've slipped into a negative mind-set.

The message pumped out always has the same theme: the odds of you making it through are just too great for X, Y or Z reason.

Notice there's always a justifying reason offered. It's often eloquently constructed, usually believable and may be based on 'real' data, commonly dredged up from the Red-Tops.

That nag might be a partner, friend, acquaintance or relative. Such nags are like dementors, sucking the very life from your being, until there's nothing left but an endless void. They'll have you mainlining on their negativity, if you let them.

Such people are worthless. They seem to believe that their only hope of personal salvation is to find some other poor so and so to grind down into an even worse state than the one they themselves are presently in.

Faced with such a person, you only have one chance. Start how you mean to go on – kill them. (Figuratively, I stress, before I end up being responsible for inspiring multiple episodes of genocide.)

If you do nothing else, cut them out of your life. You have to. They're a complete drain on your mental resources. They add not one iota of value to your prospects. On the contrary, they will hoover up your life, if you let them.

Your action is clear - dump the chump, or ditch the bitch. Get them out of your life, be they friend, partner or relative.

There is no better solution, whoever they are. If you struggle to do that, at the very least, simply do not talk to them about work or job applications and do not listen to one single thing that they have to say on the subject.

> "Do you have anything positive to offer? If not, fuck off."

That might get your message across. At the very least, it might cause someone to think twice before barfing up yet more negativity.

Dumping your chump or ditching your bitch will improve your mind-set and thereby considerably improve your prospects of winning the type of job you're really looking for.

Understanding the numbers

So, while we're in a killing frame of mind, let's put to rest that other hoary old chestnut – the statistics. As they're presented in news reports, they're often about as accurate as trying to use a shotgun to trim your toe-nails.

When do you ever hear a news story say something like, "Actually chaps, things really don't look so bad, today there's some good news"? Instead, they tend to be just like your blood-sucking Dementor 'friend' that you've now hopefully laid to rest with a stake through their heart and a patronus up their jacksy.

The media like nothing better than the shock value of a nasty number. Indeed, it's those nasties that sell their rags. It doesn't take long until you begin to believe that the whole situation is hopeless. Accuracy is often a casualty in news reports.

Let's take this example. On the 28th of June 2013, the BBC's website reported that British teenager, Dwayne Ward, holidaying in the Marmaris resort in Turkey, had been stabbed at least 10 times, late the previous evening. At the bottom of the page were links to The Daily Mirror's site, where he'd been stabbed 17 times, and the London Evening Standard's site, where he'd been stabbed 20 times. It is possible that various hospital staff continued to set about Dwayne as the day wore on, but somehow I don't think so.

Media reports on the subject of employment statistics are often no more consistent.

It's possible to step back from the, often twisted, interpretation of numbers and see a much more useful picture. The big question to always ask yourself is, 'What really lies behind some of these numbers?'

To see this in action, let's firstly look at some figures quoted on a major news website in September 2011. Although slightly historic, this example provides a perfect illustration of two ways to look at the same information.

The article was written following a snapshot survey of 49,065 students, who'd left university back in 2007, conducted by the Higher Education Statistics Agency (HESA) on the 29th of November 2010.

The headline was, "Increase in unemployed graduates, survey suggests."

The leading, attention-grabbing, set-in-bold, first paragraph ran: "Almost 28% of UK graduates who left university in 2007 were still not in full-time work three and a half years later, figures have suggested."

If we take this at face value – OMG! That's it, we really are all doomed. I mean to say, that was then, now the whole economy has had another couple of years of stagnation and the prospects of real recovery in the near term are low. Even worse, the European Union might break up and our economy will take yet another dive and since Europe is our biggest trading partner, it really does look bleak for jobs. We're definitely doomed and it must be more than the previous 28% now, mustn't it?

Even worse than that, we've all heard that 20% of school leavers are unemployed a year later. (Actually, you can substitute any number you like there, I've seen 'em all reported.) But anyway, doesn't that mean that if you take a degree, your prospects of employment actually decrease by another 8% and now you're even paying for the privilege? What was the point? We really are all on a one way trip to oblivion, aren't we?

Help!

Deep breath … let's pull ourselves together and dispose of this negativity.

Looking deeper into the figures, the actual breakdown of the 27.7% who said they were not in full-time work is:

- 8.8% were working part-time or voluntarily;
- 5.3% were working and studying;
- 6.5% were just studying;
- 3.6% gave their response as 'other',
- leaving 3.5% considered as unemployed (up from 2.6% in 2005).

Doesn't seem quite so horrendous or hopeless now, does it? And it certainly doesn't mean that the 3.5% 'unemployed' have been that way for the whole time.

Okay, some people probably haven't got exactly what they want out of the whole university and job exercise. Some people have probably taken far longer than they expected to get to where they really wanted to be. However, some people may have considerably exceeded even their own wildest expectations. If you look again in ten years' time, you might well find that some of these people have reversed their positions. Hey, that's life.

Bear in mind you are not powerless in this situation, otherwise you wouldn't be reading this. You are the best placed person to make a difference to your real prospects of employment, so let's not get hung up on the daily melodrama and the doom we're supposedly all subject to.

Even if you take, say, the 20% unemployed school-leavers' figure at face value, it means that 4 out of 5 people actually do have jobs. So why couldn't that be you? Undoubtedly, the proportion of young people who never get work is considerably smaller. Furthermore, there will be a reducing number of some people floating in and out of work, as everyone moves forward.

Secondly, let's now take a look at some more recent data, on the overall UK employment position.

In September 2012, the Office for National Statistics came up with their latest employment figures. Although public sector employment has fallen by 628,000 to 5.66m, private sector employment had risen by 1.07m to a record high of 23.9m since the coalition came to power in May 2010. There are now 29.56m people in work, 431,000 more than a year ago. Also, the number of people working part-time is 1.42m – the highest figure since records began.

Those numbers are quite positive, even more so if you think that every one of those people has to leave employment at some time and each time that happens it creates a vacancy. That's great for you.

Annual churn is hard to estimate, but obviously creates a substantial number of opportunities each year, even if the economy were to utterly flat-line.

We clearly need to take a more holistic view of the whole 'prospect' situation.

Thirdly, and more recently, High Fliers Research published a report entitled "The graduate market in 2013", based on survey data gathered in December 2012 from the UK's leading employers, who were defined as those listed in The Times Top 100 Graduate Employers 2012 survey, conducted amongst 17,737 final year students.

Reading source reports, such as this one, will give you a better picture of the real employment situation than a headline-grabbing press article might.

The survey found that leading organisations reduced graduate recruitment by 0.8% in 2012 but that they collectively expect to increase graduate recruitment by 2.7% during 2013. (That figure was revised upwards to 4.6% half way through 2013, in the light of the next survey.)

That's good news but it's even more interesting to look at the sectors within the overall recruitment market:

- there were big cuts in the number of graduates recruited during 2012 in the categories of media, accounting & professional services and banking & finance (perhaps all unsurprising);
- significant growth in graduate vacancies was seen in 2012 within the categories of public sector employers (up 25.1%), retailers (up 20.1%), engineering & industrial companies (up 14.8%) and IT & telecommunications (up 34.0%).

So even in a slightly contracting market, opportunities abounded in the right sectors. Don't take my word for it, browse for the report, examine the data and draw your own conclusions.

Bear in mind that such data doesn't suggest that, if you're an engineer, your prospects are good but if your intended career is as an accountant, things are bad. Even engineering, industrial, IT and telecoms companies need accountants, lawyers and media professionals.

The huge message to take away is that you absolutely should not stick with the spoon-fed headlines. Understand where the real numbers are coming from and figure out how you can best find opportunities that suit you.

If you do that, you'll have the first shoots of a strong career in your hands.

Taking action

Let's get three actions underway that will clear out the fluff from your head-space and help you develop a much more positively focused approach.

1. Ditch the bitch, dump the chump. That really is action number one and hopefully you're well on message with it after my previous comments. It really is easier to do than you think and, when there is no longer a lead weight dragging you under the swamp, you'll feel so much lighter.

But take things a step further – consciously talk with people who have a positive outlook on what can actually be achieved and why. Ignore people who talk about what can't be achieved and why not.

Even better, begin to consciously associate with people who are achieving progress. Talk to them about how they've done it. People on the move tend to be more than happy to help those coming along behind since there's no element of direct competition involved. Nine times out of ten, if you show a real interest in someone, they'll be thrilled to tell you how they did it.

2. Focus on information, not disinformation. Read all the reports, surveys and news articles you can, but focus on the positive weight of any data that acts in your favour and ignore the fictitious negatives that falsely present the case against you being successful at finding a job.

If you do that, then the absolute worst case scenario is that, even if the 20%-type figures are at least partly right, you've now shifted yourself mentally into being with the 4 out of 5 people who will win that job. You're no longer part of the 1 in 5 group who've chosen to define themselves as on the losing side.

3. Develop a sense of successful persistence. Be positive about your prospects. Start now. Even the unemployed are unlikely to be unemployed forever. The chances of you not getting onto the career ladder are actually quite remote if you persist, step by step.

That's not to dismiss the challenges you'll face, especially in the current climate where desirable places may be fewer and competition more intense. But let's look at another worst-case scenario – let's say you are, at best, average.

Gasp. OMG, how terrible. (FX: Sound of hysterical crying.) Quick, where's the Kleenex? Thinking about it, damn the Kleenex, where's that high building?

Well, let me tell you a highly personal secret at this point – I'd take being just any old Joe Blow average chief executive of a public company any day of the week. How about being just an average millionaire? Bring it on.

If you're an average whatever-you-aspire-to-be, you're somewhere around the middle and that puts you very firmly NOT in the 1 in 5 group. And from there, it's within your power to work to improve.

Now who wants to be average? Yeah! Define the group you want to be in and then work to ensure that you're not at the losing end of the spectrum.

Look around your chosen group. I'll bet you can spot the ineffectual ones. Well, they're doing you a very large favour because they're going to fail first, thereby leaving you in the winning group. It just doesn't get better than that.

And, well done, you've just scored another bunch of kills.

To be clear, I wouldn't ever recommend storming into an interview and screaming the words, "Hey, look at me! I'm average, pick me. Pick me!" It's not going to go that well. However, simply knowing you've just moved further up the pecking order is a great boost for your confidence and your chances.

When something goes right for you and you feel good about it, it's amazing how much easier your next few steps are. You seem to glow inside. It's a tad on the glib side, but it is true – nothing breeds success like success and people give things to people they believe are winners.

Develop the 'Electric Monk' habit, courtesy of Douglas Adams. Believe. Deeply. You are moving forward. Even if it's just a tiny bit, focus on it.

Get stuck in.

Feed off it.

Pump it up.

Go to it, girl!

Go on my son, give it some!

So, let's move forward. Hopefully by now, you've got a much better perspective about things, you've got a couple of tricks of the trade under your belt, you've tasted first blood and you've developed a more optimistic outlook.

Continuing to take stock: where are you now? Today?

Choosing your direction

Picking up on the "Ready … Fire! Aim." issue, it's vitally important that you don't waste your time attempting to chase down positions which you have no hope of winning unless the recruiter is your dad. If you are that person who has now shipped out 823 applications and got nothing but silence in return, I have some advice for you – accept that you're doing it wrong.

I'm sorry if that hurts. I don't know what your problem is, but something needs to change and the only person who can make that change is you.

Accept responsibility, take charge and put the past behind you. Look forward – tomorrow's another day. Let's make it better than yesterday.

To set a more positive course there are three things to get straight.

- Where do you want to be?
- Where are you now?
- How are you going to move forward?

A. Where do you want to be?

What's your destination? To put it another way – what's in it for you? Okay, you want a job, but why, what does it bring? If you change things and suddenly get a whole lot of progress going on, what does it mean for you? Money? Satisfaction? Status? Prospects?

- **What's your dream job or career?** What do you want to be doing and in what field or industry? What can you feel truly enthusiastic about? Is there any job or industry you really don't want to get involved with?

- **Do you just need a job?** In other words, in the short term, would any job do just to get money coming in? Does it have to provide a certain level of income? Does that narrow your focus down to graduate-level positions or would work as a checkout operator in your local supermarket solve your problems just as well for now?
- **Or do you want a very specific job?** Are you aiming at getting on a graduate management training programme with a large employer in, say, the aerospace industry? Do you care where it is, geographically?
- **Or do you need to get some key experience** over the next several months before you try for the real job you want? Would you live in the Antarctic if necessary? Would you even pay, just to be allowed to do it? How much would you pay, and in what currency (time, cost, delay)?

Working through even this small bunch of questions generates a tick-box template for you, against which you're quickly able to assess the suitability of any potential role you come across.

This is important because the biggest waste of time in your life is spending it doing things that don't need to be done. If a role isn't for you, don't waste your time applying for it. You won't get it if your heart isn't really in it.

Worse, there is a danger of becoming discouraged. Instead, spend that time teasing out other opportunities that do fit your profile and that you can feel truly enthusiastic about. Enthusiasm shows through, it gives you an edge.

We'll come back to enthusiasm later. At this stage, make sure you define the range of roles you're able and prepared to look at and note the limitations on the acceptability of those roles (in terms of money, status, location, longer-term prospects, risk, social acceptability, etc.)

B. Where are you now?

Obviously, this is a very individual thing. Perhaps you're just starting to search for a job whilst you finish off your course. Perhaps you've already finished and you've been chasing for a while. Maybe you already have a job, but it's only a stop-gap and you need to move on.

Whichever it is, this is your starting mark from which you can set a clear line to where you want to be next – your destination.

If we see it as journey you're going to undertake, what have you got under your bonnet? What are the key points in your favour that qualify you for the role or position you want (skills, qualifications, experience, etc.)? What are the areas that give you cause for concern? Where do you think you are weakest, relative to the likely competition?

On balance, is your destination entirely believable? Is your journey rational and attainable step for someone at your general stage of development?

C. How do you get there?

If you can believe, with certainty, that your next step is entirely attainable and that you have all of the qualifications and experience you need but you just need to go through the process, then your confidence will carry you a long way, with a higher chance of success.

But what if it isn't? What if it's possible, but it's a stretch? Then you've got some work to do.

- Firstly, note down each and every reason why you feel that you might not easily attain your goal of winning that particular job.
- Next to each reason, write down what you can do to strengthen your position and overcome those barriers.
- Out of this, distil an action plan for yourself. For example, let's say the problem is a lack of work experience. Then what can you do to get some? Do you need general work experience or does it need to be specific? What are your options? Could you take a vacation job? Would someone let you run a short project? Can you volunteer somewhere? What action are you going to take and when? Who will you contact? How? What will you say? Why should they help you get what you want? And so on, for each problem area you've identified.

We'll dig into a lot more detail around this in later chapters. At this stage you should be looking at the broad-brush issues and avoid getting bogged down in time-consuming detail. See this as a quick and dirty exercise to take stock of your position, the direction you're going to go in, the logistics of your intended journey and your fitness to make that journey.

If you were making an expedition in the car there are preparation steps that you would automatically go through, like: packing your bags; deciding what equipment to take; checking over the car; carrying out any servicing needed; making sure it's clean, fit for the type of journey and fuelled up. You'd also get yourself a map and plan the route.

Your journey to winning a job, via a search, an application process and an interview process is just like any other journey. Start with a defined plan, prepare and then adapt to circumstances en route.

Shouting "Hey, there's a job I really want!" and firing off a quick application without analysing what's being asked for, where you do and don't match the requirements and how you should present yourself, is the direct equivalent of the "Ready … Fire! Aim." problem presented at the start of this chapter.

Many people do it, thinking they're shooting from the hip and being really dynamic. Don't be one of them. They might be shooting from the hip, but they'll be putting the bullet straight through their own foot. Of course, that's excellent for you – such people are improving your chances all the time.

Developing a personal perspective

Whilst we're taking stock, let's try and develop an overall perspective about the processes you're going to experience on your way to winning that job.

1) **It's a numbers game.** You cannot absolutely guarantee that you will win that first and one specific job you're applying for, no matter how good a match you are. All sorts of things can go wrong – from you not being on form on the day, to the interviewer being unprofessional, to the candidate having been pre-selected (yes, it does happen). Don't beat yourself up for failing when in fact the interviewer unprofessionally chose the person with the cutest buns. You're in a war of attrition. In a year, X% of people make it through to win that job, and you'll be one of them, but it might take one, five or ten attempts. Like guerrilla warfare, learn what you can from each fire-fight and move on. Every time you rise again, you're a whole lot tougher and one step nearer.

2) **Your odds improve with your every action.** We said earlier, some people are just hopeless. By that I mean they're a poor match for the requirements of the job they're applying for. Great, they're automatically shunting you further into that X% who make it through in the year. Some people shoot too soon with a poorly prepared application. Brilliant, that adds another few per cent to the pile of bodies (sorry, I mean rejected candidates). Some people will turn up to interviews presenting themselves as God's gift to the world only to find out that God will smite them down in revulsion. Marvellous, that makes even better odds for you. These are all easy wins, so stay sharp and things automatically get better for you all the time. Drop your attention and the snipers will pick you off in the blink of an eye.

3) **Being too specific can be counter-productive.** By all means decide overall what you you're aiming for, but be flexible about the details. The more specific you are about such things as: exact location; starting level of salary; starting job title; a named company in your target sector; etc., then the more your odds narrow as a consequence. Victor Kiam, American entrepreneur and owner of Remington shavers, said that starting salary should never be a consideration when taking any new job because, once you've got the job, you can show how good you are and the money will follow. I'll let you into a personal guilty secret here – I thought he was a nutter. Eventually I found that he was exactly correct. The message is – get a job, then do what you can with it. Don't hold out for the max at the start and risk everything for what would be, in reality, a very small short-term gain. Equally, don't let them kick sand in your face. If a potential employer is taking the mickey and planning to screw the eventual candidate down to the ground, just because they can in this climate, then you're better off walking away and finding a better quality employer. Have confidence in yourself, your ability, your suitability and your prospects – if you don't, no one else will.

4) **Careers are like cats.** They too can be skinned in more than one way. I think my career, or at least the conventional part of it, went well. In my thirties I ended up running a market-leading subsidiary of a FTSE 100 company. That was a goal I always had in mind (one of them, anyway) and I achieved it. However, in advance, I could never have predicted the exact route by which I actually got there. I found that a sense of general direction was much more useful to me than an exact path, to keep me moving forward. Having a longer-term goal for your career is excellent, but as you target winning your first or your next job, just keep in mind that you are unlikely to find a perfect match with what you think you

need. It's definitely a form of guerrilla warfare: take the victories where you can and keep moving forward.

5) **Invest in yourself, even just once, and you can bank it forever.** If you develop a new skill, it's just like riding a bike, you'll never forget how to use it. Each and every skill you develop now, as you train and fight to win that next job, will stay with you for the whole of the rest of your career. No job at the minute? Well that's a great opportunity to increase your value to a prospective employer. Spend your time developing a new skill to increase your chances of making it through the selection process.

Key point summary 2 – Preparation

Key Learning points

- Headline unemployment figures reported in the media can be highly misleading and you need to avoid being negatively influenced.
- Progress comes from the process of asking yourself: where are you now; where do you want to be and how will you get there?
- The biggest waste of your time can be in chasing opportunities which you have no chance of winning. Choose your targets wisely.
- Shouting, "Ready ... Fire! Aim," and shooting applications quickly from the hip is both pointless and counterproductive.
- Every positive action you take and each step forward you make reinforces a subconscious belief in your prospects. Use that.

Signposts

- If you've sent out 823 applications for no result, accept that you're doing something wrong.
- Even if unemployment in your category is running at 20%, four out of five people therefore have jobs. You can choose to be one of them.
- With 29.3m people in work, annual 'churn' constantly generates new opportunities.
- Understand the market for jobs in your field. Some industries are declining but new ones are growing all the time.
- A goal and a general direction will be more use to you than being determined to follow a specific path.

Actions

- Decide what type of role you're suited to and really want to be doing.
- Cut naysayers and negativity out of your life. Associate with achievers.
- Be persistent, it's at least partly a numbers game and a war of attrition.
- Develop an action plan to cover weaknesses and improve your capability. Any investment you make will pay you back handsomely.
- In a job-search, know what you want but be prepared to compromise.

Chapter 3 – Searches: stalking the jungle

"I was asked what I thought about the recession. So I thought about it and decided not to take part." Sam Walton, founder of Wal-Mart, about the recession in 1980.

So, you've taken stock of yourself. You have more idea about the type of job you're really interested in and you have a much better idea about your real prospects of surviving the battle to get it. Hopefully you've truly laid to rest the ghost of negativity about your prospects, even in the current climate.

Now is the time to step into the jungle, conduct some detailed reconnaissance and choose your killing grounds. In other words, in the parlance of the recruitment industry, you need to find suitable job opportunities to apply for.

Do it boldly, do it loudly and do it thoroughly. There is no need to be afraid at this stage. You're there to flush out potential employers who are presently well dug into their defensive positions. Their flags are flying proudly atop their castles and each flag has a list of current vacancies printed across it.

Tell absolutely everyone you know that you're looking for a job. Tell the people you don't know. Tell the people in your bus queue. Shout it down the darkest avenues of the internet. The more noise you make, the more chance you have of uncovering a potential employer with a vacancy. The silent killing-in-the-dark-with-your-knife bit starts later, when you've chosen which jobs to stalk.

The only proviso I would add at this point is: consider keeping your mouth very firmly zipped whenever you find a target you've got a real shot at.

Telling your friends, relatives and flatmates might be fine, but telling absolutely everyone on your course that you've dug out a previously unidentified stellar opportunity with a starting salary of fifty large ones a year, and you were thrilled to discover they've still got one place left on this year's graduate intake, is not so smart. As you're putting together your application, armed with a self-congratulatory drink, you risk not seeing a friend standing quietly behind you filling in their own application and loading cross-hatched bullets into the biggest gun you'll never see.

A mild degree of paranoia will keep you alive longer. Couple it with a dose of schizophrenia: shouty that you're looking, on the one hand; quiet that you've found something, on the other. That will save your friends endless hours of guilty, hand-wringing angst as they try to cope with knowing that they were the ones who put you down. Avoid the problem.

By the way, you should start to practise these new skills – a twist of paranoia and a little zest of schizophrenia – with immediate effect because they'll come in very useful as you move through the later stages of a recruitment process.

Erm … conversely it should now become second nature to keep your ears open when around course-mates. Ahem.

Moving forward … why are potential employers dug into defensive positions? Because they know they have what you want and they're expecting a mass onslaught from a whole bunch of people just like you.

To their advantage, they know that the attack will be uncoordinated and they have an armoury packed with extremely efficient weapons with which to scythe down the attacking masses. They're adept at pitting individuals against each other in a blood-fest of hand-to-hand combat. It's a relatively low-stress, low-overhead approach on their part. They set the battle in motion and simply reward the fittest with an offer letter.

However, to your advantage will be the prodigious abilities you'll develop over the next chapters as you learn how to target opportunities, analyse job specifications and get past the gate-keepers. You'll be attacking employers' ramparts considerably more clinically than the next person.

Employers might be well-defended, very cunning and utterly ruthless, but if you learn to see clearly what they're after, you can calculate exactly how best to display your wares and conquer their defences at each and every stage. Your less-well-prepared peers will be cut down with every step you take.

Once over the ramparts, you'll wash off the camouflage paint, dress for dinner and transform yourself into the hottest hooker or raunchiest rent boy in town, in an effort to pass the final stage of the beauty pageant. There'll be a knife secreted about your person somewhere. It'll be a winner-takes-all contest and the losers won't even get a funeral.

We'll cover a lot more on this in later chapters. Battle only ensues once you submit an application. For now, you're just concerned with flushing out likely prospects from the jungle undergrowth, and doing so in a fairly open way.

But where do you start looking?

Search strategies

Different people tend to use different search strategies, depending upon their character type. There are three basic search methodologies you can pursue.

- **Harvesting** is almost entirely passive and involves largely reacting to what is systematically fed to you, perhaps by your university.
- **Hunting** is highly proactive and involves searching specifically for the type of role that you want, often with an employer of a certain profile.
- **Gathering** leans towards the passive and involves grazing in a less focused way to see what turns up from contacts that you make.

You might notice that only one of these strategies, hunting, requires high-octane, focused, proactive work on your part. The other two involve reviewing what generally hoves into view so you can match it against the personal template you created earlier, to see whether it's worth applying.

Certainly, whichever of these three strategies you're following, you'll need to put in a huge amount of effort once you find a position to apply for, but only hunting involves you in turning the tables and running a real selection process for yourself. Your basic character might well determine which of them you naturally and comfortably prefer to follow.

Harvesting is very easy for plugged-in, institutionalised types who are happy to follow the conveyor they've been on since choosing their GCSEs. Nothing wrong with that, you've still got to fight to win out against your peers and you'll need to be as lean and mean as the best of them.

You'll be responding to such things as graduate recruitment initiatives, perhaps organised via the milk round, but it's passive in so far as you're watching opportunities as they're fed to you in some way.

At the end of the process, you could find yourself with a nationally recognised employer and many people envying you.

Hunting requires you to be more outgoing and highly proactive. For example, your starting point might be to gather a list of all the employers in the country who recruit research chemists (if that's what you're into).

Then you might perhaps whittle those down by assessing them against each other in terms of such things as starting salary, likely career progression, field of work, geographical location, employment security, opportunity to travel, etc.

Next you might factor in information from social network sites about them, make contact with some staff and then start posing questions. And so on.

At the end of it, you will be pretty sure that you'll have found the very best opportunity out there in the jungle for yourself, in your chosen field of work.

Gathering really suits the more social beasts amongst us; those who talk to anyone and everyone in every which way and are happy to put themselves out there. Some people do it as easily as breathing.

It's an unfocused form of searching because you're basically parading the streets with a billboard and waiting to see what turns up. Again, nothing wrong with that. Your net will reach far and wide and you will trawl up random opportunities that you would never have come across any other way.

That all makes life quite exciting because you literally don't know where you'll end up. Some people will delight in that prospect, others will run screaming from the room and have an OCD paddy at what they see as a complete lack of structure to the approach. God, you might as well shake the dice, right?

Well, yes, but so what? At the end of it you'll have uncovered that golden gem of a job that will forever make everyone you ever meet go, "Wow! How in the world did you find that? I didn't know such a thing existed. Do they need anyone else, where can I apply?"

What's best?

There is no right or wrong way. What's best is to do them all, but in reality, one path will be easier for you because it will fit with your personality type or stage of development. The important thing is to be aware of that, and not neglect the others, even though they are harder for you to get to grips with.

Personally, I lived unconsciously as a harvester until I was 25 years old. It just never occurred to me that there was any other way of being, until I went to a party outside my normal circle of friends. I got into conversation with someone and went, "Wow! Where in the world did you find that job?"

As a result I went completely off the deep end with a new hunting approach. The very next morning I stepped naked into the jungle and started the search for an opportunity just like it. After some work, I emerged from the jungle into a clearing and realised I'd found exactly what I was after.

So, to reinforce the point, there is no right or wrong way, work with what works for you. Just be aware that there is more than one approach you can take and follow as many routes as you can.

Before we look into some of the major tracks you can follow to uncover potential job opportunities, let's take a look at how the size and type of organisation you want to work for might affect your overall search.

Types of employer

For the same job, different sizes of organisation offer different working experiences and career opportunities. They also operate different selection, induction and development methodologies. Very generally speaking:

- larger organisations offer narrower, well-defined roles and a more structured development path, with wider opportunities within the same organisation;
- smaller organisations offer wider roles involving more day-to-day task variability but often have limited in-house career development scope. They are not necessarily any less professional.

Let's look in more detail at how the size of organisation might affect the choices you may need to make and therefore your job-search.

Very large scale organisations. We're talking here of organisations already employing many thousands, tens of thousands, or even hundreds of thousands of people. They're likely to be at least widespread nationally, probably multi-site, with a significant proportion of exports, but often they'll be true multi-site multinationals, operating regionally or globally.

To some people, in these anti-globalisation days, such organisations are the foul and blasted spawn of the devil, born from a diabolical experiment allowed to escalate beyond the control of mere mortals. Some organisations are considerably bigger than countries, certainly more powerful and much less democratically run.

To hear the anti-globalists, you'd imagine the chief executives of these organisations wring their hands daily at their lack of access to a decent death-star. In truth, not all of them insist that their employees turn up dressed in a Darth Vader cossie, kill their relatives and commit to the path of darkness. Some of them do actually wear white hats and can point to a great deal of beneficial work around the planet.

From your point of view, if you exclude this whole category of potential employers, you're cutting off about 10% of your opportunities. Worse, depending upon your longer term ambitions, you might well be excluding the best 10%, from a career development point of view. So, instead of worrying about the poorly-behaved ones, focus instead on the ones that do fit with your morals and ethics. They are out there.

Such organisations tend to run highly-structured graduate selection, induction and development schemes. They will typically follow the milk round, supplemented with: existing university connections; a national advertising campaign in the big dailies and increasingly, the use of internet and social media advertising.

Primary eligibility tends to driven by: the relevance of your degree; whether you have at least a 2:1 and usually on whether you have good A level grades (sucks to be me, then), even if you have got a good degree.

What else makes a difference to your prospects? Good people and team skills, directly related work or project experience, transferable skills or experience and longer-term career potential, either technical or managerial, will all tend to add to your score.

As with all of these things, you might score high in some areas and low in others. The real key to unlocking a door in this category is to see whether you can realistically put yourself into the frame, assuming you want to. Long term prospects tend to be good (at least until you reach late middle-age and have to face The Great Slaughter, but that's another story), hence the stiff competition to win a place.

Larger organisations will also tend to run a 'fast-development track' for people they consider to have exceptional talent. Your prospects are good even if that's not you but if you're a late developer (sucks to be me, again), it can be very hard to later accelerate your career up the hierarchy, unless you're prepared to change employer.

Small organisations. This is the other end of the scale and, boy, are things different in this category. In terms of numbers, we're talking about a spread from literally a handful of employees up to around two hundred and fifty or so.

There are no fast-tracks marked out for you here, but career progress up the hierarchy can easily be an order of magnitude faster than within a large organisation. For a given seniority level, salaries tend to be lower but you might get promotion earlier and compensate that way. You need to decide whether the trade-off might work for you.

Large organisations have a department for everything and the majority of your time will be spent working within your particular job function or speciality, supported where necessary by people from other departments.

In a small organisation, within a very short time of starting work, you're likely to personally know all of the directors or heads of the primary functions – sales, accounts, operations, IT, facilities, communications, etc. You could put forty years into a really large organisation and not even know or care who these people are.

In small organisations you'll typically be spending less time on your primary job function and more on peripheral issues. For example, if you have staff under you, hiring and firing will fall much more on your shoulders than it would in a large organisation where HR provide huge support. In addition, you'll be much more exposed: if something doesn't get done, it's easy to see who didn't do it. Conversely, of course, if something is achieved, recognition tends to be swift and spectacular.

For some people this is a nightmare scenario. For others, the flexibility required adds massively to the job interest. Career progression in a very large organisation will be a highly-structured and well-supported affair. At the small end, climbing the ladder can be surprisingly swift with sudden changes and with a wide range of responsibility coming to you very early in your career.

On the down-side, career progress can be considerably more haphazard. You might have to change employers to get a job with more responsibility as a small organisation just may not be able to offer sufficient opportunities for progress. Career development will be left in your hands and you'll need to self-manage training and personal development.

There's also the question of risk. Getting in at the ground floor with a ten-person business, looking at high growth prospects, can see you right at board level within a year or two, feeling like a stallion and riding your career like you stole it.

Equally, it can leave you shattered, broken, piss-poor and unemployed over the same time-scale as chickens come home to roost, finance dries up and castles in the sky undergo catastrophic nonlinear structural exasperation and implode into a black hole as they realise that Newton was right about gravity after all. Shooting for the stars does carry the risk of doing a head-plant, as small organisations have limited resources.

That's less likely to happen in a very large scale organisation and if it does, there could well be a safety net organised to catch talented people like you, unless you happened to take the piss out of Darth Vader in his hearing, of course.

Total wipe-out is less likely to happen with an organisation employing over a hundred or so people that's been around for many years and has a more conservative approach which doesn't bet the ranch on world-domination every day.

Unsurprisingly, these factors act to strongly influence an employer's selection criteria and they should make you think carefully about what's best for you.

It's important to remember that small does not equate to unprofessional. You'll find the whole gamut of recruitment behaviour in this category: from the owner-manager who won't have you unless you're also a heavy-breasted, dwile flonking, beach volleyball player, through to the overly zealous corporate wannabee, entirely driven by procedure, who will have you and your parents psych-profiled and demand that samples of your bodily fluids be analysed and kept for a rainy day.

Prime eligibility for recruitment tends to be driven by:

- the relevance of your degree;
- technical competence for a specific role;
- having a demonstrable hands-on approach;
- personality fit with existing people (chemistry, in the parlance);
- a driven interest in the offered role or the organisation's products or services.

Things that make a difference to your prospects of winning that job offer are:

- relevant work experience;

- specific vocational skills;
- practical skills;
- team-working skills;
- your personal character and general level of enthusiasm.

The successful candidate here will be more independent, highly flexible, resourceful and can show that they'll hit the ground running on day one.

In terms of prospecting, these organisations are unlikely to be joining the milk round and they are very likely to advertise but less so with large boxes in the dailies. You might find them in the line-ads. Advertising is more likely to be in trade magazines, locally targeted and field-specific. They may also exploit any local connections they have with universities, local industry and with people they know, including family members of employees. Increasingly today, they'll be making use of online advertising and social media, if for no other reason than because it's cheap and their target employees have ready access.

If they have a post to fill, they'll typically want to do that now, this very instant, because they have a current vacancy. The recruitment process can be measured in weeks, rather than the many months common with the very largest organisations who bucket-fill graduate programmes.

Middle-size organisations. Note the word 'middle', not 'medium', as the previous category includes what are commonly called SMEs – small and medium-sized enterprises. Instead, we are talking here of organisations employing a few hundred to several thousand people.

In terms of recruitment processes, these organisations will tend to be well structured and systematically organised. They are quite likely to be advertising nationally, especially the larger ones. They're also likely to be using contacts they already have and be making good use of social media.

They are less likely to run full scale graduate training and development programmes but the larger ones are still likely to suck in an intake of new cannon-fodder each year, putting them through a shorter induction programme. Recruitment will be almost entirely driven by and linked to vacancies, present or anticipated.

As a function of their increased size, these larger organisations can inevitably offer more internal opportunities to you as your career progresses, although you are unlikely to travel the world with them and are less likely to be asked to change your working location periodically.

Any role you take up, and the responsibility that goes with it, is likely to be more precisely delineated.

On the other side of the coin, there will be much more of a departmentalised supporting structure around your role, allowing you to concentrate more on your primary job function with less distraction.

That may all be a plus or a minus for you; it depends what you're looking for.

In fact, that statement holds true across all of these three categories of organisation. Also note that there can be significant blurring between them. It's not unheard of to find large organisations with abysmally sloppy and unprofessional recruitment and personnel management practices that would be more typical of a ten-person outfit run by a crack addict with an attention deficit disorder.

You'll need to adapt accordingly, but it helps to have an idea what you might or might not get from an employer, depending upon their scale, as it may influence your application strategy and consequently your search strategy. Different actions on your part will flush out different types of employer and different types of job opportunity from the undergrowth.

Don't take the above generalised information as chiselled on tablets of stone.

A small organisation may be owned by a large PLC and that may or may not have a big impact on recruitment and your career progression. They might be constrained by a corporate straightjacket, or the chief executive might be entrepreneurial and fiercely independent. Either of those two extremes can be good or bad, depending on what suits you.

Speaking personally again, I've worked both sides of that particular fence. I've worked for a small organisation for several years with two hundred people and it was an absolute delight.

Equally, I've worked for a small organisation that drove me utterly nuts and the owner manager should just have been put out of his and our misery IMHO.

I hated every single last solitary minute of my work at the latter but both were brilliant experience and highly beneficial for my career.

I've also worked for a couple of large PLCs, one national and one global, and exactly the same feelings prevailed when considering one against the other. Again, both were highly beneficial for my career. Use the employment situation you find yourself in to best advantage.

That's why the more you can dig up about an organisation, its situation and its managers, the better you can figure out how working there might be made to work out best for you. If you think a place looks like it's run by a bunch of chicken-killing Satanist lunatics even before you start, don't make eye contact and step away.

Having said that, if you think you might well have to bite the bullet and work with the Devil himself, be aware of what you might be walking into and that it might not be long-term. Get out of it what you want in terms of experience and career growth but when you leave, make sure you take your soul with you.

Think I'm kidding? Not a bit of it.

Sector choice is a further consideration for you.

Do you know whether you prefer to work in the private sector, the public sector or the community and voluntary service (CVS) third sector? Salary, job function and subsequent career route, indeed the very fabric of your being and the future nature of your thoughts, will all be significantly affected by your choice.

Heavy.

You may already have a very strong preference that may be based on your philosophical or political beliefs, or you may be entirely open to any of them at this stage. Just be aware that it's not impossible, but it can be challenging, to change sectors later.

Having said that, the third sector can be quite useful initially to help you build up some generic work experience, which you can use as a springboard into the other two sectors when an opportunity arises.

Once you've been in a sector for a time, a bit like an actor, there is a risk that you'll get type-cast by prospective employers. They might need a great deal of convincing as to whether you can really jump the fence into their arena.

Opening up your options

So, are large or small employers best to look at, or should you perhaps look for something in between?

If you're asking yourself this question with an open mind, perhaps even for the first time, you're markedly improving your odds of finding and winning a job that's right for you.

Typically, institutions push students down the major employer route.

As a group, the major employers in the UK have a thirst to fill over sixteen thousand graduate-scheme places each year and will each take dozens, sometimes hundreds, of graduates. Universities and other institutions have a need to help thousands of graduating students find work.

Putting the two together and creating a milk round, albeit partially online these days, makes obvious sense, but do the numbers balance?

The motivations for students to chase a graduate-scheme place with a major employer are obvious: high starting salaries; golden hellos; professional training; higher perceived job security; international travel and better imagined career prospects all abound.

The result is inevitably heavy competition for the places available.

The High Flyers Research graduate market report shows that the top employers currently expect to absorb perhaps around 5% of graduates onto their schemes this year. Add in the additional larger employers, who also engage with students via universities, and that number obviously rises.

However, a very large proportion of graduates end up chasing a minority of those toughest-to-get positions. Most will obviously chase several to improve their personal odds but unfortunately, a very large proportion of graduates must inevitably lose out. They'll end up scrabbling and playing catch-up, when they finally exhaust their graduate-scheme options.

Don't let all of this put you off. A graduate development scheme with a major employer may be exactly the right route for you. If it is, go for it. Just make sure to take on board as many lessons as you can from the remaining chapters of this book. They'll help you to strongly improve your odds and win through against the tough competition.

Someone has to win a place offered, why not you?

If that route is not for you, what alternatives might you have?

In November 2012, The University of Newcastle Business School produced a report entitled, "Graduate Employment in Small and Medium Sized Enterprises: Results from an AGCAS member survey."

The study identified a need to not only encourage graduates to consider and apply for employment in SMEs but also a need to encourage SMEs to consider, engage with and recruit graduates.

Think about that situation for a moment.

It suggests that whilst the bulk of graduates are steered down the easy-to-follow route of chasing graduate-schemes and major employers (with many losing out), small and medium sized employers are being ignored by students and graduates and they don't know themselves how best to draw them in.

Surprised?

Well, no prizes for now guessing what to do if you want to expand your employment-prospect horizons then.

Slip into the jungle, find SMEs and talk to them.

If the mountain won't come to Muhammad ….

Seize the initiative. You need to be proactive if you're going chase SMEs because, to quote the report, "… these companies tend not to have enough recruitment flow to warrant extended interface with students."

Do you need more convincing?

The Federation of Small Businesses identifies that SMEs account for 99.9% of all private sector businesses in the UK. Furthermore, they account for 59.1% of private sector employment.

Do you need even more convincing?

Started in 2007, app company Songkick was named as the 7th best start up in the UK by Wired magazine. Songkick is an app that tracks the bands a user likes and alerts them to concerts, using social media and personal data. It now has more than a million users a month.

Songkick doesn't advertise jobs. Instead, they effectively let people self-select by seeing who manages to find a way to their door because they're interested and enthusiastic. Their three month graduate placement scheme became popular as news spread organically, not through advertising.

My suggestion, if the SME route is appropriate for you, is to start chasing down it sooner rather than later. Even if you're also attempting to secure a place on a graduate scheme, don't wait: try and cut ahead of the pack.

The message is clear: keep your eyes, mind and options fully open.

Institutions can sometimes neglect to put across the wider picture of potential employment opportunities. Don't be blinkered by the comforting, easy-to-follow, milk round route, because it's loaded with risk.

Let's move on now and look at some of the pathways you can follow through the jungle to start flushing out some potential employers.

Search-paths to explore

There are a multitude of ways to search for jobs.

- Cold-calling to get yourself onto a shortlist of one is hard work, but can pay big dividends.
- Friends and family and personal contacts may be able to put you forward for a role that hasn't yet been advertised.
- Job adverts offer low odds, unless you select the ones to apply for carefully.
- Networking need not be a dirty word and helps you to search both wider and deeper.
- Social networking is a powerful tool, but hide your skeletons.
- Talk to existing and previous employers as they already know your capabilities.
- Local employers are reachable and may be able to offer valuable experience.
- Recruitment agencies require you to build personal relationships with them after the initial contact.
- A website and blog can be useful, but don't expect people to just turn up: hustle for visitors.
- Online job sites can be useful but may be swamped with opportunistic employers looking to sell a cheap deal.
- Head hunters are unlikely to be relevant to you yet.

There are others, but those are the main routes to follow. We'll look at them in detail through the course of this chapter. Two are regarded nervously by newbies so, YOLO, let's tackle them head on. They are: getting yourself onto a shortlist of one; and the phone-a-friend route.

Head down, let's go for it.

A shortlist of one is best, so get yourself onto one. In other words, target an employer and talk them into giving you a job.

Sceptical that this is possible? So was I. Let me tell you a story …

I was on a highly-selective, heavy-duty management development course. It had the objective of helping me make the transition from being a nerdy engineer into a responsible manufacturing manager capable of leading a staff of hundreds. To complete the eighteen month programme I needed an employer who would let me run amok in a position of responsibility for a year inside their business so that I could get certified, CV-able, experience.

You'll spot the obvious catch-22 problem here – I had zero person-management experience. In fact, I had zero experience of anything managerial at all. A bit like your stage of development now, I was big on potential but short on experience. I had spent the period leading up to this writing welding procedures which explained how a grunting Neanderthal with an electric rod and a gimp mask could bodge up bits of the Thames Barrier.

Worse, it became clear that the method of finding such an employer involved me finding them and persuading them I was a good bet. Obviously there'd be no adverts to look at since only a maniac would actually advertise in an attempt to fill a vacancy they didn't know they had, with a self-confessed incompetent.

I arranged to meet with the course director and my tutor.

"Erm … my experience of this approach is nil, chaps," I said.

"Good luck then," they offered.

Yep, this was all going to go well.

The Yosser Hughes, "Go on, giz a job," approach I could just about buy. As when you're out clubbing, if you keep asking, you're bound to get somewhere in the end. But the, "You didn't know you wanted me and I don't know if I can do the job but go on, give us a go guv," approach seemed just a teensy bit of a stretch to little old negative me.

I'm telling you all this so that you get a sense of perspective about the worst-case-scenario-shortlist-of-one attempt I was about to undertake. It was clearly madness but unfortunately I had no choice. I'd quit my previous day job as a well-paid engineer to come and do this course. Bugger. It all made Everest seem like it was a hill with a nice view to trot up before breakfast.

"Drive around industrial estates and see what you can find," was the instruction. "Knock on a few doors. Introduce yourself."

OMG. I knew I was going to die. I knew people in factories. They made the Vogons look like social workers. At the very least, I needed chain-mail underpants if I wasn't to face being battered senseless again by people with office furniture at their disposal. I could just imagine how it would go.

Knock knock.

"WHAT?"

"I just wanted to ask if …"

"Wait here while I get the furniture."

Deep sigh. Better remember the pain killers. My heart was heavy, but then I had a stroke of luck.

I was driving over to a friend's and saw a factory on the edge of an industrial estate. I'd driven past it loads of times but never really noticed. The lucky bit was that it was a Sunday, so there was absolutely no chance of anyone being there.

It looked alright, as these things go. It was a fair-sized building, so a big enough company for my needs and it looked well kept, modern and had a nice array of glass windows along the front and down both sides.

My last office had been deep in the bowels of a half-mile long Victorian workhouse in Trafford Park, with absolutely no windows. I never ever saw daylight in the winter months. Friends had begun to notice the bulge in my forehead where evolution had kicked in and my body was trying to grow a small dangly light on a stalk. This looked like luxury.

I pulled in, parked up and peered through the windows. I could see assembly benches, racks of components and chunky bits of green machinery standing around, partly assembled. It looked good.

I walked around to the front door, got down on my hands and knees and flipped the letterbox open, as you do. It smelled divine. Actually it just didn't stink like a thousand year old barrel of burnt oil, which my last place did. There was even carpet in reception which ran up the hallway and through to offices with quite posh wooden desks in them.

Excellent, I thought. It didn't look like the legs came off the desks very easily. I might be able to leave off the chain mail. My mood brightened even further, so I took down the address details, made a few quick notes and roared off into the sunset.

The letter I dropped through their letterbox was short, direct, said what I wanted, said what I thought I could achieve and included a CV. I didn't enclose a picture.

Whilst I felt very enthusiastic, I can't honestly tell you that I was very optimistic. The odds were surely against me?

But, hold the front page, they came straight back. They were expanding, needed to appoint a new manager, were just about to advertise but hadn't yet, so why didn't I come along for a chat?

Blow me down and ride me sideways, I got the job: Works Manager running a CNC machinery-building factory with fifty staff reporting to me. No blackmail, no bribery and no battery-with-furniture involved. I was astounded.

So, dear reader, not only can it be done, it should be done. By you. Now. Your odds are colossally better than you might imagine.

I accept, I was a bit lucky in pulling it off on my first attempt. I also accept that mentally it would have been hard to keep trying it over and over if I'd kept being rejected, but that would have mainly been because I wouldn't have known that it could actually be made to work.

But it did work and the great news is that now you know that it's possible too.

So get yourself onto a shortlist of one. Dig out your glad rags, tart yourself up a bit and see if you can step straight through the jungle and up to the ramparts in one giant leap. Book yourself space at that last-stage beauty pageant, secure in the knowledge that no-one else will be around to get in your way.

It's a technique I've used on several occasions now, albeit with varying results. That first time was spectacular, others less so. Knock-backs are inevitable and you will have to recognise that it's a war of attrition. Pick yourself up, have another go. And another. You've got nothing to lose and literally everything to gain if you pull it off. The more you try, the easier it'll get.

It requires guts at the start, but mainlining on the adrenalin surge will become so addictive, you'll be cutting your way through that jungle before anyone else even knows you're there. It's the ultimate in going commando – stepping naked into the jungle, on the hunt and with your weapon ready. You can pull it off, if you're willing to try hard.

So where do you find a shortlist of one? This approach clearly fits in very well with a hunting style but note that your 'gathering' work also complements any hunt for a shortlist of one. You need to know what type of role you're after and what type of organisation might be able to offer it. Then it's down to search and recon work to hunt out suitable places, followed by your approach.

This all used to be a bit of a slog through directories and trade magazines, supported with a lot of trudging through town centres, retail parks and industrial estates. Today, a near-ubiquitous internet makes searching much faster, considerably wider in scope, geographically unlimited and a great deal more efficient in helping you to sift out the dross from the delightful.

I do still recommend the trudge as well. It's character-building, especially on rainy days. If it's snowing, you might even get a sympathy-shag type meeting. The following example from July 2013, reported on the BBC's news website, provides the perfect justification for you to embark upon a good trudge.

Luisa Downey, a then-unemployed graduate from Colchester, had been spending her time boarding local trains and handing out CVs to passengers, requesting that they employ her. Caroline Seear, Managing Director of the Maldon office of Red Recruitment was 'impressed by her get up and go' and, after more formally meeting up, offered her a job and a place on the firm's graduate training and development programme.

Up to that point, Luisa, who had graduated from Essex University with a 2:1 in 2011, had been unable to find suitable work in advertising and public relations, her chosen field. Red Recruitment had just such a role to fill and were thrilled to find someone with real initiative and a highly positive attitude.

Cold calling and getting on a shortlist of one really does work. Start now.

Friends and family. Even if you're on the mother of all murderous hunts for a suitable target organisation, the opportunistic importance of proactive gathering, using the friends, family and personal contacts route, should not be underestimated.

Another quick story for you.

I sat alone at my desk, depressed. It was ten o'clock in the morning, I was in Yorkshire and my employer was corporately psychopathic. I hadn't been with them long but I felt that my whole career was sliding down the pan and someone else's hand was inching toward the chain. I was seriously contemplating buying a croft in the Outer Hebrides.

I really struggled to find even one iota of motivation for another job hunt. It seemed pointless. My CV was polluted so badly I may as well have been working for BP and calling Tony Hayward mate as we sailed together through a black Gulf, filled to the brim with choking seabirds and badly marinated fish.

Bollocks, I thought. Time to phone a friend. I rang Lynn in Watford. He worked at what was then the Engineering Industry Training Board. I told him where I was working, what it was like and that I was going to toss a match in and walk away. I was putting myself on the job market and if he heard of anything cropping up, would he kindly let me know.

He was supportive, but very clear that there was little or no chance of him coming across the sort of role I was looking for: he just didn't come in contact with the people who'd be looking to fill that sort of position.

Double bollocks. I got a cup of coffee but as I sat down again five minutes later, wondering if there was a way to fake my suicide, the phone rang.

"You won't believe this," Lynn began.

I didn't.

Somebody he hadn't spoken to for years and years had called him that moment, purely on the off-chance. The chap owned a large manufacturing business in the north of London, one of his managers was coming up to retirement and did Lynn know anyone he could talk to about filling the post?

"I gave him your name and I've got his number here for you."

I could have kissed him, even if he'd been smoking Cuban cigars and coughing up pints of lung-butter. But five minutes? That was all a bit scary.

I made the call, trying not to sound too keen and failing, and went down for an interview a couple of days later. The job was perfect for me and yet again, no furniture was involved in the interview process. I trotted back gleefully and resigned my current post before the week was out, two fingers up.

Score.

That experience perfectly illustrates, yet again, the immense power that flows from a shortlist of one but it also shows that you absolutely must talk to people because you just never know what's around until you kick a can down the street with someone.

The job in north London served to strongly reinforce this point. The business employed several hundred people and whenever we needed to recruit, we spoke to employees first to ask if they had suitable friends or family currently looking for work.

It wasn't especially that it was cheaper than advertising but it was massively faster and more effective as a recruitment method. We could be sure that anyone we met was both capable and being vouched for, so it kept the criminals, communists and cretins well away from our doors. Well, most of 'em.

Most places that I've worked for since have used this same technique to very good effect, so the message is clear – step straight into the swamp of your contacts and thrash around. Plan to eat alligator for breakfast.

You remember all the bullshit you've seen written where it says in recruitment-agency adverts, "Most jobs aren't advertised," and you should, "Tap into the hidden job market"? Well, it's true.

Up to 60% of jobs are filled without the vacancy ever being advertised, or even announced. Employers very often prefer to take on people who are a known quantity or who have been vouched for by someone else, even if they don't know much about them. The simple fact that you're referred through by someone who knows you're not a violent, drunken, homophobic thief can be enough to tip the scales in your favour, even if other candidates are applying.

You've seen the extra bit in online adverts where it says, "…so plug into the unadvertised hidden job market with us?" That actually is bullshit. More often than not, anyway. How could they possibly have access to knowledge of the jobs of which no one has knowledge? Step around the trap, cut their throats and wade on into the swamp.

Okay, that's two things under your belt: hacking down a path on a focused search and a trawl through the swamp. Note that both are active. If an opportunity suddenly leaps out at you, then you'll need to jump forward to the next chapter. In reality, things can take time and there are no guarantees.

So, where else should you look in the meantime?

Let's swing entirely the other way to look at a more traditional source.

Job adverts. That's a nice and easy route to follow, isn't it? People pay for you to read about the jobs they have. All you have to do is pick up a publication, subscribe to relevant lists or visit appropriate web pages. Now this is a form of job-search everyone can recognise. How hard can it be?

Actually, it's a mean mother. This following example comes from the States, but the same exercise could have been carried out almost anywhere.

Eric K Auld posted a job advert on Craigslist and he got 650 responses on the first day. The job paid $13 an hour plus health benefits for work as a full-time administrative assistant in Manhattan. Unfortunately, the advert was fake.

Awesome. I wonder if he's still alive?

Interestingly, applicants had anywhere from forty years of experience down to zero and ranged from school leavers to graduates to pensioners.

What can we learn from this? Even had the advert been genuine, as at least 650 people obviously believed it was, it's clear that there are a lot of people wanting that type of work. Replying would have resulted in you having a 1 in 650 chance of landing the role. Actually, it was probably less than one in a thousand, depending on the cut-off date for the advert.

Even if we assume that you're a good candidate with the right qualifications or experience and that you could present a decent application, correctly structured with good spelling and grammar, the odds were still mind-blowing.

It does look as though the idea of researching before applying was an alien concept to at least those 650 people, otherwise they might well have spotted the fact that they'd be wasting their time.

It's easy to see how people get trapped in an endless cycle of reading, replying and waiting. When they reach that magic number of 823 they have the evidence to 'prove' that the world is against them.

I would suggest that adverts are only useful to you where you can be sure of three things:

- firstly, that you're a very good match to the requirements;
- secondly, that the ad is sufficiently targeted, making it unlikely that the overall number of applicants will be mindlessly huge;
- thirdly, based on some quick analysis on your part, that you think you can prop up at least one thing in your favour that should give you an edge over the vast majority of other applicants, if not all of them.

If you do this, let's look at how your odds can improve.

To start, there may be only a hundred applicants for a targeted job, requiring specific qualifications and experience, focused on a specialisation. Still high, but nowhere near the one thousand level, and that makes a big difference.

- Commonly, over fifty per cent of applicants (the chancers) will be self-excluding with an inadequate match to the requirements.
- Another large percentage (the amateurs) will be dumped because of poor technique. Their application won't clearly demonstrate their value.
- Yet more (the feckless) will fall at the first fence due to piss-poor spelling, grammar, punctuation and presentation.

By surviving the CV / application cull, with targeting, you can easily be down to one of only ten people being seriously considered for interview. Since they might invite between four and six people to attend, that's pretty good for you.

Well done, you just killed a lot of people, about ninety-ish, and they never saw you coming. You didn't even know who they were, but you can rest easy at night knowing that they really are now flatter than Paul McCartney at an open air concert.

This approach potentially means that you're applying for less jobs overall, but so what? Do you really want to waste your time, energy and optimism applying for hundreds of jobs that you have virtually no chance of winning, or do you prefer to focus your energy and make a better job of attacking the ones that you do have a really solid chance with?

Bear in mind that your only objective is to get serious consideration of your application and win an invitation to an interview. You'll never get the job offer just from your application. So at this stage your odds of landing an interview now lift to a roughly 1 in 2 chance if they're going to invite in, say, five out of the ten survivors.

By choosing your ground carefully you've got the odds of being the one to win the job down from 1 in a 1,000 to 1 in a 100 to 1 in 10 and then finally down to perhaps 1 in 4 or 5 or so (at the interview stage).

Doesn't look so bad now, does it? It's perhaps a bit simplistic to say that you have a 20% chance of winning any job you apply for, but you get the idea?

We'll cover more about improving your odds during the application and interview stages in the next chapters. For now, take on board the point that adverts are not worth excluding, but you need stop the madness. Be analytical and have the confidence to step around the advert traps and walk away so that you can fight the battles you have a chance of winning, not waste your strength on those you'll probably lose.

Choose the adverts you will spend time on carefully. Adverts are absolutely not worth a relentless pump-action approach – save that for your networking.

Speaking of which …

Networking. Some people like it, some people loathe it, some people feel threatened by it, some are terrified of it and the term seems to mean different things to different people.

Add the word 'events' after the word 'networking' and a fairly high proportion of people begin to panic, get angry or seek medication, depending upon their disposition.

A certain class of individual will begin to glow with pleasure at the very mention of the idea – avoid them at all costs.

A quick web search will pull up varying definitions of the term 'networking', when used in a business context. The businessdictionary.com website defines it as, *"Creating a group of acquaintances and associates and keeping it active through regular communication for mutual benefit."*

It's not a bad definition for our job-hunting efforts so let's keep things simple, diffuse some of the emotive feelings and add some clarity.

If you ring your mum and mention that you're looking for a job in your chosen field of golf ball design then, effectively, you're networking, albeit casually. If you extend that and systematically mention it to friends and colleagues, then you're serious about it. But if you actually start hunting out new contacts who might be helpful to you, then you're on fire.

All of this is useful activity and none of that seems too bad or threatening in any way, even though it's called networking. That's unlike attending horrific speed-dating style business networking events, where you have to make pitches individually to a room full of strangers.

Or those revivalist-type 'opportunities', where the only people who benefit are the organisers or 'professional' people: the, as yet, un-jailed Ponzi scheme pyramid sellers, in other words. They'll be pushing herbal remedies, fatal dietary solutions or suppositories that make orgasms last for a day and a half.

At these, the main protagonists bang on about 'building your network' when they actually mean you building *their* network and paying them for the privilege.

Quite often there's a pin-striped, orange-brown, desiccated spiv at the front, whipping the crowd into a frenzy by pointing out that he earned fifty grand on Monday alone, he bought an island with last month's pay cheque and the only thing he had to do was learn how to thrash kittens to death with a golf club.

It's not uncommon to accidentally find yourself at one of these 'events', sitting at the side of a slightly distant relative or friend who rang you out of the blue because they happened to be nearby and thought you could catch up and they know this nice bar in a hotel and would seven o' clock be okay? Sharp?

It's these types of events that have given networking unfortunate connotations and now cause us to have such appallingly negative feelings, whenever we hear the word. Personally, I would rather attempt to use an angle-grinder to clean my teeth than voluntarily attend one of those again.

But let's put those feelings away and take on board that networking can be fun, it can involve doing only what you enjoy doing anyway and you only have to do it in ways that you feel comfortable with. Do it in the way that suits you and ignore the unsavoury side of it.

If networking is about engaging with a (growing) circle of other people, then to actually make networking work for you, I'd suggest that you need to be doing it in a proactive way for it to be worthwhile and effective.

So, if you want to let people know that you're looking for a job, talk to friends and family. Talk to every contact you've ever met. Talk to everyone you meet that you've never met before. Hustle to get referred to someone.

Target a key individual you've dug out and then follow their path through the jungle: meet their friends; hang out at their gym; travel the same routes; join the same clubs; buy your bondage gear at the same outlets. Figuratively speaking, make Hannibal Lecter look like an amateur.

Whatever it takes, hustle people (as nicely as you can) until they give in and help you, refer you onwards or blow you out.

- **Be objective-driven.** You need to have a specific purpose in mind when you engage with people, not just be intent on adding them to your total number of contacts. An example might be: I'm going to tell everyone I know and everyone I meet that I'm looking for a job as a golf ball designer on the off-chance that they can put me in touch with a person at a company, who is looking for just such a person.
- **Actively search out people.** You need to be structured in your approach when you come into contact with new people. After the pleasantries, be upfront and direct about the fact that you're looking for a job. Keep it short, simple and interesting. Avoid making a sales pitch. Aim for a conversation both sides can enjoy. Exchange contact details and move on. The less pain they suffer and the more interested you can leave them, the more chance you have of them coming back to you.
- **Engage with contacts.** Don't just add them to a contact list you never look at, in the vague hope they'll come back to you one day. You need to maintain your contacts, strengthen your relationships and remind people you're still looking. Do this through periodic dialogue. However, contacting people every half day might be considered stalking.
- **Ask for things.** Many people are too embarrassed to do this, but there is no shame in it. Asking for help, advice, referral or the name of a contact is perfectly acceptable, provided that it's not an onerous task for the other party and that you're happy to reciprocate in the future. If things work out, remember to say thank you later.

47

- **Feed your contacts.** Update your contacts when you've moved forward, achieved your objective or changed tack. Don't keep them in the dark. Contacts tend to get pretty irritated when they come back with an excellent opportunity for you, only to be told you picked something up four months ago.
- **Keep your networks separate.** Especially your online networks. Whilst proactively updating your friends and colleagues about the fact you're still looking for a new job is most definitely useful networking, having your bestie update your entire professional network about the details of her latest squeeze and exactly what they got up to and with which animals, isn't.

Social networking. Picking up on the last point, if we add the word 'social' before the word 'networking', then we're into a whole different picture involving the likes of Facebook, LinkedIn, Twitter, Google+, etc. Most people don't think twice about adding someone to their network in this way so I guess most of us are quite comfortable with that.

In terms of job hunting though, sites such as these are effectively just tools to use under the whole networking banner, so it's worth thinking about your use of social networking more widely. It offers you unprecedented opportunity and the perfect way to connect with potential employers.

Some recruiters are targeting social networks and using them to advertise vacancies. Social recruiting across LinkedIn, Facebook and Twitter enables organisations to exponentially increase their reach by encouraging employees to share job opportunities with their relevant contacts.

Prospective employers encouraging this claim that this social referral process is faster, less expensive and often produces a better cultural fit at the end of the day. Sound familiar? It should do, it's an updated version of the friends and family path.

I have another secret to let you into … you're not paranoid, they *are* actually watching you. Potential employers, that is. Or at least they will be, once you start trekking through the jungle on a search to flush some of them out.

What will they see? Well, obviously not Mother Teresa, but some of your dirty linen might well need tidying up, scraping and ironing flat again before employers start running their fingers through your hair and taking a close look in your underwear drawer. Creepy? You betcha.

You'd be well advised to ensure that what you post for your friends is not something that will later bite you back when a potential employer looks at it as part of their vetting processes. Alternatively, run two accounts, one for your private life and one for your professional and keep them well separated.

If in doubt about a post, the acid test is always: if you were sitting at an interview, would looking at it increase or decrease your chances of winning through? If there's any risk, don't post it or make sure you delete it later.

It can however be somewhere between difficult and impossible to be absolutely certain that you've completely eradicated a previous posting.

Often, all you can do is try and clean up your act and move forward, hoping to leave your steaming pile of skid-marked linen quietly behind and hope it's swamped by your more recent, more responsible, online behaviour and either doesn't get noticed or gets ignored for being historic.

It might or might not work.

That glorious image of you holding the blood-soaked chainsaw on that drunken weekend where four of you cut two legs off a Welsh donkey for a bet and watched it try to run around the field might have been hilarious for several weeks afterwards. Unfortunately, it does look a tad callous when you're applying for a job as a social worker. It won't be explained away very easily.

If potential employers and agencies continue to follow the social networking route further, then you will have to be even more diligent in ensuring that you appear to be fully respectable. Pictures of stupidity, drunkenness and party japes will have to go and be replaced by acts of courage, caring and conscientiousness. Sorry.

As part of your active searching, follow or connect with organisations that look interesting and might be able to offer you the experience, job opportunity or internship that you're searching for. Understand what their products or services are. Find out what others think about them. What is it about them that interests you? What sort of opportunities might they be able to offer you? Keep up to date with their current news and views.

To break the ice and start getting your name known, try posting comments or posing questions on any online forums they run. Get to know about specific people at the organisation and what they do there.

Don't try to connect with everyone, but do try to connect with someone relevant. You need to give them a reason to connect – what's in it for them? Can you step things up to email exchanges or, even better, a phone conversation? If you buy them a coffee and a bun, can you meet up with them to talk about what it's like inside their organisation and to do that type of work? Or could you arrange a visit to look around relevant departments and improve your experience? Can you volunteer to help with something?

If you don't ask, you won't get. You'll be surprised what's possible if you are truly interested and look like a member of the human race. People welcome others taking an interest in them and their work. It can be useful for them to be seen to be making positive external contacts too. Perhaps, in return, you may be able to provide them with some useful information or an introduction?

Keep in mind what it is you're after. Who is the person in the organisation you really should be talking to? Can the person you've managed to connect with refer you on to them, along with some positive comments? Can they possibly even recommend you?

All of this on-going engagement provides an excellent reason to consider running two online personas. If not, there's the obvious potential problem of your Adolf Hitler Avatar being served up on forums. Unfortunately, there's a less obvious, but considerably more damaging risk that it'll be served up without you knowing. Some email clients now pull in information and images from Facebook and LinkedIn.

Having finally been introduced to that key person, what will they think when they see your email address as sheep.shagger @ outlook.com and they're looking at a picture of you naked, donning wellies?

There are three key messages to take on board:

- always make a good first impression – you only get one chance;
- don't bang on endlessly about yourself and what you want – think what can you do for the person you're in contact with;
- your network is your net worth – build it wisely. Remorselessly.

A survey published by careerbuilder.co.uk found that over half of employers specifically used social networks to check out a candidate and 43% had rejected a candidate as a consequence. That survey was published in January 2010 so things have undoubtedly stepped up since then.

The main causes of rejection seem obvious no-nos but that clearly didn't stop people doing dopey things, although possibly because it didn't occur to them at the time that someone would later use it as evidence against them. Key causes of rejection following a social network trawl by the employers were:

- mismatches between qualifications and experience listed on an application versus those listed online. Lying, in other words;
- obviously poor communication skills. spilling grammer punctuation's, and Sentence structure were judged to be beyond the abilities of 31% of candidates. Think that's unfair? Tough shit, that's the way it is. Why get someone on board who causes fifteen queries on the meaning of every email they send out, simply because they're too bone idle to punctuate it correctly? In the real world, people actually die because of mistakes in communication but, at the very least, professional and business credibility can be instantly lost when people see your incomprehensible garbage spewed forth in something as simple as an email. If you cannot or will not follow normal conventions when writing and posting, you deserve everything you don't get and slow death is inevitable;
- inappropriate comments or behaviour. This was grounds for rejection for a massive 49% of candidates. Inappropriate pictures and abusive discriminatory statements are obvious problems but so too were bad-mouthing previous employers, betraying confidential information and abusing co-workers.

Even winning a job and starting work does not mean that you're necessarily clear of your old online dirty linen. The recent case of the seventeen year old Kent youth police and crime commissioner deciding to quit her job, as a result of previous tweets she'd made, serves to sharply illustrate the point.

On the other side of the coin, over half of organisations found evidence that caused them to look more positively on a candidate in comparison to their peer competitors and hire them. Top influencers were:

- a strong, positive profile which supported a candidate's professional image, qualifications and ambitions;
- rock-solid communication skills;

- a well-rounded personality, judged to be a good fit with the organisation in terms of attitudes and behaviour towards others and
- good references about the candidate, posted by other people.

Very clearly, every minute you positively and proactively invest in your public profile, via your social networks, will pay you back in spades once you've managed to engage with a potential employer and start to follow the application and selection processes.

Don't hang out online in the same section of swamp as a collection of other like-minded golf ball designers. It's easy to do. There's probably a group and it's tempting to join. You imagine potential employers will flock to it and pluck you out. Unfortunately, doing this is about as mindless as introducing Gary Glitter to your kids at a pool party and getting Jim to fix them afterwards. If you do, to a potential employer you risk looking just like all the others in the swamp and your odds shrink back to 1 in a 100 or worse.

Instead, hang out in places where the potential employers who employ golf ball designers hang out. Get yourself known to them by plugging in quietly, understand how things work and then raise your head above the parapet with a quiet call of, "I'm here and I've got something intelligent to contribute."

Make sure that all of your supporting social network ducks are in a well-disciplined row so that, if people click links, they see what you want them to see – evidence of your professionalism. Your odds will rise instantly back to one in a few. Maybe even to that holy grail shortlist of one.

Okay, we've covered the big five: shortlist of one; friends and family; adverts; networking and social networking. What other paths can you beat through the jungle to flush out potential employers?

Ask at your existing place of work, if you have one. If you're looking to move up, assess whether it's possible and desirable with your present employer. Even if you're only a part-time casual worker or a volunteer, there is no harm in putting yourself forward and making your ambitions known.

Know what you want and plan what you'll say, carefully.

This obviously works better with larger multi-site organisations, but if you're a valued and reliable existing employee, why wouldn't they want to keep you and help you towards more responsibility, better pay and improved prospects?

In my experience, although it's a risk, it's comparatively rare for a mean-spirited boss to hold you back because they value you too much or they see you as a threat. In any event, even if that occurs, you can bet more senior people will see it happening and come hunting for them at some stage.

Ask at previous places of work. This is a frequently un-mined vein of pure gold. If you've worked somewhere previously, check to see if they're currently recruiting. If they're not, make contact with someone inside the organisation and ask about opportunities that may arise for which you might be eligible.

Why is this so important a route to consider?

According to the High Fliers Research report mentioned earlier, recruiters amongst the top graduate employers expect that one third of all their vacancies will be filled with people already known to them.

One third.

These successful recruits will have worked within the organisation, either as an intern, on an industrial placement, through project work or during a period of vacation work.

The report identified that, of the UK's leading graduate employers:

- over 80% offer paid work experience programmes for students and recent graduates;
- 50% provide industrial placements for undergraduates, commonly for 6-12 months and
- 50% run paid vacation internships which last more than three weeks.

There is obviously a fair amount of opportunity to gain work experience with those leading employers (and others), whether or not you're presently able to apply for a permanent position with them.

Regardless, the fact that employers look more kindly on people they already know provides a very strong indicator for you to consider actively talking to the places where you're already known.

The issue of work experience is clearly an important one. More than 50% of the recruiters who took part in the research warned that graduates with zero work experience anywhere, "… have little or no chance of receiving a job offer for their organisations' graduate programmes." Take note.

Talk to local employers. Look at town centres, industrial estates and retail parks. Many of the retail chains and local bars and shops post details of vacancies on their windows or notice boards. They might also post these online, but there is no substitute for smiling, face-to-face, human contact.

Even if they don't have a notice board, walk in and ask. What have you got to lose? Anyway, the staff often have useful background information or know of what else is around. Quite often they'll point you to head office, in which case you might well have collected two names – the person to contact who can actually help you, plus the name of the person who is referring you. It's a small step, but a useful one and it all helps.

Whilst, with a degree, you're likely to be looking further up the tree than shelf stacker, checkout operator or bar person, bear in mind that the hotel, restaurant and retail industries, amongst some others, are famous for enabling bottom to top long-term career progression for good people. Got a third or worse and struggling to clamber onto the greasy pole? This is a way. Got a first and you're a complete rebel? This is a way.

Beating the system from the inside is a tough mission but no-one on earth can say you don't understand how things really work as you move up into management. When you're in a hotel room trying to change the sheets for the third time that day, whilst the police are collecting evidence, the manager is wondering whether to redecorate or put a frame around the blood stains and call it art and people are waiting to rent the room for the next two hours, you'll really know how that business works.

You'd need to be prepared to stay focused and keep pushing over the long haul but hell, you have to do that anyway. The money won't be great at the start but it's a real job which covers your arse, the experience will be invaluable and you never know what opportunities to develop your career will crop up in that organisation. If you're good, recognition eventually follows.

Remember also, counter-intuitively, it's always easier to get a job if you already have a job. It demonstrates that you are potty trained and can actually get up in the morning and do something in a disciplined way.

Recruitment agencies. Different agencies will tend to focus on their own specific areas of expertise such as office work, the building trade, accountancy, administration, manufacturing and engineering, managerial work, executive recruitment etc. Some focus on temporary work, some on supplying people for permanent positions. They've all got their own niches.

Look at each carefully to make sure you're not pinning your hopes on one that has zero chance of finding you work because it's not their speciality.

However you are obliged to submit your details, try and build a personal relationship with as many people as you can inside the agency. Try and get in to see them but at the very least, talk to them on the telephone. Use Facebook and LinkedIn to connect with them. Keep your name, face and needs front and centre of their attention. After a while, they'll feel guilty for not finding you something and consequently feel obligated to put your name forward first.

This approach works well for getting you fed with regular temporary work; it's a question of building up trust and reliability. Although your objective might well be to find a permanent position, temping experience can prove invaluable when you are finally able to apply for what you're really after.

A personal website and / or a blog. This is a great way to pitch your virtues to potential employers if you can get them to look at it. It would be optimistic to expect that droves of employers will be trawling the net to look for potential candidates just like you, so it's not worth getting hung up on search engine optimisation (SEO). Instead, you need to engage in activity that herds willing people towards to your pages.

Note that emailing an entire industry with a link to your site and a demand that they use it will simply alienate you from that industry. However, posting intelligent comment elsewhere and providing a link as part of your signature will self-select potential visitors for relevancy. Visitors may be small in number but if they are highly relevant, your odds are considerably better.

A brochure-ware style of site design is the entry point for you, enabling you to summarise your qualifications, experience and virtues. The bottom line is that, if you can use a word processing programme, you can design and update your web pages.

Customisable templates make it ridiculously easy to adapt the style, colours and imagery, so that the content you add looks thoroughly professional. Often you can get easy-update hosted web-space and templates for free.

Note the word 'update' in that last sentence. For God's sake update your pages regularly. It doesn't have to be a massive mish, just ensure that 100% of the content is still relevant and add a couple of fresh bits now and then to make it clear that your site is not rotting from the inside. Nothing puts visitors off faster than landing on your pages, only to find tumble-weed blowing past the dead skeleton of your once ambitious expectations.

A step up is to consider writing a blog. If you've got the time, something to say and you can write intelligent content, running a blog from your site is a great way to encourage both more, and repeat, visitors. Again, your emphasis should be on updating at least weekly, so if you're going to do this, make sure you have a theme that you can run with for an extended period.

Setting up and adding regularly to your blog is quick and easy with sites like Wordpress but there are many others that enable you to do that just as well.

A good, well written blog is an excellent way of increasing your chance of building your reputation and getting noticed by potential employers, if you can get them to look at it and engage with you. In this respect, a blog is more valuable than flat web pages because, every time you update your blog, you have a valid opportunity to post the fact to relevant discussions on forums.

You've also got a good excuse to re-email people, thereby keeping yourself uppermost in their mind. Just beware of over-doing it. The second you're seen as a spammer, you'll be floating face down in the swamp for a long time.

You can step things up even further by running your own subscribe-to email lists, discussion boards, forums and news feeds. It's well within the capabilities of one person to do that, provided that you have the time and the dedication to keep it fed. It's not a step for everyone, as you must have a strong enough theme or purpose to build it all around.

Drupal is free and easy enough to operate; just beware of the steep learning curve and the longer time needed to get things set up.

Clearly, a web site and blog will dovetail neatly into your social networking activity and complement each other perfectly, since each can feed visitors into the other. As tools to encourage engagement with you, they're invaluable.

Online job sites. This is an obvious port of call, but therein lies its problem. It's so obvious, everyone registers, even when they're not actually really looking for a job. The sheer volume of applications from half-hearted hangers-on may swamp any advertised position. Remember the Craigslist example earlier? You have a very high chance of your application being tossed aside because it only gets ten seconds of attention, if that. I'd suggest your chances of being selected for interview are almost, but not quite, random.

I'm over-generalising, but the knock-on impact is that such sites can attract adverts for low-quality positions, offering poor pay. Fagin-style employers may be trying a punt to see if they can get slave labour that they can sadistically use and abuse. Career prospects for such roles may be low. Nevertheless, they are a route and you never know what might turn up.

As with press adverts, the more specialised the requirement, the better your odds are, if you fit the profile and can find an edge. If you can find a job site which specialises in a particular industry, job function or field, your chances of finding a real position with sensible employment terms will increase markedly.

If you have a particular employer in mind that you'd like to work for, watching the jobs section of their website can be highly worthwhile. Be aware that you can usually elect to be notified of job opportunities by email but you should still browse their site regularly as things can get missed.

Getting head-hunted. I felt I ought to mention something about pond-life at this point. There is a category of malignant predator floating in the swamp that you need to beware of, if you don't want to get sucked under. I don't mean head-hunters per se. There are some very professional outfits about, but they normally need to work on roles offering well upwards of 100k a year to make a living at what they do.

Nationally operating recruitment agencies, and their job-sites, normally spend their sales budget finding potential employers with vacancies and they spend their marketing budget encouraging people like you and I to register with them. Apart from straightforward advertising, they can match people on their database to jobs coming up and look for a best fit. Works well, nice one.

The fly gets stuck in the camouflage paint when the agencies are starting out and have neither sales nor advertising budgets, or when they just think they've found a cheaper way of doing things. They stalk big employers' listed vacancies and, for any given job, they then trawl LinkedIn for suitable candidates like me and thee. The upshot is, you get an email or a phone call telling you how absolutely stupendous you are and they claim they have a client gagging for what you've got packed in your lunch box.

> "Can you just drop us a suitable updated CV?"

Then they head off to the big company.

> "Hey, we've just got a great gal onto our books and she's perfect for a role I just happened to notice you're advertising. Can I send her details through?"

Of course there's a fee-proposal that goes with that so, unsurprisingly, there's a loud bang as the agent gets the good news down the phone from the verbal equivalent of a Glock. Then he comes back to you and you get the same hole through your head from the ricochet.

Oh well, c'est la vie, but seems harmless enough? In fact it can be quite a large waste of your time if you've been doing your bit professionally by studying the brief, researching the organisation and tailoring your CV accordingly. That can, and should, take between half and one day, but in this case you have almost zero chance of getting anything out of it.

Okay, you've registered with an agency who might come back to you but you could have done that in less than a minute online, with a more generic CV. The agency gets to build their database on the cheap and has started the first steps of relationship building with potential big-company clients, largely using a chunk of your life as currency.

They sound awfully like the networking hustlers we met earlier, don't they? Is there anything you can do to spot them? If you could meet face-to-face you'd notice straightaway that they have truly huge, leathery balls covered in massive callouses, grown from being repeatedly kicked full-force in the crotch.

As you won't get to meet them, you have to be a bit smarter. Common sense is a good first line of defence. I mean no disrespect, but who the hell in their right mind is ever going to head-hunt you at this stage of your career?

Unless you finished a PhD in earth-worm husbandry last week and Worms-R-Us have such a vacancy but the job's in Afghanistan and they consequently have no applicants and had to resort to head-hunting, it's just not going to happen.

Secondly, reading the brief can often give you a good clue that something's not quite tickety boo. It'll be too brief. No pun intended.

Online adverts usually offer up the barest minimum of information. A proper brief is normally a very weighty document indeed so the dead give-away is when there are minimal details about the package inside the brief given to you. It leaves you with more questions than answers, and that's quite handy.

So thirdly, after reading the brief but before wasting your time, ask a few well targeted questions of the agent and see if you get credible answers back.

Another dead give-away will be when they have to 'go back and discuss it further with the client'. No client will ever provide a brief to an agent and not include full details of the job, the organisation, the candidate-profile and the package. If they do leave these out, they'd just spend their entire life on the phone answering the same questions over and over again. If the agent doesn't have this to hand, he's either the world's sloppiest moron or he simply doesn't have a relationship with the client yet.

Fourthly, get the name of the person making contact and look 'em up on LinkedIn, Facebook etc. Turning the tables is always fun, and usually informative. If they've had this job for only six weeks and their previous job was milking cows in Dullardshire, then it would seem just a teensy bit unlikely that they're actually hobnobbing it with a major plc in London, Chanel in Paris or the EC government in Brussels.

If it looks too good to be true, it probably is, so step around the trap but, for a change, let's not leave a body behind. There's no point in being rude because you never know what's around the corner. If in doubt, your best bet is probably to say that it's not the job for you, but ask if you can register with them for future opportunities.

To tart your details around, they don't need to come back to you unless a real opportunity hoves into view. You never know, they might get lucky one day and therefore so might you, but at least now they're working for you and not the other way around. Cunning, huh?

Jobcentres. The government run 'Jobcentre' is another traditional path to tread, either physically to their office or metaphorically online to their site and online database,

'Jobcentre Plus'. The relevance to your ambitions may be limited, but take a look and see if you can make it work for you.

Networking. Did I mention networking? Not fully? Well then, talk to your family, your friends, your (ex) workmates, your distant acquaintances, the postman, the local garage attendant, the vet who just treated your cat, anyone in any address book you can steal, people you meet out and about, your friend's friends, charity collectors, door-to-door salesmen, the people who ring up trying to sell life insurance, the policewoman who's just pulled you over for speeding (after you've been booked, of course), Jehovah's Witnesses, the guy who's come around to unblock your drains, shop assistants, lollipop ladies, people sitting near you on the train and the guys lowering your dead granny into the ground on a rope (good odds, four in one go, or five if you catch the vicar's eye).

You get the idea, but keep it short, sharp and interesting. Keep a note of how many people you speak to each day and who they are so that, if you re-contact them, it's easy to pick up where you left off.

Social networking. Did I mention social networking? Oh.

Shortlist of one? Okay, I'll get my coat.

So, the above are some of the main paths you can hack through your own part of the jungle. Some are likely to work better than others for you, depending upon your background, preferences and likely career direction.

Job-search actions

Whichever path or paths you're choosing to follow, there are some generic actions that you can undertake to improve your chances.

Create a job-search action plan. Plan to get not just a job but *the* job you want. Write down the outcome you expect from your job-search.

Obviously that's a job, duh, but be specific:

- what type of job;
- at what level;
- with what type of employer;
- at what salary range;
- in which preferred locations;
- in support of what longer term career direction?

For each job-search path you intend to follow, list out the significant milestones along the road between where you are now and where you'd like to be. For example, let's say that you're after work as a graphic designer and the first path you're going to follow will involve an internet trawl and direct targeting of organisations to ask if they have any opportunities.

The major milestones you might set could be:

- define the scope of the job you want (as above);

- identify an organisation to contact;
- make an initial enquiry to find out about possible job opportunities;
- find the right relevant person for specific information;
- exchange initial information between the two of you;
- perhaps even meet relatively informally to exchange more information;
- submit an application;
- attend an interview;
- agree an offer.

Setting milestones in this way for each opportunity you identify keeps you moving forward and allows you to track progress in a meaningful way.

Bear in mind that you might naturally jump past a few steps with some organisations, depending upon how their recruitment practices are structured. With others, there may be many more steps involved in what turns out to be an arduous, byzantine process. Adapt your milestones accordingly.

With every step you take, be clear what you hope to get out of that step and what you want the next step to be. If you don't have clear objectives in mind when you engage with someone, you're just passing the time of day with them. That's nice, but useless.

Think of it this way: no-one is going to offer you job unless they've met you so you need to keep pushing your contacts down a line of growing involvement with you. When you start dealing with someone, always aim to get to the next step, probably in the following sequence:

- emails;
- instant messaging / SMS exchanges;
- telephone / Skype conversations;
- meetings.

No-one wants to just drink tea and catch-up with you so, if you move up a step, you can be pretty certain there's an opportunity somewhere down the line. Keep going until you get to it or the road comes to a dead end.

Incorporate these forms of contact into your milestone plan, if it will help.

For each opportunity you identify along each of the job-search routes you intend to follow, concentrate on your next milestone and note down:

- what actions you're going to take to get there;
- when you'll take them;
- what you expect to achieve.

Monitor your progress by recording:

- the results so far for each opportunity;
- the details of every contact you make;
- follow up actions to take with each (with dates).

That's all very simple to do but masks a substantial amount of work. Being systematic in your approach will save you a lot of time, enable you to learn faster and strongly increase your chances of success.

Prepare yourself. Plan for interviews, even at this stage. When you put yourself out there, people will ask you questions. The closer you get to a job, the more sharply focused will be the questions. Aim not to get caught on the hop and have to give unrehearsed, glib or even damaging answers.

You need to do some basic preparation work, just in case you get a phone call out of the blue, or bang into someone unexpectedly who can help you,.

For the specific job you have in mind:

- list ten questions you think you're most likely to get asked;
- construct the outline of an answer for each;
- write a concise version of each answer out longhand;
- rehearse speaking them until they're second nature to you.

Conversely, also:

- construct ten or so intelligent generic questions to put to the people you're likely to be meeting and talking to.

The better the questions you have at your disposal, the smarter you'll sound. People like talking about themselves, so you'll have instant relationship-building tools to hand if you've got questions people can respond to well.

Be prepared for the eventuality of a potential employer calling you for a 'quick chat'. Plan how you'll handle the situation if they call when you're in a meeting, in the bath or legless in a bar somewhere.

Be prepared so that, regardless of the timing, you can come across as someone who is controlled and copes well with the unexpected. Avoid sounding like your brain has just nipped out for a while or you're in training for a national 'like'-using competition.

Build your perceived value. When you're beginning to zero in on a particular role, check what the role and package on offer look like.

- How does the role compare to your originally defined ideal?
- Where do you score and where would you lose out?
- What's the minimum and what's the maximum they'd be likely to offer?
- Where do you feel that you could / should be in that range?
- What would make you happy?
- What's the level below which you'd feel hard done by?

It's not uncommon for employers to list a wide pay range but declare that offers will be dependent upon the candidate's ability and experience.

Right. So they're prepared to pay bottom dollar if only they can find a numpty for the post? On planet Earth, employers want the best they can get so such an approach is clearly crap and the employer is just looking for a cheap deal.

There are several things you can do to overcome such strategies.

- Maintain a sense of perspective. There is no point in getting your hopes up by wasting time on an opportunity that you'll be disappointed in, when they offer you a bowl of gruel and a box of bog roll each week. If you do have to compromise, perhaps on salary, location or prospects, make sure it's your choice to do so, or not.
- Develop a positive mind-set. Know why you're following an opportunity, what you want to get out of it and what your limits are. It will strongly help your motivation, focus and prospects if you really want a certain position. If you're just dragging yourself grudgingly through the motions and not that enthusiastic, it will show and harm your prospects.
- Avoid underselling yourself. In any discussions, maintain a clear sense of your own worth right from the get go. Simply being clear that you know you are a strong candidate will underpin your application and remove any expectations that you can be had for a knock-down price.
- Subtly imply that you're a valuable proposition with several irons in the fire. It will markedly enhance your perceived value in the mind of the potential employer.
- Avoid early discussions about salary. You risk accidentally pitching yourself into the cheap seats or pricing yourself out of the market. If you're asked about your salary or package expectations, try asking what range the organisation expects to be able to offer. Make it clear that, due to your strengths, you'd expect to be towards the top end.

So, head people off at the pass by making it clear you're confident of your own value and you know what's reasonable in the circumstances.

Make contact with people. Organisations can't help you, but people can. You have to find them, reach out to them and develop a proper relationship.

It's the reaching out part that most people have a problem with but have confidence, they won't bite you. If you've got the name of someone relevant who can help you, make contact any way you choose but get to the point where you can exchange a meaningful dialogue with them.

Contact might perhaps start with email, but never forget the telephone. It's a powerful weapon, particularly with the near ubiquity of mobiles. Speak directly to people at the first available opportunity.

Once you've moved from being just a contact to being a human being in their mind, you've made a big leap forward and have someone on your side.

Call with a purpose. No-one minds answering a call if it's interesting, relevant and beneficial; everyone resents the intrusion if it's a waste of time.

Call at an appropriate time. Put yourself in the shoes of the other person. If you can, pre-arrange a time to call using email or IM etc. Don't make it a mish, just ask when's a good time because you'd like to talk about … blah blah.

Apart from when you've already got an on-going relationship, the phone can be useful to open doors. It's good for:

- chasing your way into the hierarchy of an organisation to find out who's the correct person to talk to. Start with the main switchboard but be ready with what you want to say when you get put through to someone;
- when you can't get a response by any other means, such as via email;
- when it becomes mindlessly cumbersome to persist with long emails;
- moving your relationship forward to the next level.

You can learn so much more about someone by talking to them.

As a relationship building tool, the only thing that will beat the phone is a face-to-face meeting, so there's your next objective. Just make sure not to push too hard and come across as a stalker. Be sensitive to the time pressures others may be under.

Don't waste time waiting. Things can be slow to move, people have other priorities and decisions might be slow to get made so use waiting-time by:

- finding more opportunities;
- adding to your experience;
- learning another language;
- developing further value-adding skills;
- doing part-time or voluntary work;
- improving communication skills;
- running a blog;
- extending your knowledge on core subjects.

Anything that keeps you growing will ultimately move you forward.

Doing something meaningful will keep you feeling positive.

Always pursue the three 'B's. Be positive. Be enthusiastic. Be optimistic.

If you want to wallow in misery, fearing that the light at the end of the tunnel is the oncoming one-way-only unemployment express train to hell and Old Nick himself has the hammer down, consider killing yourself now and do the rest of us a favour.

Why?

Because you never know what will turn up next week.

If you look, you'll eventually find. If you're positive, people will give. If you're negative, people will walk away. Who wants to employ a miserable bastard?

If you're lying in the gutter and moaning for Britain, people will leave you to it. If you're lying in the gutter and trying to get up again, somebody will help you. The majority of people love those who just will not quit.

If a potential employer rings you out of the blue for a 'quick chat', excusing yourself as being a bit down because you've just been kicked in the teeth with a rejection letter will see the person on the end of the phone lining up their right boot for a good go as well. Who wants a loser? Get a grip, be positive.

So, let's say you're in one of those situations where it's all gone badly wrong for you. You've just had a rejection for something you were certain you'd get. You're mortified because in a fit of anger you kicked the cat inside out. Your flatmates have had to sedate you to stop you hacking at your wrists with the metal top from a bottle of Stoli.

Bummer.

I sympathise, but I would rather attempt to shave my own nuts with a chainsaw than choose to listen to you moan about it. It's tough but your strongest tool is resilience. You're a soldier: get up, move on.

If the devil wants to take you down, give him one hell of a fight because tomorrow really is another day. You'll always win in the end if you just simply will not stop. Rise from the dead; who knows what the day will bring?

Key point summary 3 - Searches

Key Learning points

- It's essential to clearly analyse any job opportunities that you flush out. The more you understand about the organisation's requirements, the more successfully you can portray yourself as a good match to them.
- Understand the three main search methodologies you can use: harvesting; hunting; gathering. There's no right or wrong way but understand which works best for you and work hard at it. Remember not to neglect the others.
- The size of organisation tends to influence how they'll search for candidates and advertise available posts so adapt your own search paths and application strategy.
- Knowing and therefore believing that a particular search path really can bear fruit makes a significant difference to your likelihood of success. A prime example is the cold-calling 'shortlist of one' search path.
- Fortune favours the proactive. Never underestimate the potential value of opportunistically discussing your search with people you know and meet. Very many jobs never reach the point of being openly advertised.
- Adverts are only truly useful if: you're a very good match; they're tightly targeted; you can see an edge for yourself.
- In a job-search, your first challenge is to win an interview. Trying to win the job outright is counterproductive.
- It's important to engage with your contacts regularly, ask them for help when appropriate and keep them updated on your progress.
- Talk to everyone but don't try to connect with them all, only the people and organisations who prove to be relevant. Aim for quality, not quantity.
- It's important to try and build your perceived value when you engage with people. Avoid underselling yourself at all costs.
- Whatever happens, no one wants a loser so don't behave like one. Get a grip: be positive; be enthusiastic; be optimistic.

Signposts

- Organisations can't help you, people can. Reach out, it's easier than you first think.
- Search openly, positively and thoroughly and tell people clearly what type of job you're looking for.
- Large organisations tend to run highly-structured and well-defined selection, induction and career development programmes, making it easy to understand what you'll be going through.
- Small organisations vary considerably in their approach to recruitment. Career development may be more haphazard but progress through the hierarchy may be faster. Small does not equate to unprofessional.
- The sector the organisation operates in (private, public, third) will govern their values and recruitment methodology. You'll need to adapt your approach accordingly.

- Job adverts, online or offline, are more valuable to you if they have a narrower scope of requirements and you can match them. A very wide scope makes for a considerably more random selection process.
- Responding to a tightly targeted advert can give you odds of a one in two chance of being invited for an interview.
- Networking is creating a group of acquaintances and keeping it active via regular communication for mutual benefit.
- Aim to keep your online presence professional and positive because many employers research potential candidates online.
  - Top influencing positive factors are: a professional profile; a well-rounded personality; positive references from others.
  - Key causes of rejection are: mismatches between real-world and online data; poor communication skills; poor behaviour.
- A personal website or blog can enhance your reputation and provides a reason to keep in contact with your network.
- If you use an agency, build a personal relationship with them.
- Online job sites get swamped and can be discouraging to use.
- Pick up the telephone to step things forward and help build relationships.

Actions

- Create a well-defined job-search action plan which includes the significant milestones along the route to winning a job.
- Tell absolutely everyone you know and everyone you meet that you're looking for a job and what type of work you're after.
- Use the following major search-paths:
  - a shortlist of one;
  - friends and family;
  - job adverts;
  - networking (real world);
  - social networking (online);
  - current and previous employers;
  - local employers;
  - recruitment agencies;
  - online job sites;
  - personal website or blog;
- Engage with your contacts regularly, ask them for help when appropriate and keep them updated on your progress.
- Avoid hanging out in online groups full of people who are similar to you. Hang out in places where employers hang out, instead.
- Move forward with useful contacts by stepping up your engagement from emails / IMs to telephone conversations and on to meetings.
- Prepare yourself early on for discussions, meetings and interviews, just in case something crops up unexpectedly. Avoid discussing salary.
- Never waste time waiting, use it to improve your capabilities.

Chapter 4 – Applications: killing the opposition

"Remember chaps, there's a war on." Edmund Blackadder.

In the jungle, how do you out-run a tiger? Who cares? You only need to out-run that person standing next to you. Can you do that? A good pair of trainers would help, but much better, even if you're wearing clogs and a pink onesie, is to know that you can pull a sub ten second hundred metres out of the bag if you have to. Even allowing for an adrenaline rush that would make Niagara Falls look like the last shake before bedtime, you're simply not going to make it if the other person is fitter than you, trainers or no trainers.

Staring into the tiger's eyes and smelling its fetid breath is not the time to be planning a training programme to up your game a tad. The world isn't going to stop whilst you get yourself sorted. A breath of modest I-don't-like-to-be-seen-to-be-trying-too-hard amateurism will be your last. There'll be no opportunity for a second chance once your head comes off and there's a beautiful rainbow arcing through a fountain of your own blood.

So, here you are today, ready to ship off an application, perhaps several, in the hope of getting an invitation to meet the tiger so that you can be judged against the other applicants. How do you think it's going to go? Will you be the one to escape being killed by your peers and eaten by that tiger? Who knows, but if it were me, I'm shit-scared of tigers so in the meantime I'd be training sixteen hours a day and sharpening my knife.

Let's put interview preparation aside until the next chapter and for now let's focus on your prime objective: preparing an application that will get you selected as an interview candidate for the particular job you've flushed out.

We'll work through the following major topics:

- understanding your challenge;
- application selection processes;
- understanding what employers actually want;
- preparing to apply;
- putting your application together;
- proofreading your application and submitting it.

Applications can take different forms so we'll look at the various elements that may go to make up your entire submission:

- a curriculum vitae (or résumé as it's sometimes called);
- paper application forms;
- online application forms and
- covering letters.

How you approach each of those also depends upon the type of organisation to which you're applying. Applications for public sector and third sector posts need to be completed very differently to private sector ones so we'll look at the differences between the two and how best to approach each.

Some questions you may be asked during the application process could be competency-based and we'll take a look at how to deal with those in detail.

You won't be warned when one is asked. Failure to spot such questions will severely reduce your chances of making a successful application as they require more highly-structured answers than you may be used to giving.

Don't feel daunted, forewarned is forearmed.

You can turn all of the potential pitfalls to your major advantage if you know how to spot them and your peers don't. The bigger the challenge, the more you can swing the odds to your favour.

Right then, let's get started.

Understanding your challenge

The very first thing to be aware of is that you are not trying to actually win that job at this point. Your objective is only to make it through to the next stage. This is vitally important. Yes, your application needs to cover the whole territory requested in the job specification but the person reading your application has only one function – to operate the first stage selection process. You therefore need to appeal directly to them, to maximise your chance of making it through.

Secondly, what actually is the next stage after application submission? Traditionally, that would have been a face-to-face first interview with the recruitment agent running the search or with the prospective employer directly. In the name of efficiency, recruitment processes today typically break selection down into several stages, so make sure to find out what the next steps might be, if they're not stated. The more you understand about how you'll be assessed, the better you can prepare your application.

Thirdly, your application may or may not elicit a positive response but if it does you need not to be surprised and gormless-sounding when someone makes contact with you. Remember, the person running the next stage in the process has only one objective – to whittle down the list of potential candidates. You therefore always need to show the best of yourself if someone makes direct contact with you.

Fourthly, who are you actually trying to beat? Who is your enemy? It's tempting to focus on the recruiter but your job is in fact to seduce them, not kill them. He or she is simply the gatekeeper.

There are two elements to first-stage selection once you've submitted your application. Meeting the criteria laid down in the person specification is obviously one of them. It's a matching exercise. It's that simple and you need to tick all of the boxes. If you don't have what it takes, you don't make it through.

However, if you don't make the first cut, it's largely your fault. Either you just didn't score highly enough against the requirements, (in which case why are you submitting the application?), or else you didn't manage to fully convey that you really are an excellent match.

It's here that you can easily cruise up to that magic number of 823 rejections without even breaking into a sweat. You can apply for a job as a bio-weapons designer every day of the week but if all your experience is in childcare you can forget it, unless you've managed to systematically poison everyone you've ever looked after.

The second element is comparative. It's you against all of the other applicants. The hordes who want to kill you, in other words. Your prospective employer wants the very best they can possibly get, so all of the people meeting the advertised person specification are then further compared against each other to see who is 'best'. Whether that will be an objective or a subjective assessment depends upon the professionalism of the reviewer.

It's a very simple fact that, provided you match the base level of criteria laid down in the person specification, if no one else applies you will ultimately get the job. Hence, in the real world, you need to seduce the assessor whilst silently slaughtering the horde. It's a nasty job performed against an enemy you can't see but can imagine. Dallas had it easy in the ventilation shaft of the Nostromo with only one unknown enemy. At this early stage, you've possibly got hundreds of ruthless people trying to hunt you down in the dark. Every single one you stand above in the ranking is one you'll stand victorious over on the battlefield. Stay alert or die.

Application selection processes

Let's move on and take a look at some of the most common selection processes used against you by the gatekeepers. Once they've received your application, they have to decide who to shortlist for face-to-face interviews.

Software robots are likely to be the first line of defence you have to crack. For larger employers, or agencies who find themselves vetting people regularly, your application will be one of a bunch lodged in a database and the text of it will be scanned by a search-bot. It will be looking for key words and phrases, within your application, that tie in to the person specification and the job description created at the outset.

If you fall below a minimum score, you fail. You may or may not get a rejection note to let you know. Not getting even an email is common, but pretty poor IMHO. It creates a very bad impression about the potential employer, even though it may be the recruitment consultants who are the guilty party.

It's tempting to parrot all of the words and phrases from the job advert and brief. Unfortunately the software will also be programmed to reject any application that obviously includes blocks of text pasted across. Additionally, it does make for remarkably boring reading and your application will have to be read by a human being sooner or later, if you do get through the first cut.

Your best route through is to write your CV and application normally and then return at the end to check if it has the right key words in the right places.

An example might be where a job advert asks for candidates to have, say, a basic knowledge of Drupal running on an Apache web server. The software is likely to search your application and CV for the keywords 'Drupal', 'basic', 'Apache' and 'web server' in close proximity to each other, perhaps collectively somewhere near the word 'experience'. Understanding how this works and practising your technique is the surest way to improve your odds.

We'll cover more on how to analyse briefs and what to subsequently put in your CV and application later.

A human being is likely to be next up. They'll review the pile of applications that made the cut. Their objective will be to sift out the dross to leave a hard core bunch of highly credible potential candidates. If software search-bots are not being used then in fact the human will obviously be first in line.

Stories are legion about the alleged length of consideration time each CV or application might get and it varies from four seconds to around a minute. The reality is that each will get the attention it deserves. If you imagine a pile of one hundred CVs, it's likely to be attacked in two or three stages.

The first will be to sift out the definite no-nos. From experience, I can personally do that in less than an average of ten seconds for each. Note the word 'average' and be afraid. In rough order of looking, out will probably go:

- hand-written applications (too much of a ball-ache to pick through);
- poorly formatted CVs and covering letters (ditto);
- anything with spelling, punctuation and grammatical mistakes (if you can't be arsed to check it, why should someone be arsed to read it?);
- anything without the required qualifications (why did you send it in?);
- anything without the requested level of suitable experience;
- anything really unsuitable (a fourteen year gap year, for example);
- any weird hobbies and interests (what are these saying about you?);
- anything with an attempt at humour (seriously);
- anything with an appalling introductory paragraph (attempting ingratiation, for example);
- anything obviously unfocused (a random ramble through the irrelevant forests of your life);
- anything boring to read (life's too short) and
- anything that just makes the reader want to hurl.

Note that the reviewer is not supposed to be discriminatory. That's quite ironic when you think that the whole selection process is very clearly an exercise in discrimination. Even age is not supposed to be used as a judgement factor but it's pretty obvious that if the person specification is calling for someone 'dynamic' and you're eighty five years old, with no legs and lashed up to an iron lung, you probably won't get through even if you have got the world's best experience.

You could have put a whole day's effort into your application, the whole course of your future life can hang in the balance, and yet inside a few seconds you're nothing but a small red stain in the dirt. Harsh, but here's a tip for when you submit your application – do it right.

Note that the first run through is purely to find reasons to dump your application, not to find reasons to keep it. Be aware and dodge the bullets.

The second run through will be more thorough. The reviewer will be attempting to grade the pile into 'yes', 'no' and 'maybe' categories. It's here where your seduction of the reviewer begins. They will be trying to assess the quality of the match of each application against the criteria. The maybes will only get a look in if the pile of yeses is too small and causes anxiety.

The third and more detailed run through will be to cut the yeses down to a target number. Here the reviewer will be looking for 'extras'. What marks you out as a star candidate, relative to the brief and your fellow applicants?

It all sounds daunting, but simply knowing how these selection processes work and adapting your applications accordingly will improve your odds from less than one in a hundred to better than one in ten for winning that job.

Theoretically, if you submit ten high-quality applications, your odds of landing a job are solid. You might, however, be viewing the effort necessary to get yourself on to a shortlist of one slightly more enthusiastically by now.

Survivors are marched forward to the next stage in the selection process.

Profiling may well be next. It used to be applied later in the selection process due to the time, cost and controlled-environment face-time needed. Now, the internet provides a low-cost and convenient delivery, analysis and feedback platform, enabling profiling to be used much earlier in the selection process.

The objective of using profiling is to try and recruit candidates that are likely to succeed in their role, should they win through. Various surveys have suggested that only around 40% of recruitment decisions turn out to be fully successful in terms of job performance, judged against the original recruitment objectives. At best it's half and, at first glance, that suggests you may as well pick qualifying CVs at random with the toss of a coin.

Profiling tools try and improve those odds for the employers and the type of profiling tests used will depend upon the role being advertised.

Various 'intelligence' tests can assess ability in terms of numeracy, literacy and reasoning, usually by means of a fixed range of multiple choice questions set against the clock. When scored, there is likely to be a cut-off mark, below which your application will be bumped off the table.

Use the 6 Ps – Perfect Preparation Prevents Piss-Poor Performance – and practise these tests so that you are thoroughly familiar with the various types and formats of questions. You can take sample tests online for free, or you can buy booklets online or at large high street stationery stores.

Personality profiling tests are different and aim to uncover and explore what type of person you are and help predict your likely behaviour in certain circumstances. For example, if your basic personality dictates that you will always seek to avoid confrontation, then working as a prison officer, security guard or policeman are jobs that you are highly unlikely to be any good at.

Conversely, if you are the sort of dictatorial maniac who makes Joe Stalin look like a social worker, then a career as a primary school teacher is likely to go very badly wrong for you. If you have a personality inclined toward impatience, coupled with a low boredom threshold, you are extremely unlikely to make it as a forensic scientist. And so on.

It's generally not possible to fully practise these tests beforehand. In fact doing so would potentially reduce the value of the result if you did. What you can do, if you know the name of the test beforehand, is to familiarise yourself with the objectives of that test and understand how it relates to the real world.

When you sit a personality profile test you are normally asked to think of yourself in a specific situation, for example in a work setting, and answer the questions with that in mind. The result should be a profile of your personality as it would be in that setting. So, for example, if you were applying for a job as a management trainee, then there are certain qualities that would stand you in good stead in such a role and some that would be unhelpful to you. The test will expose the areas where you're a good fit and the areas where you're not.

How effective can such a test be? If applied as a rigid recruitment template such a test can be staggeringly bad. At least one major industrial plc applied a profile template to their managers and replaced the ones who didn't fit the designated profile adequately. That organisation is no longer with us.

The reality is that all organisations benefit from a range of personality types working within. The personality traits required for, say, sales are completely different to those required for a safety-critical role, such as that of engineer. Applying a standard 'management' template to both roles is mindless.

Using your resulting profile as a vehicle to jointly explore your suitability for a role works very well, provided that the interviewer is trained and is able to spend sufficient time with you on it.

I've sat many such tests and I've always found the results to be pretty accurate, if occasionally a little disturbing, and the insight that I've gained into my character has undoubtedly enabled me to achieve at a higher level than I otherwise would have. It's certainly helped me to develop my career in the right direction.

How honest should you be with your answers in a personality profiling test? After all, you're in a competition and trying to win that highly valuable job, aren't you? Well, I'd suggest to you that the last thing you want is to end up doing a job for which you are chronically ill-suited.

For that reason, answer honestly. Don't try and second guess 'the right answer' because there simply isn't one. Don't try and skew your result in a specific direction to suit a role because multiple questions are designed to be self-checking and you risk truly weird results coming out.

Do be honest with yourself about the results. Be accepting, rather than confrontational, with an interviewer. I'm not suggesting you agree with everything, taking the negatives right on the chin, but I am suggesting that you accept that you may have weaknesses. You're only human and being honest builds trust during an interview.

You can obviously talk about your highlighted strengths and how they will help you to do an excellent job, but if you can show that you accept at least part of a highlighted weakness, you can talk about how you can take account of it during your work and how you propose to consciously adapt your behaviour.

That makes you appear stronger than a candidate who is sitting there still banging on that the test is a load of inaccurate, slanderous crap. The result might easily be benchmarked against the thousands of people who sat it previously so your chances of arguing that the test is defective in your case are slim. It's true that your feelings on a particular day can skew the results but your basic personality traits will still be there, if you've answered honestly.

If you've answered dishonestly, you've got the devil's own job of talking your way around a weakness, because you simply don't own it and the results have no meaning for you.

If your personality profile is very clearly completely at odds with what would be useful for a particular job and you have no hope of explaining your way around it all, you might want to consider whether a career in that direction is really the right one for you and choose something more suited to your characteristics. Turn the negative into a positive.

The extent of profile testing used, indeed whether it is used at all, will largely depend upon the size of the recruiting organisation and the budget at their disposal. It is commonly applied where very large organisations plan for the long term and recruit for graduate development schemes.

Telephone interviews are increasingly being used as an early-stage selection process, to sift out the no-hopers and distil a shortlist of potential interview candidates. It may come before or after profile testing, depending upon the preferences of the organisation and the selection process they've chosen to operate.

The telephone interview may be introduced to you in the form of an 'informal quick chat', or it may be pitched as a more highly-structured and formal exercise. Either way, you need to be on the ball, as it's a do-or-die event for your application.

The next chapter deals with interview preparation, including telephone interviews, so for now, just be aware that the purpose of a telephone interview (and any other selection tools deployed) is to identify whether you are worth the time and cost of that crucial face-to-face meeting.

What is actually deployed will depend largely upon the size of the recruiting organisation and the budget at their disposal.

For a small organisation, just one person might select you for the interview shortlist, based on your CV, application and covering letter only. That may well be the same person you meet at interview. They might be from HR, your potential line manager or the head of the organisation.

With larger organisations, it's possible that the person running each stage will be different, making it harder for you to build up a rapport before the main interview. It's also possible that several people may be used separately, to assess your application, so that multiple perspectives can be developed and everyone's needs satisfied.

Understanding what employers actually want

If you understand what the brief is calling for and what the employer actually really wants in the way of characteristics, you'll know exactly how to tailor your CV and will be able pitch your application accordingly.

Unfortunately, in this tighter economic climate, employers are tending to be much more prescriptive about the qualifications, experience and skills that they require for particular roles. That can make it challenging to ensure that you fully match the requirements of the person specification.

It's pretty obvious that employers hire on a mix of:

- skills;
- experience;
- attitude and
- potential.

Now that you have an understanding of what application selection processes your application will be up against, let's see what you can do to seduce the gatekeepers.

The base level of requirements are likely to be that you'll:

- come across as interested;
- have a degree;
- have at least undertaken some relevant project work and / or
- ideally have relevant work experience from holidays, a working year out or from post-degree work.

If these don't meet the requested standards, to the level laid out in the brief, then your application will fail. Let's presume that they do meet that standard and let's also say that you've been very diligent and not committed any of the faux pas referred to earlier. That only keeps you in the game, it won't necessarily directly help you onto that final shortlist. So what will?

Employers often complain that most graduates lack the right skills.

This is a bit rich as many employers have deliberately cut back or eliminated training that they traditionally provided and yet universities have little or no means of delivering the real-world training, skills and experience that employers say they need graduates to have. Indeed, some universities would insist that preparing students for work is most definitely not part of their role.

Catch 22 rules. It's one of the contributory reasons why we simultaneously have a shortage of 'suitable' candidates, an unemployment issue and a productivity shortfall. Employers simply want someone else to pick up the tab of getting young people into a more employable, higher value-added state, whereas the government suggests that if an employer wants recruits to have particular vocational skills, then they should provide the training.

Great.

There is good news. This situation can be extremely useful for you since, if you can find a way to show that you do have the right skills and experience, even if it's a bit of a stretch, you're right in there with a free shot at an almost-open goal.

Let's look at the four key areas of skills, experience, attitude and potential in more detail.

Skills. What skills are employers asking for, in addition to the field-specific ones required for the role they're advertising? Employers' complaints about a lack of graduate skills can be summarised down into four main problem areas.

- Graduates lack an understanding of basic business functions such as accounting, operations, logistics, marketing, customer support, etc. Really? Wow, it's a shocker, isn't it? So you only get that understanding if you've had a suitable job but you can't get a suitable job because you don't have that understanding yet. Hmmn … how does that work then?
- Graduates lack a real-world perspective (heavy sigh) when it comes to understanding cost, time and resource constraints.
- Graduates lack relevant IT skills in a working environment.
- Graduates lack the ability to understand how teams function and how to work well inside one.

So, on the plus side, employers have just provided you with some free consultancy by listing those issues and showing you that they represent your four main opportunities – your challenges, if you like.

A primary action point is to ensure that your CV or application clearly demonstrates as many of the skills in those problem areas as you can muster. Even if, at first, you don't think that you have them, the chances are, if you work through your history carefully, you'll be able to cover each of them.

This is a secret-weapon moment for you.

Why the use of the word 'secret'? Because most adverts and briefs won't explicitly list those particular skills as requirements. Emphasis in the advert will appear to be more on the role-specific skills needed. That gives you an excellent opportunity to uniquely show some added value. You can stand out like a shining beacon in the midst of a grey crowd.

So if you're able to demonstrate some of those commonly-missing skills, you're much more likely to be selected for an interview. Furthermore, they will also go on to stand you in excellent stead during the interviews themselves.

Plan how to expand your experience in ways which will allow you to add these skills to your added-value armoury for future applications.

Do note that it is absolutely useless to have certain skills but fail to show an employer that you have them. Also, it's not enough to simply and baldly state that you have x, y or z skill – you really do need to show that you've gained or used those skills in real-world situations.

If you feel that you're struggling to prop up evidence of these real-world skills, don't become despondent. Next, and also later in this chapter, I'll show you how to draw on your more diverse experiences. You might be surprised at what you've already got under your belt that you can dust off and use.

Experience. I'm taking it as read that you can roughly match the core role-specific requirements requested by the brief – at least enough to justify putting in a serious application – rather than an, "Oh well, we'll see," application.

We're going to look deeper now, at trying to find previous experience which will enable you to show some added-value skills.

To get the ball rolling, think about anywhere you've worked previously.

- What work you did you do and for which departments?
- What business functions did those departments fulfil?
- Who were their internal or external customers?
- What services were delivered?
- To what standard?
- Did anything change during your stay there?
- Did anything improve?
- What were the benefits?
- What was your function there?
- What might you have contributed?
- Who did you work with?
- What were your responsibilities?
- Did you have any authority?

And so on.

It doesn't necessarily need to be big-company style employment experience that you have. Part-time work in a farm, factory, filling station, supermarket, drinking emporium, restaurant, charity shop, sandwich bar or cobbler's kiosk can be just as useful, if not more so.

Really?

Really.

A very small business has to operate all of the same functions as a mega-corp. It's purely a difference of scale. If you work part-time with a small employer for a while, the chances are very high that you'll have contact with most of the primary business functions within it.

The skills that you can show therefore depend a great deal upon how you think about the experience you've had and what you can distil out of it.

In a supermarket, for example, even as a shelf-stacker, you might get at least some exposure to all of sales, stock control, marketing, customer service, supplier management, facilities management and operations. Try getting that breadth of experience inside a very large organisation anytime soon, during part time, holiday or even project-year work.

Let's take the case of some part-time working experience gained at a small provincial supermarket. Everyone knows what that will have involved.

Or do they?

You can list your work experience as, "I worked in Joe's Mini-Mart as a shelf-stacker, part-time, for a year", and leave it at that. Your statement implies at least some real-world work experience and proof you do actually get up some days, presumably on time.

Is it really worth saying much more than that? It was work experience, what more does anyone need to know about your life as a shelf-stacker?

Well, you could add some information on the functional work that you undertook, in order to increase the perceived scope of your experience.

> "I worked in Joe's Mini-Mart part-time for a year where, apart from re-filling shelves, I helped with order planning and stock control as the company worked to implement a new stock system."

That's certainly a step forward. It suggests that your experience is wider than might be first thought from your previous basic statement.

However, to really hit home, you can distil out of your time at Joe's the deeper benefits you gained and explain more about your positive achievements.

> "During twelve months of part-time work at Joe's Mini-Mart, I gained detailed experience in all aspects of stock management, operations and customer service. I was directly involved with three other people in developing and implementing new stock-handling procedures in support of a promotional marketing campaign. We only had three months and a limited budget but didn't overrun either. I was asked to lead on improving supply-chain order planning and built an Excel spread-sheet to do that. Sales lifted by a sustained 23%, something that would not have been possible without the better processes we jointly implemented to support the marketing campaign.

> "I also opted to be trained as a first-aider and personally administered the kiss of life to a pensioner in aisle three, after she'd swallowed her false teeth."

So on the one hand you had a cheap-labour job inside a tin-pot, cowboy rip-off joint in darkest Dullsville, or on the other, you got a breadth of real-world experience, personal responsibility and achievement that a big-company employee could only dream about. Now who rocks?

All of that says so much about you that is positive. It ticks so many boxes that the poor person reviewing your application or CV is going to have to phone out for more sheets of paper to write it all down on.

- Primary business function experience – check.
- Understanding of cost, time and resource constraints – check.
- Application of IT in a real-world situation – check.
- Working effectively within a team – check.
- Plus – willingness to take on responsibility – check.
- Plus – dealing with the unexpected and coping in a crisis – check.
- Plus – delivering measureable benefits where you worked – check.

Who's ever going to remember to ask whether you got there on time? You've got a whole array of transferable skills to bring to the party; you're awesome.

Okay, it's in a small-town small-employer environment, and maybe even Joe would never think of his working life in those terms, but there's no reason why you can't look deeper and paint a bigger, more vivid, picture with which to surprise your potential employer.

The experience very clearly shows your potential. If someone put you in a bigger pond and gave you more responsibility, who knows what you could achieve?

The point is not that your experience is necessarily better or worse than your peer, who worked in a big-company environment. It's to show that you understand the wider requirements of the job and have more very real and relevant value-added skills that you could bring to bear, given the opportunity.

You stand taller than the horde because you're showing that you offer better potential than the other people applying.

Putting down "I worked in Joe's Mini-Mart part-time for a year" is an exercise in hope. It's better than nothing and you might get lucky, but you could just have been shelf-stacking, whilst doing a pound of grass a day, for all anyone knows. In fact, that's probably as much as they'd expect from someone working to get drinking vouchers and pay off some uni debt.

Note that there is no point in attacking the competition with a head-on salvo.

>"Pick me because everyone else is rubbish."

That may even be true, but no prospective employer is ever going to be truly comfortable, just selecting the least-worst choice. They prefer to go with positives, rather than being driven by the negatives, so keep your wits about you. You can actually have a lower quality of previous experience, but if you can successfully show the benefits of it, by putting it in the context of the role you're applying for, you'll be heading for that number one preferred candidate slot. This way, you're killing the opposition silently.

>"I worked as a volunteer in an Oxfam shop every Saturday for six months towards my Duke of Edinburgh Bronze award."

That's not bad. It ticks a few boxes. But what else did you get? I bet you worked on the tills for at least part of the time?

Trustworthy position – check.

People skills – check.

Sales skills – check.

You probably had to sort incoming donations, deal with the waste, price up goods, load up the racks and shelves, make things look attractive, organise sales discounts and promotions, keep the place clean, remove the drunks, and so on. That's all highly valuable experience if you show it and link it to the requirements of the job on offer.

And you did all that for free as a volunteer at a charity?

Motivation – check.

Social responsibility – check.

This is not all just an exercise in bullshit, designed to help you con your way up the food-chain. It's all very real and massively valuable experience. However, if you don't think of it that way, how are ever going to convey that value to a potential employer?

Explaining what you really did and putting it in perspective means that you're stalking through that jungle loaded for bear. You're clearly demonstrating that you see a bigger picture than your peers do. You're proactively managing yourself and you're on a higher plane.

To illustrate this point, we can look at another example.

I was providing outplacement support to an employee at a charity that was closing down due to a lack of funding caused by local government cut-backs. (Go Big Society.) He'd been there twelve months and was a graduate but hadn't been able to get onto a graduate training program. He'd taken this position, as an administrator, as it was the only thing he could get to fend off starvation. He was deeply worried that he was now valueless to any employer at a graduate level.

And this from a person with a 2:1, who presented himself very well and thought and acted in a mature and well-structured manner. His self-esteem was low and he was convinced that this was now curtains for his entire career. If, fresh out of university he couldn't get a job, what hope was there after twelve months, when there was yet another shed-load of more up-to-date graduates pouring out of uni?

Let me put a question to you. What did he have that they didn't?

The answer is:

- work experience;
- evidence of real-world personal responsibility and
- a track record of achievement.

He had all of those in spades.

After reading through the Joe's Mini-Mart example, you'd hopefully worked that out. If not, read it again.

By changing his thinking, re-focusing his approach and re-applying for graduate programmes, he immediately began to get selected for big-employer assessment centres. He was very quickly taken on by a large, globally-operating employer, without even a break between positions.

Solid.

Bear in mind, that it's not essential to have a year's post-degree work under your belt to build that sort of experience. It can be shown from any part-time or vacation work that you've undertaken.

Obviously project work gained during a sandwich degree, or from a project-year out, is really great experience, but you'll only get the most from it if you can show that it boosted your real-world skills and experience, relative to the role for which you are applying.

Even if you've only ever served in a student bar, break out what you did, what you've experienced, what you've learned and what you've achieved along the way. You may well be surprised and so might a prospective employer.

This is why it is so important to get any work experience that you can, paid, unpaid or voluntary. Imagine how much harder the person above would have found things if he'd said, "I'm not taking an administrator's job, I deserve more than that".

The message is – dig ditches, sell brushes door-to-door or clean toilets if you have to but, for your own sake, at least do something.

Assessment of attitude and potential is more subjective and these qualities are more easily shown at an interview. We're most of us able to quickly gauge another person's attitude after spending only a few minutes, or even seconds, in their company. However, we're seeing an attitude that is driven by relatively immediate-term events.

When someone is feeling particularly affected by something, for example their bank losing their student loan, they will be stressed, possibly angry. They may act out of character, they will complain a lot and may be perceived as a highly negative individual, if that's all we ever see of them.

And there's the rub. That's all a prospective employer will see of you – a snap-shot gathered from a CV / application, or a snap-shot gathered during an interview, at which you'll be under stress.

What will they see and how will they rate you? A complaining negative individual, or someone with enthusiasm, triumphing over adversity and therefore someone highly positive in their outlook?

It takes a lot of effort to convey a positive attitude and that work can be devalued with even one comment perceived as negative. People want to recruit winners and they use a positive attitude as a strong indicator of that potential. Negatives break the mood and put a downer on things.

Rule number one is to not say anything negative about anyone or anything on your CV or application. Ever. Run a final check for this. There should be no negative comments about previous employers, bosses or colleagues. Make everything you say into a positive.

Showing that you left a previous employer on such and such a date is simply a fact. Leaving because you were angry about being passed over for an improved position and felt you could do better somewhere else is reality. Unfortunately, putting that on your application presents the information as a negative and demonstrates that others thought you weren't a winner. That sends a flag up and the safest option will be to just bump your application off the table and into the shredder.

Instead, stating that you left to address a better career opportunity is a big proactive positive. Adding information about what you subsequently achieved will vindicate your decision and declare you a winner.

With a hundred CVs to go through and limited information available to you, would you select the positive, or the negative, person? The answer is obvious.

Secondly, irony and dry humour will not come across well on a CV, application or covering letter. Recruiters are used to reading straightforward, business-like documents. That's what they expect and that's what they'll see. Attempts at humour will be seen as inappropriate.

Moving to the positives, make sure that your experience demonstrates that you have a strong work ethic, as this is another key concern that employers have about recent graduates.

Employers also feel reassured if they can see that you have the character traits of adaptability, loyalty, trustworthiness, commitment and a sense of personal responsibility. Try to make sure that your experience shows as many of these as possible. Note that making a statement such as, "I am loyal," will cut no ice whatsoever. Anyone can make flat statements like that and you'll come across as shallow, if not actually manipulative. In your experience, try and find a way to show or directly imply that loyalty is one of your traits.

Potential fits into the same category. "I have potential," is only going to make the recruiter laugh as he shreds your paperwork, whereas it's hard to doubt the potential of the person in the Joe's Mini-Mart example earlier. It shines out like a beacon because the simple experience shows so many unexpected things about the candidate.

If you can meet the person-specification, you have the same potential as everyone else who submitted an application and meets it. After that, the more boxes you can tick against the 'extras', the better your chance of standing out.

Again, it's not necessarily what you've done, it's what you've got to show for it and whether you do in fact show it, or not.

Preparing to apply

So, if that's what employers want to see, what are you going to show them and how are you going to put across that you're a better bet than most?

Your application will ideally need to do three things perfectly:

- match the requirements of the advert or brief;
- exceed the implied extra personal requirements;
- demonstrate your higher potential, relative to your peers.

For a generic process, to keep yourself focused on a particular job opportunity, the following are the steps for getting yourself organised.

- Dissect each advert or brief in minute detail, word by word.
    - Identify what the candidate profile demands, making two lists – a) the openly stated requirements and b) the implied personal requirements.
    - Understand what the job will entail, by way of duties.

- o Recognise what doing the job excellently would produce in the way of outcomes and results for the department or organisation.
- Do background research on the organisation.
  - o Where does it fit into the industry?
  - o Who are its competitors?
  - o What's the history of the organisation?
  - o How is the organisation doing?
- Do background research on the role.
  - o Where does such a role fit into the industry?
  - o What type of people have done well in this role?
  - o How does the role fit into a career and what could be next?
- Point by point, now match yourself against the lists of requirements you made earlier, making bullet-point notes of your fit, by each point. Dredge up your whole past and really make it work for you.
- Make a separate list of the points which you think particularly distinguish you from other applicants. Distil this down to three key reasons why they should give the job to you and not someone else.
- Draft a concise covering letter that includes why you think you're an excellent match to the role and would be successful.
- Produce a tailored CV and / or competed application form.
- Re-read the whole of your application and be brutal:
  - o does it tick every single box against the list of requirements?
  - o trim out every surplus paragraph, sentence and word and
  - o make formatting, spelling, punctuation and grammar perfect.

That's tailoring for you. One simple word, one hell of a lot of ball-aching work. Still, what else would you be doing? With practice you'll inevitably get faster at pulling together ultra-high quality applications but in the short term, I'd suggest that each application is going to take you a full day to complete.

That probably breaks down into:

- half a day for the research and list making;
- half a day to draft your covering letter, CV and / or application and
- half a day to check it and re-edit it all again.

You might well find that the drafting work takes more than half a day to complete but do still force yourself through the checking phase at the end.

You may have noticed that's three half days there? Well, I did suggest spending a full day on it (which is up to twenty four hours long) and either that same evening or the next morning is a good time for checking, whilst it's all thoroughly fresh in your mind.

As an aside, remember our colleagues who've diligently fired 823 applications into the void? This process would have taken them almost five years to get them all out, assuming they took the weekends and Christmas off. I cite this as evidence that they undoubtedly didn't follow a proper process, paying only lip-service to the idea of tailoring.

In the light of this, how much more targeted can you make your next application and how many people will you silently cut down as a result?

Analysing the brief and the advert for its key requirements is fundamental. For the 'technical' aspects of a role, essential skills are normally listed in detail and are fairly easy to set about matching yourself to.

From the whole of the advert and any brief provided, make a list of each skill or type of experience stated or implied as required. Against each one, note down any qualifications, training, experience and items of background you have which support that point.

When you've finished, re-summarise your list and supporting notes so as to try and eliminate the duplication. Saying the same thing three times against three separate skill requirements won't reinforce your point, it'll make it look as though you don't have enough to say and have to keep repeating yourself.

Try and have a different supporting point or evidence of experience from your background against each requirement. It may not be entirely possible to avoid duplication but be conscious of it and try.

This is all hard work but these notes will be invaluable as you later pull together your CV and / or application. They will save you hours of time and considerably ramp up your chances of surviving the onslaught of the hordes.

After that, go back and re-study the advert or brief. There are usually phrases littered through both, sometimes dressed up in a dramatic style, about the characteristics of the person required. They may be very general and come across almost as padding, or they may be more specific and have a direct bearing on the selection process.

Let's have a look at some typical phrases used in ads or briefs and consider what they're asking for and how you can present yourself. Again, make a list of each phrase and then add notes about you, against each of them.

" … organised … ability to juggle multiple projects … work with minimum supervision … ."

It suggests the working environment is going to be fairly hectic, boundaries of responsibility may be grey and there'll be a need to often get by on your own, as your manager may be too busy to help you. It's quite possible that objectives and priorities may change at short notice. Organised panic rules?

It helps to set these words and phrases in the context of the actual job being advertised. That would give you more of an idea what you're in for, in this job.

In support of your application you'll need to weave in examples from both your education and work experience which show your ability to prioritise your workload, when you're being pulled in different directions simultaneously. Try to show instances where you either took, or were given, responsibility and you distilled an ordered plan out of the madness around you. Try and illustrate that you have an objective-focused mentality and that you cope well with self-management.

Try using words and phrases that include things like: "I was entrusted with …"; " … handled numerous projects …"; " … allocated resources according to …"; "… balanced the conflicting demands of A, B, C and D …".

"... a passion to work in ... a keen interest in ... enthusiastic and hardworking ... ."

These terms may be intended purely at face value to suggest that a person, truly interested in the field, would sit well within the role and the team. Alternatively, they may be implying that you'll be working long hours under a degree of pressure and will need a good background in the subject and your enthusiasm to get you through.

This is why your background research into the organisation, the industry and the typical duties involved in the role is so important, as what you find out will help you to put such comments into a meaningful context.

In any case, employers always prefer candidates who can show a real interest in the role, the organisation and the industry so your application needs to show this about you. Dig deep into your personal life and areas peripheral to your normal work or study for relevant experiences to show your interest.

Your covering letter can be useful here to state why you really want this job and, without creeping, why you're particularly interested in working for them.

Elsewhere, try and highlight your level of personal drive in this area. Use phrases like: "...I volunteered for ..."; "... additionally, in my own time, ..."; "... wanted an opportunity to ...".

Show your determination to get a job done with phrases like: "I pushed to ..."; "I vigorously pursued ..."; "I dedicated my efforts to ..."; "I had to develop my skills in the area of ..."; "I overcame ..."; "I exceeded expectations by ..."; "... exceeded targets ...".

"... self-starter ... proactive ... leader ... ."

These terms suggest you'll be bridging the gap between being given an objective or direction and how you end up getting there. They imply that there is unlikely to be a lot of help or guidance along the way. They further imply that you'll ideally be a fairly outgoing person, able to approach others from cold and win them around to assisting with your tasks.

Your CV or application will need to show how you've exhibited these traits in the past. Cast the net as widely as you like across study, career-related projects and work, non-career work and other personal interests.

Membership of clubs and societies can be useful if you've been particularly active within them or taken on positions of responsibility and addressed a particular challenge.

Especially useful would be any example of where you formed a group and led the way forward. Try and use words and phrases like: "I started ..."; "I originated ..."; "I launched ..."; "I instigated ..."; "... organised ... headed ... directed ... initiated ...".

Try and show the whole story including what you needed to achieve, how you pulled the situation together, what actions you took, how you interacted with others, any difficulties you experienced, how you overcame them, what the final result was and what difference it made. This doesn't have to be presented in a bound volume as less is definitely more. With practice you'll be able to distil such a story down to an efficient, short paragraph.

" … enjoy working in a team environment … excellent interpersonal skills … good communication skills … ".

The emphasis here is obviously focused on your ability to interrelate with others but don't stop at thinking it's all in the context of your peers. Teams, especially cross-functional and cross-hierarchical teams, can also include people considerably more senior to yourself or subordinate to you.

In an environment where you're working with more senior people, you may have an excellent opportunity to showcase your abilities but that can be a double-edged sword. Anyone appointing you will want to be sure that you'll be able to conduct yourself in a mature way, keep an open mind at all times, roll with the punches and be inclusive rather than exclusive in your dealings with people and their contributions, good or bad.

You might want to shine but bitching, back-stabbing and butt-fucking others in your team is the surest way not to do that. Some people unaccountably never actually realise that fact.

A few years ago, a friend of mine was working for one of the best known, globally-operating, blue-chip organisations in the world. He explained that the culture was such that he spent almost exactly a third of his time being stabbed in the back, a third stabbing others in the back and the final third actually doing some work. Understandably, that organisation dropped substantially down the world rankings until someone finally set about correcting the culture. My friend did a runner and found a better career path well before that.

Today it's much more widely recognised that such an environment will be unhealthily destructive, rather than constructive, as used to be thought. Anyone appointing you will need to be sure which way you'll swing.

Some people just are loners, bad in peer-group situations and achieve most when left entirely alone. That's not wrong, unless someone drops them into a situation that calls for a high level of team working, at which point madness prevails. Thus, there's a need to assess potential recruits carefully on the way in so that they don't end up in roles that won't suit them.

Try to show situations where you've had dealings with people and ideally try to illustrate a mixture of examples where you've not just worked in a team situation, but you've had to manage all of upwards, downwards and sideways.

Use phrases like: "I worked closely with xyz in order to …"; " … I co-ordinated activity …"; " … together overcoming the challenge of …"; "… liaising with …"; ".. kept people up to date …".

Your experience will obviously be limited at this stage of your career but you're looking to present yourself as comfortable dealing with people at all levels. Show that you're capable of putting yourself into others' shoes to understand their point of view but that you then have the confidence to do the right thing for the result. Show that you don't tend to ride rough-shod over the toes of everyone around you and show that you're aware of the need to influence others rather than dictate to them.

" … thrives under pressure … in a fast-paced competitive environment …".

Pressure means different things to different people at different times. If you've been held hostage by the Taliban for six months and were only freed by the SAS launching a dawn raid, during which three of your peers died and you lost a foot, then hearing the words, "I know it's impossible. I don't care how you do it, just get it done yesterday or don't bother coming back," from your boss at work is unlikely to even raise your pulse, let alone cause actual stress.

On the other side of that particular coin, there's a risk that your interest and motivation in that task your incompetent boss has just told you about will be low. It just won't push your buttons and lift the blood stream into a trot, let alone a gallop. You need a buzz, otherwise you're simply doing the minimum because you're paid to. If you want to develop, you have to push.

Ideally, you want to be facing a challenge that is sufficiently new, with a level of difficulty that will get your attention and cause sufficient anxiety to motivate you and keep you focused. In an ideal world, your employer wants just that for you, so that you're always pushing at the envelope of maximum achievement.

Different people will react differently to the same potentially stressful situation. Some will be bored, some will cope admirably and become high achievers and some will shrink to a blubbering wreck and chug valium, just at the mere prospect of the late delivery of a box of paperclips needed for a task.

Where do you sit in all of this? Do you enjoy pressure and lots of it with lots happening all around you constantly, or do you want a nice, quiet environment where you're left alone to face unrelenting pressure in your own way? What type of person is this role calling for? Any research you can do around the role you're applying for, particularly within that specific organisation, will enable you to steer your response correctly. Try and talk to people who work in the same organisation for clues.

Show examples where you managed to achieve a result in a difficult environment. Bear in mind that pressure comes from even simple things, like limited time and resources, not only from some yelling maniac on the verge of losing it big time because his departmental figures and career prospects are both heading south in a hurricane. Show that you've had to think on your feet.

Use words like: "… adapted to the situation …"; ".. responded to the highly challenging demands of …"; "… had to balance …"; "… exceeded expectations by managing to …".

During the recruitment process, it can be very difficult to assess someone's capability to withstand pressure. The bottom line is that the recruiter wants reassurance that you won't panic under stress and that you can keep your head, stay focused and turn the pressure to advantage, not meltdown.

"… good academic background … high-calibre graduate … excellent attention to detail …".

These phrases might suggest that the organisation is looking for a candidate with good 'technical skills', in the loosest sense of the word technical. In other words, a high degree of subject knowledge may be required in order to best fulfil the role. It's quite likely that selection will require a 2:1 or above. It's a fair bet that the role will involve a relatively high proportion of analytical work.

If you feel that your academic results may not be sufficient, look at these phrases in the context of the whole job advert. If the role is a very isolated and inward-looking research post, then you may struggle to establish your suitability. However, even research-based roles may involve teamwork and people-interaction and require communication skills, general IT skills, resource management skills and practical skills, amongst others.

In those circumstances, if you're very strong in those other areas and you can perhaps offer a USP (unique selling point), say through having worked on a very successful project in the exact field before, then you may feel that, on balance, it's worth a punt on your part. If so, I would say either do it to the max or don't do it. If you go in with an 'oh-well-we'll-see-what-happens' approach, you'll get wiped out because you won't put sufficient work into it. Your lack of determination will show through. Don't waste the effort.

If you are academically very strong, give your educational achievements a high prominence. Show additional, supporting project work that you may have undertaken in that field and highlight notable achievements. Don't forget any awards that you may have. Look at what broader experience you might have and what may best directly add to your credibility and desirability.

If you're academically nearer the bottom of what you think might be acceptable, put the emphasis more firmly on which skills, experience and achievements you might have, which support the broader list of candidate requirements. Don't hide your qualifications, but try to ensure that the recruiter gets to them after reading all of the other paragraphs which demonstrate in spades that you really are truly ideal for the role. If they are completely rigid on the level of academic qualifications required, then sadly you'll be shot.

Research is clearly a vital part of your preparation once you've picked apart the brief and understood what is being asked for. The more you can put the advertised role into a wider context, the better you'll understand how to present your strong suits.

For example, if you're applying for an advertised role in the printer division of a large organisation, stressing your absolute love of inkjet-printer design and your determination to work in that field until you die is all well and good, but if the organisation is in the throes of reversing out of that part of the market and is looking for suitable talent to bring on board and train for 'the next big thing', then your pitch is misdirected.

Research will help you avoid such pitfalls. If your research raises concerns about the medium-term viability of the advertised role, then you have some excellent discussion points to raise if you make it through to interview. In this example, if your research enabled you to understand the real position, your application would ideally illustrate your potential to develop as the organisation changes. That would also allow your sense of ambition to show through.

The recruiter is likely to have an insight into the organisation's plans. It's clearly not an exact science, but the closer you can align your CV to those anticipated developments, the better your chances of selection. By showing or implying the depth of research you've conducted, you're demonstrating that you're someone who is prepared to go the extra mile.

The results of your research will depend to some extent on the size of the organisation and how well it engages with the wider world. If you can find almost nothing about them, it doesn't necessarily matter as it's the same for everyone. In fact, it still tells you something. Either they're working in a highly secretive industry, they're in a sensitive commercial situation or perhaps they'd benefit from upping their marketing and PR efforts. Again, useful points for discussion, if you can get the chance to mention these things and find a way to illustrate that you've done some legwork.

Two things to avoid are, firstly, saying things like, "I have undertaken lots of research," and secondly, criticising the organisation as a result of it. The former comes across as naivety, creeping, narcissism or insecurity and the latter as complete arrogance. In reality, even if you could gather sufficient information to make an informed judgement, what would give you the insight into the organisation's real situation since you don't actually work there and have no vested interest yet? The world is full of back-seat drivers and the last thing they'll want is to recruit another know-all.

Your research will need to go well beyond a relatively passive drift through the organisation's website. You'll need to widen your research to take in websites which provide more general sector information and sites which focus on competitors, customers and suppliers for the organisation. Social network sites will help to extend your reach but don't forget the general media, including newspapers, trade magazines and research reports. Start from the general and then move towards the specific. Compile notes as you go.

- **Organisation.** Begin with the organisation itself. What does it do? For a large organisation, this could be a considerable number of things so how are the divisions organised? Which part would you be working in? Where does the organisation operate? What do the results look like? What're the backgrounds of the senior people? What are their vision and mission statements for the organisation? Does the organisation make its values public? What latest news are they reporting?
- **Sector.** Then take a look at how the organisation fits into the 'industry' in which it operates. Who are the main competitors? What is the economic climate like? What are the main industry trends? What pressure is the organisation under? What future opportunities does it have? What do external people say about the organisation? How does the performance of this organisation compare to others in the sector?
- **Job.** Move on to research the role. What's the main purpose of the department you'd be working in? What duties and responsibilities come with the job? What are the expected outputs? Do any service levels or key performance indicators (KPIs) relate to the department? Where does the role fit into the overall hierarchy of the organisation? Who would you deal with in doing the role? What would their expectations be? What are the three biggest challenges involved in doing the job well? How might work in this particular organisation compare to a similar

role in other organisations, in the same industry? What career opportunities might flow from the role?

- **People.** Finally, give your research a 'people' focus. Can you find people who actually work at the organisation? What are employees saying about the organisation in general and, ideally, the site, section or department you might be working in? What's the mood like? What's the culture – positive or negative? Can you engage with anyone quickly and get an immediate view about things? Is anyone talking about the selection processes that applied to them, perhaps from last year's intake? What do third party news and press articles say? Are opinions generally aligned, or are there conflicting views on issues?

You need to get your application in so you will obviously be time-limited in trying to find and engage with people. Exercise caution in any comments you make, or questions you pose: you never know where your words might end up. Be enthusiastic in your questioning but neutral in expressing opinions.

Bear in mind that you're not looking to build a thesis out of all this research. Keep it short, sharp and focused. Go for the headline aspects. Only drill down into real detail if there's a special reason to do so. More detailed research can come later, if you're invited for interview. In your attempts to dig out people-info, you can fairly quickly trawl up historic comments, if any are available, and plug into the various networks to see if anything's happening.

Don't let your hopes of getting a response from people hold up your timetable for collating and submitting your application. You can put any late responses towards interview preparation, if you make it through that far.

How soon should you submit? As soon as you possibly can. There's always a closing date listed. Do not miss it. If you do, you're finished. It's unprofessional for a shortlist to be drawn up before the closing date but it does happen, so the earlier you get your application in, the better. Inside twenty four hours is a great target to aim at. Don't leave it a few days if you have actually got the time.

Compile and summarise your research so that you can draw out highly focused conclusions against which to fit your experience as you later construct your application. Here are some steps that help.

- List out three to five positive things you've found out about the organisation and its place in the world. In your application later, try to dovetail your experience and achievements into these.
- List between three and five things about the organisation and the role that specifically attract you. Later, make your views clear somewhere within your CV, application and covering letter. The latter is very often the most useful for more directly conveying your personal feelings.
- Identify the major opportunities, goals and problems that the organisation faces. Use a SWOT analysis (strengths, weaknesses, opportunities, threats) to start. Note how your experience, abilities and potential could contribute to the future of the organisation. Later on, as you compile your application, you can show your

willingness to stand shoulder to shoulder with the organisation as it addresses those issues.

The latter point particularly will help to make clear your commercial awareness, a key factor in the eyes of employers today. Showing an in-depth, commercial understanding of the factors driving the real world can help strongly distinguish your application and slay a fair proportion of the horde.

If you want to test whether your research is really hitting the target, a good guide is to ask yourself the question, "Can what I've written apply to more than just this organisation?" If the answer is "yes" there is scope to dig further.

As an example, let's say the application process poses the question, "Why have you chosen to apply to MegaCorp?" A typical reply might be along the lines of "MegaCorp is one of the leading producers in this field." Fair enough. This shows that you're aware of the wider industry and implies you've performed some research (unless you're just repeating the blurb from the ad or MegaCorp's own website, in which case it's a low-grade comment).

However, the comment is pretty generic and could apply to a whole bunch of organisations. So, is the implication that you don't really care about MegaCorp and that any of several companies would do, so long as they're near the front? Does the comment also imply that your sole interest is in yourself and what you can take, rather than in the organisation and what you can give? Are you therefore the sort of person who will grab what you want and then leave, rendering the organisation's investment in you a busted flush?

It will depend a great deal on the person reviewing your application. They might not see it that way but they need to whittle the numbers down and that's one way of doing it, so why take that risk? If the best you can hope for, from your comment, is that the recruiter jumps over it without spotting the potential negatives in it, is it worthwhile making it in the first place?

To focus more tightly, you could say, "MegaCorp are established as one of the leaders in the industry but have an opportunity to be *the* leader when they launch product XYZ and I would very much like to be part of that initiative. I feel that I can strongly contribute because … ."

That very definitely shows that you're up to speed on where they are, where they're going and where you might fit into the equation. Better still, that comment can only really apply to MegaCorp. Even better, you're really saying that no other organisation will do and that MegaCorp are the only organisation at the present time who can give you that opportunity. You're grateful for it and want to contribute in return.

Not only have you removed the risk from the comment, you've turned it around to show why you should be the one standing on top of the corpses of your peers. Your application will go into the 'yes' stack. Pity the people who get theirs read after yours because, by comparison, they suddenly suck.

That's the real value of research and that's the very real benefit of getting your application in early.

Of course, not every potential employer is number one in their field, so your words will be different in each application, but your intent should be the same.

For example, "GigaCorp are third in the industry for sales of XYZ products but listed growth projections suggest that they have the ambition of seizing the number two spot within the next two years. I would be a strong asset in support of this goal because ..."

Again, such comments make it clear you've done some research and more importantly, you've got the wherewithal to understand what it means. You'd clearly be a valuable asset compared to a lot of other applicants.

So, in preparing to apply, that covers sweating the brief to within an inch of its life and researching the opportunity until it haemorrhages blood. Is there anything else you should do to prepare? As it happens, there is ...

Make things happen. Showing your past achievements is highly useful to demonstrate that you're worth having.

However, showing that you identified what to do, chose to do it and then made that result happen, regardless of problems on the way, is a whole order of magnitude further up the value chain. You're showing that you personally created something out of nothing.

The crux is, if you hadn't done it, it would never have been done.

That is radically different from, say, getting exam results by plodding along life's conveyor. It rates higher than being given a task by your boss, even though it's still you achieving that result, because if you hadn't done it, someone else would have been tasked. One way or another it would have got done.

If someone says to you, "There's a hill, conquer it," you're a foot-soldier.

If you think to yourself, "Looking at the bigger picture, I think we need to conquer that hill because blah blah and we need do it in such and such a way and by three o' clock on Sunday," then you're in charge. You're making decisions and making things happen.

People recruit graduates for their initiative and future potential. If you can show you've made things happen, then you're showing both of those.

In your application you can show achievements, just like the other applicants no doubt can (if they think about it in that way). Can you also reach further and show that you chose the direction and the actions to take so that you could make those achievements possible?

If you can, who shows the most long-term potential? Who's the stronger candidate? Who goes on the 'yes' pile? Yep, that will be you.

Who will catch a glint of light from the knife as the cut is made? Right, the rest of the pack, sitting on the wrong side of that cut.

Now, you've analysed the brief so that you know what's required for the role. You've researched, so that you understand how to match yourself to the role. Now work out how to show that you have a talent for making things happen.

At this stage of your career, no one expects you to have instigated programs which cured cancer, put people on Mars and solved world hunger. In reality, people don't expect much of you at all, except that you're educated in a field, you've got some limited experience and you can show a bit of ankle to express your potential.

That's why, if you can surprise the recruiter by showing that you're the type of person that makes things happen, you've got a clear shot at the target and can take a sure step over to the 'yes' pile.

As an example, listing personal achievements in public debating, amateur dramatics and script writing is an utterly weird and dangerous thing to do if you're looking at a job in waste disposal and recycling. However, if that job, or a significant part of it, involves a lot of internal or external communication, suddenly your wider background and skills slot neatly behind the role.

If you can then show that, whilst those things were obviously of personal interest, you recognised that you could proactively use them to develop your personal skillsets in a direction that would benefit your whole career and you made it happen, then that makes you a much more interesting candidate.

You made something happen that just wouldn't have, unless you'd seized the initiative.

Although that's a simple example developed from personal interests, exactly the same philosophy should drive your whole application as you consider your training and experience to date. Your achievements are highly valuable but more importantly, what did you do to make things happen? Who did you have to strangle until they gave in and let you do it. How much ass did you have to kick to get to the result? What sacrifices did you make?

This is so important because an organisation employs you with the full expectation that for the whole time you work with them, you'll spend your time making things happen. This is such an obvious expectation that it's barely thought about and it only becomes expressed through the job description, which in turn is broken down into lists of duties and responsibilities.

Having run several companies, I can tell you that you could not have listed my duties and responsibilities, in any of those roles, on anything less than a whole truck load of paper. The list becomes meaningless because, as the head honcho, I was ultimately responsible for all of it. If the loos didn't get cleaned, I carried the can, so to speak. So anyone who has run an organisation could offer the exact same experience of duties and responsibilities as me.

So what makes a difference? Making things happen.

Let's take a look at two young ladies reaching the back end of uni last year. They were both pushing hard at the job market and shipping out well-worked and quite tightly-focused applications.

The first was able to show that she'd been a Sunday employee of a high street retailer for the last two years of her degree. By virtue of being on the permanent staff, she'd been through the full induction programme. She'd gained some solid work experience in a professional world and was able to show some good achievements. That's a big score.

Let's focus on the second. She had it tough. From the outset of her degree, she'd wanted to make sure she'd get high-value work experience whilst studying, so as to make herself more employable at the end. She was terrified by press accounts of a dismal job market for graduates.

She'd worked out the generic skill sets that would stand her in good stead for the future and decided that, even though pay rates were lower, part-time retail work was the best way to develop those skills. She realised that she needed to target the area's major employers like Waitrose, Marks and Spencer and Boots because they would be able to provide quality training and a professional working environment. All of that would be better for her CV.

Researching, she found out that to receive full training she would need to be taken on to the permanent part-time staff rather than be employed as a casual. She made sure to tailor each of her applications, but getting a post was much harder than she expected. She was surprised to get repeatedly knocked back and had to take time to figure out why.

Her problem was the volume of competition. It was huge. Everyone, not just undergrads, wanted the same jobs, albeit often for different reasons, money being the most obvious one. Her experience was limited, she had nothing with which to really distinguish herself from the hundreds of other applicants.

She knew that she would stand a better chance if she applied to just any old retailer but realised that would devalue what she was looking for.

Instead, to get the relevant experience she wanted, she chose to take a gamble, side-step her main ambition and volunteer for six months in a charity shop.

That gave her the valuable experience she needed and as a direct result, she managed to win her desired post with a professional high street employer. The result was exactly as she'd planned. She ended up with a very valuable set of skills and experience that firmly supported her applications for a job in engineering.

What's retail got to do with engineering? Those wider skills she'd developed, especially the people-skills, came up trumps for her.

If it were you making the recruitment decision, which of those two applicants would you pick?

They both had the same experience, they could both show additional skillsets and they could both demonstrate achievement. However, the second young woman showed she'd worked it out and made it happen. It wasn't just a situation of bagging a job and then working hard – she'd chosen and re-chosen her direction. She'd sacrificed, she'd persisted and she'd won through.

And that's the key. She'd not just achieved something, she'd shown she could make something happen and for a reason.

Maybe in the early stages they'd both make the 'yes' pile but when the killing started to cull applicant numbers down to fit the shortlist, the second would have a significantly higher chance of making the cut.

In fact these two people were one and the same – someone I was coaching to improve their application hit rate. As soon as Jane added some backstory to show how she'd had to take the initiative and she'd made things happen for herself, she immediately began to win interview places.

An organisation or department will employ you to do something specific. If you don't do that you're excess baggage and ultimately, come the day of the Great Cull when times get tougher, you'll be toast. Certainly, an employer can make use of the skills you gained as a customer service operative (checkout operator, in other words) but to improve the odds, what an employer really wants is a customer service operative with teeth.

Show that's you by showing you make things happen.

There are your three kick-ass preparation actions that will make you a winner.

- Fully understand the brief's requirements so that you can match them.
- Dig for gold with your research and use it to push the right buttons.
- Show you're the type of person who makes things happen.

Putting your application together

Let's move forward and look at the various documents and forms that you might be asked to submit as part of your application. These may comprise any or all of:

- a curriculum vitae (CV) or résumé;
- a written application form;
- an online application form;
- a covering letter.

Whatever form your application ultimately takes, it should be:

- as short as possible, typed in a readable font, using a clear layout and be well titled so that it is easy to scan, as an aid to selective reading;
- written in the first person using short, sharp, easy to understand sentences and paragraphs;
- tailored to the role, the recruiting organisation and the 'industry' or field of work so that it directly addresses the requirements listed in the person specification.

First impressions and ease of reading count, so type and print your application. If you handwrite the documents and out of the envelope drops something that's all over the place like a mad woman's knitting, your application will be seeing the shredder in short shrift, no matter how good you are.

So, let's have a look at the individual documents.

Your CV (or résumé)

This a very simple document but extremely difficult to get right. When you apply for a position, its simple purpose is to present a factual summary of you and your career to date. You may have drawn one up even before finding a position to apply for and thus a CV usefully doubles up as a form of calling card.

Unluckily there is an absolute wealth of guidance available to you. Unluckily? Yep, there are more books on writing a CV than you could digest whilst doing the thick end of a ten-stretch in Strangeways for major fraud.

I just typed the term 'CV' into the 'books' section of Amazon and was offered 4,140 choices. Just one copy of each would collectively weigh around 530 kilos so it may be worthwhile living in a ground floor flat if you plan to read them all. If you read one a day it will take you eleven years to finish.

While you're at it, remember to buy a broadband package with unlimited usage. I typed 'CV' into Google and found I was the proud owner of 926,000,000 links. (Suspicious round number there, but that's what it gave me.) 'CV advice' gave me 113,000,000 links, 'Graduate CV' gave me 45.7 million and 'CV template' delivered a still indigestible 4.25 million links.

Four and a quarter million CV templates? How would I ever choose one?

OMG, it seems like everyone from the government, to people like Alan Sugar, are happy to bombard you with their version of what a CV should look like. I'm amazed nobody is offering a degree in the subject. Let me save you some time here. Hell, let me save you half a lifetime by giving you a working distillation of the whole field of CV writing. Here it comes …

What makes a good CV is entirely subjective and there's only one rule: write a CV to match the ridiculously simple needs and expectations of the reviewer.

There you go. That's it. Now you're free from the need to read, literally, half a tonne of books and trawl the web until your fingers bleed and you want to gouge your own eyes out, just to make it all go away.

It really is that simple. Think about it. When you next walk down to the local offy to stock up on booze, ciggies and lottery tickets, you might just notice that no-one has bothered to ram down your throat half a tonne of guides on how best to do it. Do you really need to be told how to open the door, what to choose, what you should say, how to pay and how not to get arrested in the shop or mugged on the way home? Please.

Your very simple objective is to quickly and concisely tell the recruiter about yourself in a way which catches their attention, shows that you're serious, matches the ad completely and lifts you above the competition. Along the way, don't piss him or her off.

How hard can it be? It's worth understanding what you need to do but do you really need almost a billion links of advice to get it done? I don't think so.

I just read Alan Sugar's CV. It's a free e-book for the Kindle on Amazon. On the one hand, I think it's utterly appalling. If I was recruiting to fill a post and he sent me that, I'd bin it within a minute. But I'm not. Recruiting, I mean. And he's not pitching for a job. The purpose of that CV is completely different and, read in the context of why he wrote it, it works very well indeed. That just serves to further prove the point – write for your audience.

But here's the rub.

Firstly, rarely should two copies of your CV contain the same information about you. You might gulp and go in search of chemical therapy, a stiff drink or a sit down at this point but the fact is that a CV should be tailored for best effect, every single time you use it.

When you begin to construct a CV for an advertised position, start by using your research. Your notes against each key requirement will load the bullets for you as you write, thereby automatically tailoring your CV to the role offered. After you have finished, you can easily check off the key points you've presented against the original full list of requirements so as to ensure that you've captured them all.

In theory, that's all nice and easy. All you need to do is just re-write your CV for each new application. Unfortunately, what makes a CV difficult to construct successfully is the very thing that is supposed to make it easy to read – its format. There are as many different CV formats proposed as there are pints poured in a piss-up but almost all impose both a chronological order and the physical separation of education, experience and interests.

That forces you to put information that you want to present into a specific section, somewhere within the CV. That can make it very difficult to tell a story and maintain logical continuity on key points you want to make.

By way of example, in order to best show your capability on a particular topic, perhaps leadership potential, you may need to draw upon any and all of:

- your main work experience (if any);
- casual work experience (which may be dotted around in time);
- project experiences (which may be distributed across your entire education) and
- activity within your personal interests (D of E, for example).

That is fundamentally impossible to do concisely, within the confines of a straightforward CV, since it specifically separates education, work experience and interests and imposes a roughly reverse chronological order.

So there you are. The brief calls for you to show leadership potential. Your CV format forces your leadership information into three or four separate sections.

You could handle that leadership issue more neatly by writing an introductory summary section but then you can't also include all of the other things you might need to show. If you do, that first section will fill a page and it will render some later sections redundant.

So what's wrong with that? Why not do it the way you want if that's what gets the message over best?

The problem is the reviewer. They may have a hundred CVs to get through and their first task is to check if you've got the basics of the qualifications and experience required. They rely on receiving documents in a roughly 'standard' format so they're collectively easy to scan. The reviewer certainly won't take the time to distil out the relevant bits from your endless introduction, so your CV will just get binned.

The reviewer's expectations are pretty simple. They want to easily see:

- your name and contact details;
- your education and qualifications;
- an introduction which gives an idea of the person you are, what you have to offer and why they should pick you;
- your professional work experience;
- your relevant activities or interests.

Within those very limiting constraints, you need to showcase how you match up against the list of requirements. It's just too easy to pick a standard CV format, lazily shovel your history into it and assume it does a bang-up catch-all job. Many people do. That's why they fail.

That's why you won't fail. You'll now tailor every CV you ever produce, even though it can be a ball-aching slog to do so. You'll do it even when your fingers are worn back to the first knuckle, you're sobbing with exhaustion and you've just had to bow out of a rock-solid promise for the evening. You'll do all that because you know working on your tailoring will substantially improve your odds of winning through.

Even when you use your CV as a calling card, perhaps for a cold-calling programme designed to get you onto that shortlist of one, if you can tailor it before you pass it over, you'll increase your chances of getting that all important invite to some face-time. At the very least, re-wording key sections, to talk directly to the industry or sector you're targeting, makes a substantial difference.

Having someone in the financial services sector read your CV and like it, but think that you'd stand more chance trying for jobs in marketing means that you just haven't done your tailoring work properly. By all means, have both a generic financial services CV and a generic marketing CV, but use them separately.

What about producing a CV to get you noticed? You know the type of thing – text set in a Serial-Killer font, printed on day-glo paper, with one half of a fifty pound note stapled to the corner and a photo of you looking down the barrel of an AK47, all enclosed in an envelope the size of a king-sized bed sheet.

The problem is that recruiters like to stay well inside safe territory and firstly look for the familiar. The paradox is that they're looking for that stand-out someone, but they need that person to conform with their idea of a norm.

If you go wild with your CV, you will get noticed, but in the vast majority of cases you'll simultaneously reduce your odds of getting selected. Save the weird CVs for those limited occasions where you're chasing jobs far out on the extreme edge of the creative universe. For the rest, work on the intrinsic quality of your CV's content.

Like everything we've looked at so far, a quality result flows from good preparation. However, at some point, you've actually got to construct a highly-focused CV and get it ready for submission, so let's work through a process for doing that.

Preparation. We've covered this in depth so have your lists, research and notes handy, make sure they're fresh in your mind. Have one last read through the advert or brief.

Framework. Choose the main sections and / or titles that will be on your CV and the order in which you are going to put them down. For this stage of your career, a workable set in order might be:

- name (people do forget to include this);
- contact details (ditto);
- personal introduction (summarises who you are, why you're suitable);
- education and qualifications (degree, A levels, GCSEs);
- professional work experience (reverse chronological order);
- other relevant experience;
- interests;
- referees.

Regarding the latter, you may want to choose different referees, depending upon the potential employer, so a one-liner which says "References available on request" is good at this point, if you are creating a CV for cold-calling.

Lay out your chosen headings in a Word document.

Adding content. With the points you need to score in mind, write to populate your framework. Take as much space as you like to make your points. More is better at this stage but only write something if it's of direct relevance to a requirement of the job. Fill as many pages as you like.

Obviously, it's the quality of your content (against each requirement) that will help you to win an interview place, or not, but what constitutes 'quality'?

In short summary, and in exponential order of rising weight, add content to your CV in the following three ways.

- **Highlight responsibilities.** Showing what you've previously been responsible for can help match your experience with the capabilities listed as required in the job and person specifications.
- **Display achievements.** For more impact, show how you applied your responsibility to achieve positive results in previous working situations. Simultaneously quantifying those results, and putting them into context, will lift your application yet further up the score chart.
- **Show instigations.** You will score highest if you can show that you took actions and achieved results that simply would never have happened if you hadn't been there to initiate things. Show what you made happen, in other words, as covered in the previous pages.

Think of responsibility as though it were a ladder to help you climb up the list of potential interview candidates.

When drafting your CV, if you focus on key responsibilities you've had, provided that you can match them to the job and person specifications, you are unlikely to either improve or harm your chances of selection. At best, you will merely keep yourself in the game, but on the bottom rung.

Surprised?

It gets worse. Excessively focusing on responsibilities can even see you marked down and thereby bumped off the ladder. Who will ever really care if you took on the extra responsibility of emptying the office waste-bin every Friday? You could go on adding responsibilities that you theoretically held, ad infinitum. Your major relevant responsibilities are the only ones worth listing.

Instead, focusing on your (preferably quantified) achievements significantly improves your chances of selection by at least one order of magnitude.

You're showing that, if you're hired, you are capable of delivering measurable value and you're well aware of the need to do so. That moves you several rungs up the ladder.

But don't stop there.

Showing that you followed a plan and achieved the objective set is all well and good, but showing that you identified a direction and set an objective in the first place, improves your chances of selection by yet another order of magnitude. You're demonstrating that you have initiative, in spades.

It's not easy to find and present examples that illustrate you're higher up that ladder than your peers, but it'll be well worth every drop of sweat.

With every application, remember two things.

1) The majority of people do not realise the distinction between responsibility and value and fail to show the latter in their applications.
2) Within the scope of their responsibility, even fewer understand the difference between being told what to do, and being truly responsible by proactively finding and suggesting what to do.

If you understand those differences, and can show them on your CV, you will stand out like the balls on a bulldog, compared to your peers.

The 'application forms' section, which immediately follows this one, shows you in more depth how to identify and add higher quality content. Read it and apply the same thinking to the content you add to your CV.

Still on the subject of quality content, at all costs avoid writing clichés and adding hyperbole. They serve only to weaken your application.

"I'm a highly creative individual."

Using this cliché, as many people do, ironically suggests that they're not very creative at all.

"I work well on my own but I'm also a good team player."

On applications, no one is ever going to not lay claim to being a team player. The person writing this is just saying, "Hey, I'm the same as everyone else."

"I'm hard working and highly motivated."

No? Really?

"I'm an excellent communicator."

Actually, no you're not. Sorry.

If you cross all of these clichés out, you've got space to throw in a paragraph which shows all of those qualities in the context of something you actually did.

As a catch-all guide to follow:

- avoid clichés, hyperbole and exaggeration;
- stay away from Apprentice-style self-promotion;
- don't list your qualities, show them in your experience.

Trimming down. A CV is ideally of maximum length two pages of A4 paper. (Great, now he tells me.)

For the education and qualification section, if you list every exam you've ever passed since you were sixteen, using one line for each, you can cover at least half a page in one go. Especially if you hike it up to a 14 point font size, right?

It's rubbish, cut it back. Go for three short blocks, the first being your degree (achieved or anticipated) and your university. The second block can be your A levels and the third your GCSEs.

Do list your schools, subjects and grades but you don't need a new line for each subject and grade. Save the space. With care, it looks better, it's quicker to scan and it demonstrates an organised mind. Any fool can write a ten page CV, the real skill is in being concise.

Now, cut the rest back ruthlessly until you end up with between one and two pages. Shorter stories catch more attention than drifting piffle. Eliminate waffle and all unnecessary words. Identify duplicated points and remove them. Saying the same thing three times makes you look less competent, not more.

Paraphrase prose into shorter, punchier sentences. Be positive. Be confident. Say it once and say it concisely to really drive a point home to the hilt.

Formatting.   Good titling is essential. Put your name and the words 'Curriculum Vitae' at the top of the page. Make them big, but not huge.

Make sure that your main section titles clearly stand out so that the reader always knows where they are, when they're reading.

Body text should be set in 12 or 10 point, titles up from there.

White space is your friend and more is better. Pay attention to line spacing and paragraph spacing so that paragraphs, within a section, individually stand out but clearly hang together within that section.

Use bullet points for emphasis and to focus attention but don't over-use them. Three bullet points stand out clearly from the paragraphs before and after but the reader's attention will skid over sixteen bullet points in a row.

Three is a magic number. People can remember three things. If you add a fourth, the first drops out of register. If you put sixteen, they'll most easily remember the last three, presumably the least important three, if you prioritised your list.

Use bold text to aid focus and readability. It's extremely useful for the first couple of words or so of a paragraph, to save wasting titling space and lines, but try to avoid your CV looking like a page from the **SUN** newspaper, complete with **bold, idiot-highlighted** words, **littered** across the inside of **paragraphs**. Italics work if used sparingly. Underlining risks confusion if your CV will be screen-read, since underlined words look like they should be links.

Application forms

You may or may not be required to submit a CV along with your application form. It just depends on the preferences of the recruiting organisation. Generally, the private sector prefers to down-play the application form and ask for a CV, whereas the public sector prefers to specifically exclude CVs on the grounds of running an 'equal opportunities' recruitment process. The community and voluntary sector (CVS), also known as the third sector, tends to follow the public sector in its approach.

We'll look at the differences in approach in more detail shortly. Firstly, let's concentrate on some factors common to most application forms.

Yet again, first impressions are of paramount importance. A scruffy application will not get the consideration it may deserve because it proves too much like hard work for the reviewer to distil the salient points from it. If at all possible, type your forms rather than handwrite them. If you really do have to handwrite them, practise first until you have the final copy you want to use and only then fill the final version of the form in. Write neatly or print, get the spacing correct for the amount of content you need to make fit.

If the form is simply requesting your basic details, qualifications and current situation, then filling in the form is going to be a fairly low-stress task but do not give it less attention because of that. Every detail counts. Every mistake with spelling, grammar and punctuation has the potential to trigger a tidal wave of irritation and bump your application into the shredder, as the reviewer moves over from a positive to a negative judgement of you.

If the form is to be the sole document upon which your application for interview is to be judged, then you still have a day's work ahead of you, working on the form rather than a CV.

Preparation is the key, exactly the same as if you were preparing your CV. Do your analysis and do your research. It will make the task of filling in the form much quicker and it will provide the focused prompts you can use to show you shine.

Interestingly, application forms can be considerably harder to get right than CVs and they're hard enough. The two or three blocks that give the most problems are: your current / past employment details and the request to explain why you think you're suitable and why you want the post.

Additionally, the form can force you to include some details you'd normally choose to leave out. Hobbies and interests are one such example. Leaving it blank looks odd but only being able to list reading and socialising as your interests may not serve you well.

You may also be forced to highlight any responsibilities held and activities followed across the whole of your time in education which, of course, you may or may not have. If you don't have anything to really shout about here, it's not a cause for panic but it does mean you're going to have to work hard to show how other extra-curricular activities may have been of benefit to you.

If these are areas of weakness for you, it's not the end of the earth. Some people just are more academic, non-sporting or introverted and the selection process is a balance, with suitability for the role taking core priority. Where things are close, the additional factors simply help to identify where one candidate may appear to have more potential than another.

Recruiters may decide to factor in late development or consider that you've already peaked. We all know of former head boys and girls who have spectacularly failed to live up to the early expectations of their potential and have ended up dealing or on the game. They can be said to exhibit unconventional, hierarchically-exasperated, nonlinear career paths.

Don't get stressed over your weaknesses. Recognise them and find other ways to show the traits that will put you ahead of the horde. If preparation comes first in deciding which of your good points to best portray, explicit presentation of those points comes a very close second.

So, let's get started on a worst-case scenario application form, which might typically be required by a public sector 'equal opportunities' employer.

The equal opportunities bit means that the recruiting organisation is trying its very best to give every applicant an equal shot at winning through and starts by imposing the same application form on everyone, thereby supposedly eliminating the variability inherent with CVs.

Although here we are looking at the initial application process, the same philosophy will continue through the interview process also. As mentioned, an application form can force a much closer look at certain aspects of your background than a CV would but, more importantly, it does at least force everyone applying to provide the same information.

The application form can appear deceptively easy, since there are defined spaces into which you can drop your information and, often, there isn't that much space. However, unless expressly forbidden, rather than forcing your information to fit the available space, you should plan to add as many additional sheets as are necessary to show everything you've got. This approach is directly opposite to the one you would take with a CV.

An application can easily grow, from an initial two or three sheets, into a six or seven page, heavy-weight monster. The areas likely to need additional sheets are those two mentioned earlier: current / previous employment and your suitability / motivation to apply. Having said that, at this stage in your career, you're unlikely to have a wheelbarrow-load of previous experience so things are easier now than they will be later.

Perversely, whereas white space on a CV is your friend, aiding readability, white space on an application form symbolises death. Try and fill each and every main box, even if you can't run to additional sheets. It then looks as though you've applied yourself thoroughly to the form and have a wealth of things to say in support of your application.

There is a real art to this. If what you have to say is obviously just turgid padding for the sake of it, then you may as well not have bothered. It may be an equal opportunities application you're making but the reviewer is human. Your application has to scan well, read well and hit each requirement point.

On the plus side, you do at least have the creative opportunity to string stories together to make your application readable. If you have naturally good story-telling skills, you are more than half way there. If you don't, work on them. I'm not entirely sure how that equates to an 'equal opportunities' process but there you go. Play the game, don't rail against it.

Typically, you'll need to use your application to show three things about yourself:

- how you meet the listed requirements;
- why you feel you're suitable for the role and
- why you want this particular role.

The questions you're asked on the form may or may not cover any or all of those three areas. Regardless, those points are the ones you should address.

Firstly, the beating heart of your application must be your point by point matching of the requirements. Explicitly explain how you meet each and every one, no matter how long it takes. As you would for a CV, initially write as much as you feel is necessary and then trim it back, improving its focus. Use your stories to transport and deliver gift-wrapped points into each requirement slot. Just make sure to condense and trim-back your prose afterwards. Whilst more content is better, endless blocks of unfocused text definitely aren't.

For equal opportunities applications, it really is necessary to be explicit. Write structured paragraphs against each point listed in the person specification. Do this one by one, no matter how many pages it takes. You cannot afford to be implicit, as you often can be with a private sector application.

In the latter, you can make a statement and be reasonably sure that several other things about you are implied by that statement and that they'll be recognised. You'd typically score for them in the private sector, 'because it's obvious' that you have x, y or z experience as a consequence.

For equal opportunities applications, that's completely inadequate as an approach and you'll be crucified, crushed and cremated in short order if you rely on it. You need to state explicitly that you match x, y or z.

Equal opportunities applications will literally be scored, point by point, against the requirements listed in the job and person specifications. The highest scorers will be invited in for interview, the lowest scorers will be purged. That's exactly how it works.

A private sector application may also be scored, but the assessor is likely to have considerably more latitude to interpret what's being offered and 'read between the lines' in order to score. An equal opportunities application is very unlikely to ever be awarded that privilege.

To really understand the difference in the two approaches, it might help to think about the entertainment industry for a moment. When script writing or directing for the screen, there is a maxim which says 'show, don't tell' and it can be used to starkly illustrate the difference between how you should structure private sector applications and public sector equal opportunities applications.

Imagine the following dialogue being spoken in a drama, as a young woman enters a domestic kitchen diner, in a terraced house.

> "Hello Miranda. How are you, now that you've been out of rehab these last three months and out of prison for six, after you previously stole money from your employer to make ends meet and pay your ailing mother's medical bills, so that you now stand a chance of regaining custody of your seven children?"

It's horrendous, isn't it? At this point in the play, information is being forcibly delivered to you, to make damn sure you get all of the relevant facts on board and straight. It's very efficient but it makes for turgid entertainment and the script writer would be rightly shot for producing such heinous bilge.

The dialogue needed is probably just, "Miranda?"

The scene and the acting are designed to give your brain the additional material needed to work out what's been happening, what's happening now and what might, or might not, happen in the future.

We might see Miranda looking hollow-cheeked, reed thin and dressed in well-worn jeans and a tee shirt, but dressed cleanly. The latter tells us something about her current state of mind. Bare feet, long hair and fabric bracelets give us a view on her personality. Some old tattoos could show us that she perhaps has some darker elements to her background.

She might look unhealthy, but carry herself in a proud manner. How she enters the room can speak volumes. She might look determined, triumphant even. She might be carrying papers, in a big white windowed envelope.

The tone of the short dialogue can tell us a huge amount about the relationship between Miranda and the person sitting at the kitchen table. It might also imply that there's news to come and it might be positive. In any case, we might gather there's a lot at stake.

How Miranda takes the papers from the envelope, how she puts them on the table and how she shows them to the other person all deliver more snippets of information.

So, one seven second scene with only one word spoken could take you a blink to understand but minutes to explain to anyone, because there's so much backstory obvious from what you're looking at. You may not consciously think about a lot of these points but your subconscious will take it all on board.

A private sector application is a bit like that. Imagine the following.

A reviewer reads that your job title was head of administration at a twenty person outfit called "Dagenham Digital Designers Limited". Dates show that you were there two years and you were promoted from the job of administrator six months after you started.

That probably all fits in only a line or so but taken together with the picture already building up in the reviewer's mind, coupled with her own experience and what she knows about the job she's trying to fill, it speaks volumes.

- You're in the right industry, geographically you're in the right place, you've been working in a relevant role and you have the right seniority.
- She could deduce that you're highly thought of. You were at a small company and such places can't afford to carry slackers so you've probably got a good work ethic.
- You were promoted quickly and held the job long enough to demonstrate that you're likely to be a strong and capable individual.
- At a small company, everyone wears three hats and reports to the boss so you're probably flexible and possess a high level of initiative.
- In that type of company, everyone rubs up against clients, so you've probably got a good commercial understanding.
- As head of administration, you're in charge of at least some people and resources, so you've probably got at least adequate people skills.
- It would be interesting to know why you're moving. This job is bigger, so you're probably ambitious, hungry for the next step, so up for a bit of a challenge and some personal development.

And so on, and so forth.

Okay, it all needs confirming, but that's partly what the interview is for. At the very least, the reviewer will be looking for further reasons to put you on the 'yes' pile, not for an excuse to drop you on the 'no' pile.

As we saw with the scene earlier, a huge amount of information is 'shown' about you, within the context of the environment you're applying to join.

That context is the clincher. It's all about the environment you're applying to work in, relative to where you've come from, but coupled with the reviewer's own personal experience and their extrapolated views about your personality.

Thus, a few words on an application can show volumes about you and the reviewer can immediately guesstimate how well you'll fit. (Perhaps you see why applications can often be reviewed very quickly indeed?)

Actually, of course, they don't really show volumes about you. They imply volumes about you.

The danger area lies within the reviewer's subjectivity and that's where the equal opportunities process attempts to pick up the slack and force more objectivity.

Consequently, in an equal opportunities application, NOTHING should be assumed about you, just from the line of your company, job title and dates of employment.

You will have to (turgidly if necessary) state every single last fact and property about yourself, that you want the reviewer to pick up on, from that period. If you don't, you won't score it. If you don't score it, you won't get an interview.

Let me really drive the point home.

I was asked to help a highly-competent, qualified accountant with her applications. She'd just applied for a senior management role, for which she was perfectly matched. Unfortunately, she didn't even get invited for an interview. I looked and saw that she was applying for an equal opportunities post in the public sector but, coming from the private sector, she hadn't twigged that the equal opportunities process involved more than a gesture toward fair play and a nod to diversity.

I suggested she ask for feedback and, sure enough, the recruitment panel at the council in question said that they couldn't invite her in for an interview, although suspected that she met the requirements in spades, as she was one of the lowest scorers when they went through her application. This was simply because she hadn't explicitly stated her suitability, point by individual point.

The equal opportunities process prevents them from putting low scoring candidates forward, as that would be unfair to the high scoring candidates. Equally (no pun intended), that same process prevents them from interpretation and logical extrapolation in order to calculate scores. In the private sector, she'd have sailed through with flags flying and all guns blazing.

You can think what you like about whether that equal opportunities process actually ends up finally selecting the best candidate but it's the reality you have to face. If you don't know how that particular game is played, you are well and truly bending over in front of Bernard Matthews, ruffling your feathers and asking to be stuffed.

If you do know, you have a very big advantage and can systematically offset a lot of your personal weaknesses by simply taking the right approach to filling in the form. You can, almost literally, elbow your way into an interview.

If you are in any doubt as to whether you have adequately ticked the box against a certain requirement, chuck in another paragraph for good measure. Preferably, make it interesting but at the very least, make it focused and concise with no rambling irrelevancies.

Secondly, it's no good being highly suitable for the role if the reviewer doesn't twig this fact. Can you do anything to make sure that they do? Yep, you can tell 'em. "I feel that I am suitable for this role because …," does the job, so long as you can prop up some salient reasoning behind this statement.

The best justification you can make is to identify very positive points about yourself and match them directly to each of the key requirements of the job and person specification.

Bullet points work particularly well in a summary introduction about yourself in the "Tell us why you're suitable for this role" section. They enable you to list the three to five primary reasons why you're an excellent match to the main requirements in the person specification.

This enables you to lay down the foundation of your whole pitch, by telling the reviewer what to think about you from the outset. You do then have to make sure that the rest of your application directly supports these points, but never underestimate the power of suggestion.

We are all programmed to be cynical, sceptical and suspicious but it remains a fact that the vast majority of people will trust you and believe what you tell them, unless there's a reason to doubt you. Once doubt creeps in, the situation swings one hundred and eighty degrees and nothing you say will be believed, unless you back it up to the hilt and produce a certificate of verification signed by all of God, Gandhi and Godot.

So, don't introduce doubt, don't exaggerate and definitely don't lie.

Don't be modest either. Go for the jugular but do avoid using gratuitous superlatives about yourself. Stick to the facts, state them boldly, highlight them with your concise prose and let the reviewer conjure up the superlatives for you.

"Wow, this young lady really hits the spot. She's a brilliant match with ideal experience and excellent skills. Let's get her in for interview," is what you want to be aiming for.

Definitely avoid, "This bloke says he's excellent at everything he does. Ri-i-i-ight. Has anyone fixed that shredder yet?"

Thirdly, if it's requested on the box, you'll need to address the, 'Tell us why you want this role,' issue. This can be tricky. Let me ask you. Why do you want the sort of role that you do? Here are some reasons.

> "I'm a power-crazed megalomaniac and this is the fastest way up."

> "I want to get experience before starting my own business."

> "I've seen so many jerks in this role, I'm sure I can do it better."

> "I've been refused for everything else I've tried for recently."

> "I'm desperate for the money and this is a port in the storm."

> "I'm nervous of responsibility and can keep my head down in this job."

> "You'll train me thoroughly so I can get a better job elsewhere."

"When you meet me you'll realise I just want it more than the others."

I'd like to say that these are all exaggerations but I can't. I've seen them all on applications sent to me. Maybe not always in those exact words but often those reasons clearly show through the poorly-applied veneer candidates have plastered across the top of their short-term, self-centred ambitions.

Employers are more than happy to support your ambitions, provided that they will also get a return from their investment in you. However, once they suspect that you have every intention of moving the goal posts to make them more self-serving, you're doomed.

Don't think about what you can get. Think about what you can give.

Talk about your ambitions in terms of what they would mean for the recruiting organisation and how they might benefit from your long-term commitment. Get the thought in the recruiter's mind that, by employing you, they'll be maximising the investment they'll be making in this role, relative to employing any of the other candidates.

Whatever you do, don't lay it on too thick and don't bullshit, otherwise you'll break that fragile trust and plummet down the list accordingly. The sound of flesh being flayed, a sensation of intense pain in your feet and a loud, electric thrashing sound in your ears will give you a clue that you're being shredded.

By all means play to the recruiting organisation's ego and go large on the topics of 'highly-professional environment', 'attractive long-term career growth prospects', 'opportunity to work at the cutting edge of the field / industry / profession', etc. People (and employers) like to be recognised and told how good they are but don't lay it on too thick and stay within the boundaries of truth and credibility. If the recruiting organisation has had ten years of ex-employees publically suing the arse off it for maltreatment, it is counter-productive to bang on about how thrilled you are with their HR policies.

Explaining why you want the role can really help to prop up your whole application, if you can show some depth of thinking and maturity around your points. If the issue of why you want the role is not obviously requested in this box, then you can certainly work your points into your covering letter, if it won't go elsewhere on the form. If you possibly can, without it looking odd, try and work your motivation for wanting this role into the form, since it is possible that not every member of the subsequent recruiting panel will get a copy of your covering letter, but they are certain to get a copy of your application.

So, that covers the three primary topics you need to address in that box.

Note that some application forms cover your current and recent employment and then throw in an innocuous looking box later with the disingenuous words, "Please provide any further information you may have in support of your application." Sneaky. Slip on your body armour and load up a big gun.

It's tempting to throw everything at the employment boxes and add a few general sentences into this innocuous-looking box near the end. Instead, focus heavily on this box and plan to cover all three areas of:

- how you meet the requirements;
- why you think you're suitable and
- why you want the role.

I've been shot by my underestimation of the demands of this box a couple of times and still have the scars, so beware – give it full respect.

You've no doubt realised that focusing on your achievements and what you've previously made happen is a priority for you on application forms. You may be helped to set the scene early on and pave your way forward, where 'current' and 'previous' employment are split into two sections, as it's common today for the current employment section to state, "Please give a brief outline of your main responsibilities and achievements."

This can help to get you a flying start but make sure to align your achievement points with the requirements of the post. If you recently designed equipment for automatically producing the world's best anti-wedgie underpants, it's not much cop if you're applying for a marketing job unless you can directly show how your work contributed to the consequent benefits that the company attained in terms of increased sales, market share or penetration.

The 'Previous employment' section (if this is separated) is less likely to ask for your main achievements so you'll need to work these into the 'Tell us why you're suitable' or 'Further information in support of your application' sections.

In either section you may get asked why you left, or are thinking of leaving. Steer away from such things as, "I work for a jerk and the organisation sucks." Stick with an innocuous, "To further develop my career," or something similar.

Listing redundancy as a cause is unlikely to be a problem, unlike stating that you've been sacked for gross indecency in the workplace. Try and provide an alternative answer if this is in fact the case. At least get to an interview before you have to try and explain it all away. It never looks good on paper.

There could well be a request for your salary information in these sections and this is another area with pitfalls. If you're coming out of university it won't be a problem but if you're changing professional jobs then it might be. If you flag your current salary and it's low relative to that offered in the new role, there'll be eyebrows raised as to whether you're really of a suitable calibre. If your salary is high, compared to that on offer, they'll be nervous about you taking a pay cut and then leaving as soon as you're able.

It's good to be in roughly the same frame, aiming at slightly more than you have, if it's a job at the same level as you have now. If you're aiming for promotion to a higher level, the jump up is less of a problem. If you are trying for a position with a lower salary, you need a good reason for that. It could be that your current post is under threat, which is fine as a reason. You could always fall back on the line that you're taking a longer-term, career-prospects approach and are therefore willing to take a short term hit.

It's generally best not to discuss or negotiate your salary and package expectations until you actually have an offer letter in your hand. It's certainly best not to state what you presently earn and / or what you hope to be offered but it can be hard to avoid the direct question on an application form. If in doubt, you just have to give in and go with it and trust you can sort it all out later.

If the selection process is not flagged as equal opportunities, perhaps because it's for the private sector, there is no harm in following the equal opportunities approach discussed earlier. The actions are the same:

- address each requirement with a key point which directly shows your suitability until you've ticked them all off;
- show why you're suitable and
- explain why you want it.

Once you think your content is perfect, only then fill in the application form you plan to submit.

It's not uncommon for application forms to request two references, usually one personal and one current / recent employer and / or your tutor. Make sure that you ask permission before providing their details on the form. They'd probably vouch for you anyway but they'll be much more positive about you if you haven't just taken them for granted.

Whilst you're at it, specifically ask them if they have any concerns about you. If you have any doubt about their enthusiasm towards you, find someone else to vouch for you.

The importance of references varies from employer to employer and some think they're an essential link in the decision-making chain. Others believe that they are almost valueless in today's more litigious society as more and more previous employers will sometimes only confirm basic facts, dates of employment for example, for fear of being sued over wrongful statements. Personal referees tend to be much more willing to divulge information.

At your present career level, reference-checking tends to be a straightforward process aimed at confirming your basic character and suitability for a role. Sometimes it's treated as a last-ditch catch-all trawl to check that you really exist, you're approximately human and there are at least two people on the planet who can bring themselves not to rant and rave in fury whenever your name is mentioned.

Usually such references won't be followed up unless you're actually offered a position so it would be a tragedy if you've made it all the way through, only to find that somebody either won't give you a reference, or will only provide something bland and sub-optimal for you. The latter may as well state, "This person was appalling and I'd die before I would vouch for them."

Don't ask potential referees to exaggerate for you. By all means, tell them what you are applying for, the type of responsibility you'd be taking on and three good reasons why you're suitable. Loading a few bullets is fair game (they can chose whether to fire them and some people appreciate a bit of prompting, or reminding) but asking them to lie is not. Not only will such a request compromise your relationship with them, it can bite you back later.

By way of an example, I have often worked with people and organisations in a particularly security-conscious industry and it is common for employers to determine, with 100% certainty, that candidates have no unexplained career-gaps. A few months of unemployment is not a problem but it must be shown and fully explained. Typically this is to ensure the honesty of the candidate and that they've not been doing time for such things as fraud, or racketeering.

I received a reference request from a high-profile employer seeking to verify the details of someone who used to work for me. The individual hadn't contacted me to ask if I minded acting as a referee. Worse, I was being asked to verify that we had employed this person for a lot longer than we really had.

My reply ran along the lines of, "Unfortunately I am unable to confirm the requested details for this person." To a potential employer there is no doubt what that phrase means and it's damaging to the prospects of the candidate.

These days, it's not uncommon for lies on CVs and applications to come to light later, resulting in summary dismissal. An advertising company's CEO falsely claimed he had a computer science degree on his CV. He left the company in disgrace, shortly after that fact was uncovered by someone else. Be warned, it's not worth it.

Online application forms

These are another type of application form that you're likely to be presented with, at some stage. At the time of writing, email submission of offline-completed forms is probably the most common method of application used by recruiters. Documents provided are typically in Microsoft Word or PDF format.

Online forms are typically web pages, which present pre-defined boxes for completion by the applicant. This application method will undoubtedly become more common in the future, especially for organisations that prefer to see application forms, rather than CVs.

It is already common for organisations to use a basic online form and then provide an upload button for the attachment of a CV and supporting covering letter.

Many larger organisations have moved further. They present considerably more comprehensive forms and they've reduced the emphasis on supplementary CVs.

Although similar, in broad principle, to the paper and offline versions, some interesting variations arise with full in-depth online application forms.

Your first challenge will be to fill in the form and click the 'submit' button without losing half or all of your work along the way. This can be caused by a crash, a network drop or a time-out and it will inevitably result in you exploding with a fury capable of making the Incredible Hulk look effeminate.

Whatever else you do, draft your text in your favourite word processing package with a view to doing a quick cut and paste job at the end. You'll submit a higher-quality application, you'll live longer, your neighbours will thank you and your cat will stand more chance of not ending up inside out.

Working offline cuts your risk in several other ways. You'll find that your offline-produced content is much easier to work on as you'll have all of your usual layout and formatting tools to hand. Whilst the finished text won't carry this formatting across, the improved interim readability will enable you to make a much better job of your answers. You can take all of the time you need to edit the document, the word-count facility may be invaluable and your spelling and grammar-checking tools will make a substantial difference.

Paper and offline forms tend to be roughly similar in terms of layout and requested content, but online forms show much more variation in all of these aspects. One significant change is that the use of competency-based questions is growing and we'll look at these in some detail below. They've long been used at the interview stage but are now often brought forward to the application stage, facilitated by the easier management of online forms.

Generally, all of the methods that we have covered so far regarding preparation, CV construction or application form completion should be applied here. The best three-step strategy for building your content remains the same:

- identify the key requirements;
- write lots of targeted content and
- edit it back.

Usually you'll have to edit your text back to a requested maximum word count. This can be tricky but it does force you to be both precise and concise, invaluable skills to learn and develop in any situation.

Competency-based questions

These add yet another layer of complexity, forcing you to be more structured in the way you provide information. It's possible that, as an undergraduate or a recent graduate, you may not have encountered such questions before so let's take a moment to look at the nature of the beast.

A competency-based question is used to look more closely at your suitability for a role, measured in terms of a particular skill or trait believed to be required for it. Thus there may be a number of these questions on the application form, perhaps six or eight, each looking at a different skill.

Your answers will be scored. You'll typically need to score over a certain level to stand a chance of being invited for interview. After that, your score will be compared against the other applicants, the highest people being invited in.

It sounds daunting but just like exams, once you've understood the technique required to deal with them and you've practised a few times, they'll become much easier to handle. It is at least easier to deal with them at the application stage as you'll normally have enough time to be able to get your answers straight before you write and submit them. At an interview, you'd need to give your answers verbally, on the fly and with no preparation. That can be tough.

One advantage you now have is that some of the horde will be unaware of the idea behind competency-based questions. That alone won't get you through but the odds will shift strongly in your favour if you can become adept at recognising them and responding to them. A competency-based question will typically be related to one or more key skills, some examples of which are:

- communication skills;
- interpersonal skills;
- use of initiative;
- planning and organising;
- decision making;
- delivering results;
- team working;
- leadership ability;
- creativity and innovation;
- strategic thinking.

It's important to keep your wits about you and recognise a competency-based question when it hoves into view; the application form may not have flags flying and guns blazing to signal that you're facing one or more of these.

Such questions will tend to run along the lines of the following:

- "Tell us about a time when you ...."
- "Give an example of a situation where you ...."
- "Describe a scenario when you had to ...."

Notice that such questions are typically very open, thereby giving you a blank canvas on which to portray your abilities, experiences and strengths. This contrasts with closed questions which are designed to elicit very narrow, yes or no, answers.

> "Have you ever been in prison for a criminal offence?" is a closed question, which leaves you with few options in answering it.

> "Was it you who took the money?" is another. They're commonly used to overcome evasiveness, another skill you'll develop rapidly, with experience.

So, a competency-based question, designed to look at your ability to take personal responsibility and to assess your longer-term potential, might be:

> "Tell us about a time when you had to step forward and lead."

Another, focused on your ability to overcome difficulties or seize opportunities, might be:

> "Describe a situation where you were required to use your initiative to complete a difficult task."

It's easily possible to assess and score your skill levels, against more than one parameter, by the use of wider questions. For example, to look at both your analytical skills and your decision-making skills, a question might be:

> "Give an example where you had to gather information from different sources and put it together so that you could make a decision."

Interestingly, you could use your answer to this question to also show your interpersonal skills if, for example, you'd drawn that information from different people, departments or organisations rather than from, say, different publications, databases and websites.

It should be clear that the following answer won't hit the mark. "I often had to gather lots of information when I was working at Killer Widgets Inc. and then make decisions. Big decisions." It might scrape you one mark out of five for verifying that you did, in fact, have to do that in a part of your career to date.

So what type of answer do you need to construct? To help, use a simple and well-tried tool known as the STAR technique. This stands for:

S – situation;

T – task;

A – action;

R – result.

Using this technique will help you to quickly construct responses which are both full and focused.

Firstly, study the question carefully to try and understand which skills are being examined. You can then choose a specific, relevant and recent example from your past, which relates to your use or application of that skill. At this stage in your career you may also have to draw on experiences from outside of the workplace. Next, work through the following steps:

- **Situation** - what was the situation you faced, how did it arise and how did you become involved in it? Add perspective to show the scope or gravity of the situation;
- **Task** - what objective did you have and what tasks did you undertake?
- **Action** - what actions were involved in moving towards the objective?
- **Results** - what was the outcome? Did you encounter any difficulties along the way and, if so, what did you do to overcome them? Why was this the best outcome that there could have been?

With practice, this technique can become second nature. Note that it can also help with some questions which are perhaps not so obviously competency-focused. For example:

> "What's the hardest decision you've ever had to make?"

A STAR-based answer will be more comprehensive and speak with an authority about your abilities that an unstructured answer wouldn't convey.

When you think of examples from your experience, think about the following:

- try to keep your examples specific, recent and relevant;
- think of examples which look at actions you personally undertook or were involved with. The actions of others are largely irrelevant and uninteresting. If you were a bystander, the reviewer might think you lack initiative. Avoid talking about hypothetical situations;
- always pick examples which had positive outcomes. If a question asks for an example (singular) then only pick one and
- avoid the inappropriate and use examples you would feel confident talking in more detail in an interview.

Strengths-based interviews

Larger employers are using strengths-based interviews as they are harder to prepare for than 'standard' or competency-based questions and can be used to gain a deeper insight into the real character of a candidate.

The root problem for interviewers is: how do they tell the difference between a (highly valuable) mentally flexible, creative and truly confident individual and a candidate equipped with positively bovine thinking processes but who just happens to have guessed correctly, rehearsed well and scrubbed up nicely on the day?

This happens because answers to standard questions (e.g. Tell me about yourself) can be predicted, pre-prepared and thoroughly rehearsed beforehand, helping you to deliver confidently on the day.

Likewise, questions which look at your competence (e.g. Tell me about a time when you had to handle a difficult team member) can be partially predicted from the core competencies typically required for an advertised role. They can be handled well on-the-fly by using the STAR technique, especially after lots of practice.

Enter the strengths-based interview …

Competency questions look at what you can do and how well you did it last time.

The theory is that if you've done something in the past, you're probably able to do something similar in the future. The trouble is, if you're merely competent, you may be just a journeyman, incapable of inspired work and the type of performance level really needed if things get tough.

Strengths-based questions focus more on what you enjoy doing.

If you're working in the area of your strengths, you'll be happier and more committed, you'll perform at a higher level and you'll achieve more for the organisation. Overall, work will be more enjoyable for you, your enthusiasm will be greater and you'll have way more energy.

Everyone has some innate strengths and when they use them they perform at their best. They rapidly learn new information and subsequently perform more confidently and competently. When people enjoy an activity they're more focussed, they work longer and they typically deliver to a higher level.

So, how might such an interview run?

Interviewers will have a range of strengths they're looking to appoint against. For example, the ability to work with others. Their questions will be designed to help them understand the extent to which you possess those strengths.

- Some questions will be more personal.
- Many questions will be shorter, sharper and tightly focussed.
- Interviewers may periodically use rapid-fire questions to stop you relaxing into pre-prepared answers.
- Lines of questioning may be non-linear, forcing your thinking to jump around.

What is the interviewer looking for?

Ideally, they want to recruit someone built for the role who can click fully into place, rather than employ someone who may have to significantly adapt in order to do it. They'll be trying to match the real strengths of candidates to the strengths judged to be needed, either for the role, or for the longer term. Consequently, they'll be looking for:

- prompt responses which are clearly natural;
- behaviours which point to what you enjoy doing;
- topics about which you are obviously enthusiastic;
- how your body language changes from question to question;
- a confident tone of voice and good pace of answer delivery.

You will probably have to draw on experience from all aspects of your life and background, not just any directly related previous work. Although that will make it much harder to guess questions and pre-prepare some answers in advance, it's not impossible.

Use the '**Match and Patch Process**' to prepare

The advert is unlikely to list the strengths the organisation is seeking to recruit against so you'll need to try and distil a prioritised list for yourself. Use the advert, any brief provided and your own background research to find clues.

The Match 'and Patch Process' is a simple but thorough 5 step process to follow -

1) Develop a sound understanding of the role, in context.
   - o Understand the responsibilities of the role in question.
   - o Determine the likely objectives for the role-holder.
   - o Think about what tasks will be consequently involved.
   - o Establish how the role relates to other people and departments.
   - o Be aware of the culture of relevant parts of the organisation.
   - o Only then develop a prioritised list (numbered from 1 to 10, or more) of the probable strengths required to do the job successfully.
2) Completely separately, by considering your whole history, produce a list of your own strengths, in a ranking order from 1 down to 10, or more. Against each, briefly list one or more examples from your past that supports your claim to that strength.
3) Now, against your list of strengths, give yourself a score for enjoyment. Find the strength you most enjoy working with and score it with a 1. Find the strength you least enjoy working with and score it with a 10. At the end, re-order your own list, according to the combined score. You should end up with things that you're strong at and enjoy doing toward the top of your list and things that you're not so good at or dislike doing toward the bottom.
4) Next, match your list of strengths against the list of those required for the role. Do the orders roughly match? Identify any significant mismatches and any important gaps where you don't seem to cover a strength.
5) Now begin to 'patch' your own list of strengths. Highlight your obvious weaknesses, relative to the role. Revisit your history to find support for those weaknesses or gaps. Dig deep and really work at it. There's always something you haven't previously thought about – find it.

Stay honest with yourself throughout and, at the end of this process, you should have a very realistic view of your chances of success at interview for this role.

You can now start the hard work of trying to predict questions, prepare some answers and rehearse their delivery.

Your covering letter

If one is required, your covering letter is as important to your potential success as your CV or application form. It's probably the first document from you that will be seen and it's vitally important that it gives a good first impression. Even more importantly, you can use this document to set expectations in the mind of the reviewer. Think of it as a brainwashing weapon.

> "Hello. I don't think I'm really suitable for this post but I thought I'd see whether my application might stand a better chance than I thought."

I hope by now that you recognise that such an opener is the fastest way to paint the wall red, behind you. Unfortunately, many people go straight in with a diluted version of that, almost apologising for bothering the reviewer, despite them already being paid handsomely to do little other than make a decision about your application.

Be positive. You have every right to be there, even if you really are a chancer with a particular application. Set the expectations of the reviewer so that he or she is looking for justifications to put you through, not to reject you.

How do you do that?

> "Hello. I have all of the experience required and fully match the requirements listed in the person specification. The role is exactly the one I need for the next stage of my career and I'm sure I can commit for the long haul. In doing that, I am certain that I can make a very strong contribution to the prospects of the whole organisation and everyone in it. In short, I am perfect for this role, please invite me in for an interview. If you don't, I'll go elsewhere and you'll regret it forever."

That's what you have to say.

There is a catch, unfortunately. If you do use those actual words, you'll get shot slightly more slowly (if such a thing is possible) but just as certainly as you would if you were taking a hesitant approach. The points made in your favour are flat statements with no supporting justification. By making them directly, you risk being perceived as arrogant. Using a threat at the end is tantamount to playing Russian Roulette with all six chambers loaded.

The only time you could make such statements and get away with them (except for the threats), would be at the end of an interview where the ground has already been well covered and you're asked to, "Summarise why we should pick you." For your covering letter, you need to make points which strongly engender the above positive thoughts in the mind of the reviewer so that they reach those conclusions for themselves.

Your letter needs to fulfil certain objectives for you:

- entice the reviewer to read your CV or application form;
- leave no doubt that you're suitable for the role and
- show your enthusiasm for the opportunity.

Let's get the three absolute basics of covering letters out of the way:

- your layout, formatting, spelling, punctuation and grammar should all be as good as you can get them and don't forget to include your name and contact details. Remember to proofread everything thoroughly;
- start your maximum one page letter with a boiler-plate statement such as, "Please find attached a copy of my CV in support of my application for the post of …. ."

Include the job reference, if any, in the sentence or as a title line just below your, "Dear Whoever," and

- conclude with a final paragraph something along the lines of, "I would be pleased to meet to further explore my suitability for this position and hope to hear from you shortly if you feel that I am a good match to the listed requirements."

The real action comes in between those latter two. A good start might be, "I feel that I am a good match for this role because … ." From there you need to list between three and five solid reasons which justify your inclusion on a shortlist of people to be interviewed.

This is a direct approach which doesn't waste time. Bullet points work well to focus the attention of the reviewer sharply on your main strengths. Bullet points also give you the opportunity to add short intro and outro paragraphs.

The result can be a highly-compact, no nonsense and thoroughly professional-looking set of justifications, presented in the form of a summary. Done well, this not only acts to set expectations but it entices the reviewer deeper into your whole application. You're buying both time and goodwill in their mind. Done badly, you're dead already and can start dusting off your zombie outfit.

If your covering letter is an email, not a Word document or signed letter, ensure that you still use polite forms of address and structure. Use 'Dear …', not 'Hi …' and 'Yours sincerely / faithfully', not 'Laters' and 'Best regards', not 'br'.

Beware of needlessly antagonising the recipient. For example, I personally hate the 'br' brigade. I actually want to do awful things to them, slowly. Why?

For a start, they're in such a rush that they don't mind letting you know that their time is considerably more valuable than the need to be courteous and respectful. Secondly, they can't even be arsed to capitalise it.

I will NEVER employ anyone using that sign-off because I am already convinced that they are lazy, useless, selfish, incompetent, ignorant bog-people. When I see 'br', I imagine the sender has a sloping forehead and still drags their knuckles along the ground as they walk. I wouldn't be surprised to find they're persisting with growing a thick pelt of fur up their back.

In short, I perceive 'br' as being an almost insanely disrespectful sign-off.

So, why take the risk of cutting corners in such a way?

If the recruiter wants to engage with you, frequency of contact is likely to be higher on email and will tend toward the slightly less formal over time. Always take your guide from the person coming back to you and reflect their style. If they use, 'Hi Jon' and sign off with 'Best regards' or 'Kind regards' then do the same. Don't take the risk of trying to lead on that one. You know that you've fully arrived in their consciousness when they don't use either an intro or a sign-off.

Bear in mind that, on the face of it, your main virtues should already have been thoroughly covered elsewhere within your application so you can be quite cunning with your middle paragraphs and bullet points. Where possible, include details not in your CV, in order to personalise your application, so that you're not just regurgitating bland career history.

Use your letter to link your CV to the specific requirements of the job on offer. With your first draft of the letter, at the very least, summarise the three to five best reasons why you're an excellent fit. Beyond that, layer-in as much of the following as you're able or seems appropriate.

- **Focus. Think 'AIM'** with the middle of your covering letter. Try and grab **A**ttention, simply and quickly, with something about you that stands out and differentiates you. Then raise **I**nterest by illustrating your wide competence. Finally, increase the **M**otivation to invite you in, by highlighting the specifics of the benefits that you can bring to the party.
- **Show determination.** You really want this job in that location and you're determined to get it. Don't be afraid to show that you're very positively focused but be aware that there's a balancing act involved. Showing that an ability to focus, and determinedly see things through, is in your DNA is fine. Offering as evidence the fact that your great grandfather single-handedly wiped out the last ten breeding pairs of Dodos, with a zealous determination to prove Darwin right and taunt God to respond, isn't.
- Determination is an admirable quality. Utter ruthlessness isn't. It makes the hairs stand up on the back of the reviewer's neck because allowing yourself to show ruthlessness makes it clear that you're not a team player, you're just another maniac.
- **Play through and hit a different target.** "I match all of the technical requirements for the post and in addition … ." Cue bullet points: job done. Yes, it's a flat statement at the start but you're using it as a launch pad into territory that differentiates you from the horde by saying, "Hey, I've got all that, now just take a look this." Just make sure you can back up this approach. The first part must be true and the second must be fully supported. If it is, your odds of getting through step up like a rooster to a cock-fight.
- **Pique interest in your application.** "I've waited over six months for the opportunity to apply for this post." Really? How come? You've raised interest, whop down a great reason. Just make sure it's not because you've had gangrene, your Nan died or you kind of forgot. "I've wanted to be a product designer since the age of five when I found I loathed the styling of my mother's coffin." That captures interest and shows motivation. "As holder of the unbeaten 2008 world record for organising the biggest ever get-together of people dressed as Smurfs, I'm confident that my organisational abilities are unmatched." Who wouldn't want to meet you after that? Conversely, starting with, "As you can see from my CV …" is not only outstandingly boring, it's about as presumptuous as you can get. It's akin to painting yourself with honey before ramming your fist deep into a wasp's nest.
- **Be titanic.** If you've got one fantastic thing about you that stands out like a hairy billiard ball and supports your application in spades, this is the moment to cue it up, give it a combing and punch it into the corner pocket with a clack that will shake the building. "I invited the present-day reincarnations of Mother Teresa,

Gandhi and Martin Luther King to the product launch and they all turned up. Kim Jong-Un tried to gate-crash but we locked him in a store-room until it was over." Who wouldn't want to read your application after that? Just make sure anything you put down is true and back it up.

- **Show emotion.** Draft your main points in terms that allow your enthusiasm to show through. Be excited. Feel passion for the role and let it course through your veins. You don't need to go over the top with a confession of undying love for the organisation but you do need to convey your obvious enjoyment for what you do through use of selectively-chosen, positive adjectives. It works every damn time.

- **Show you've researched.** Rather than making a direct major point about the fact that you've conducted some research (and risk sounding like a creep), show it indirectly by explaining your strong points in the context of their main issues, challenges or opportunities, which you've picked up from their website or the trade press.

- **Tailor your letter.** Do not simply re-use a really wonderful covering letter that you've previously written. This letter HAS to be tailored to the opportunity. Devote at least one sentence, point or paragraph to why you really want that job in that organisation. Use the organisation's name at least once. As you draft your letter, think about exactly who you're writing it to. Feel the emotion and generate positivity. Imagine the outcome as the reviewer reads it and involuntarily stands up to spontaneously applaud you.

- **Make three extra checks.** Are you absolutely one hundred per cent sure that you've addressed your letter to the right person? If you get it wrong, for whatever reason … you know the penalty. Secondly, make sure that you've used the correct spelling for the name of the organisation. Lastly, make utterly sure that you've haven't left in any names, job information, reference numbers or descriptions that immediately tell the reader that all you've done is a quick cut and paste job from a previous letter and you're so incompetent, you can't even check it properly.

Okay, expecting spontaneous applause is a bit of stretch but you get the idea. You may not be able to work in all of the points above but any one of them may well do the job and get you that invitation to an interview.

It can be tempting to include photos of yourself personally building an orphanage and use coloured text to show your softer side. Stories are legion of people breaking every rule in the book to get attention and subsequently being hired. However, I would suggest that for every well-publicised example you hear about, ten thousand others lay strewn like red confetti across a now silent killing ground. Beware of the paradox mentioned earlier – you need to stand out, but still fit within the boundaries of expectation. Go figure.

It's all about risk. Perhaps the above example would get you noticed for all the right reasons if you're after a job as a creative within an advertising agency and if you're appealing directly to an owner-manager intent on making an edgy reputation for themselves. But perhaps not. Generally recruiters are looking for a safe pair of hands, not a lunatic on acid likely to kidnap clients' children for a corporate snuff movie to be made in the name of 'creativity'.

In the vast majority of cases, recruiters are not paid to take cavalier risks so you optimise your odds if you aim to provide them with what they expect. It's true that the key is to get yourself noticed but you need to be noticed for the right reasons. Figuratively speaking, it's no use getting noticed for being the inappropriately-dressed and drunken, loud-mouthed jerk at a wedding.

For private sector applications, it is really important to spend as much time as possible on your covering letter because it does have such potential to help you hit the target. If your letter looks good, has a quality feel and reads well, then it is highly likely that the reviewer will associate those qualities with you.

Note that, theoretically, a good covering letter will make no difference to an equal opportunities application. Applications will generally be judged entirely on the content of the application form (and whatever else may be requested). Even so, in my opinion it's still worth crafting an excellent covering letter, just on the off-chance that it reaches someone on the selection panel and influences their thinking. If all you do is set positive expectations of you, in the mind of one or more selectors, that alone is worth gold to you.

For a private sector application, an excellent covering letter will not get you invited to an interview on its own but it will do two things: it will stop your application being almost instantly eliminated and it will encourage the reviewer to look for further reasons to put you onto the 'yes' pile.

Earlier, you may have noticed that my suggestion for a rampantly positive middle section of your covering letter basically boiled down to one simple message: "Pick me, you bastard!" Your covering letter is a call-to-action for the reviewer and your concluding sentences need to make your wish to be invited in for an interview clear.

Being too pushy with, "I look forward to you calling me in for an interview," or the over-confident, "I know you'll want to interview me," sits in the same territory as, "Call me now or I will hunt you down like a dog until you give in or die." Laudable sentiments but they're about as likely to be successful as trying to kiss someone sober when you've just done a bottle of voddie, two jars of pickled onions and three packs of ciggies.

You need to preserve good manners and, "I look forward to meeting you if you feel that I am a good match to the requirements," softens the blow whilst still being clear about your wishes. "I'd welcome the opportunity to discuss my suitability further if you feel … ," or anything similar will also do the job for you.

Those statements do, however, leave open the doubt that you may not be picked for interview. Some people (usually working in sales) would suggest closing out that doubt with a more positive statement like, "Please contact me, on 0800 8008135 or via email, to arrange for me to attend an interview."

For me, it's still too pushy. Why take the risk of appearing arrogant if the risk of being rejected with a stay-safe statement is almost non-existent? You are acknowledging the reality of the situation. Offering deference and doffing your cap to accept the superior power of another makes much more sense than spitting in the eye of your interrogator. Ask ex-SAS member Andy McNab, whose books sometimes make this point. Being proud and dead is laudable but ultimately useless. Trust me, I've been there and it subsequently took me ages to remove the splinters from the furniture I was beaten with.

In conclusion, the horrendously bad news is that writing a good letter (and CV or application) is a real art and needs a high level of skill. However, the fantastically good news is that it's a learned skill. Less than a page, short sentences, positive statements, how hard can it be?

As Mark Twain would have famously tweeted, if only he'd been up with the technology, "I didn't have time to write a short letter so I wrote a long one instead." Tidy. Take the time to do it properly and you won't regret it.

Proofreading

So, you've taken a lot of time and effort to produce everything and get it ready for submission. Now, take even more time to proofread everything thoroughly and you'll thank yourself a thousand times over. But don't just proofread to eliminate errors, proofread your whole application to refine it. Apply make-up and add a decent hair-do to it as well. Titivate to thrill, dress it to kill.

Let's start with proofreading your CV.

First impressions count. The structure, layout and formatting of your CV should draw the attention of the reader in. Sit back and take an overview to see if it does that. Centre stage should be your personal introduction. It should catch the eye and then be thoroughly engaging, drawing the reader in, enticing them to dig deeper. Keep it short, keep it sweet.

The requirements are then the next most important element your CV should address. Do you show that you match each and every requirement, at least to some extent? Are any of your statements merely implicit about a particular requirement and, if so, could you re-word a statement to be more explicit? Tick them off, one by one, to catch them all.

Run a keyword check on your CV to ensure that it won't get rejected by any automatic filters that might be used. Use the advert and brief to draw up a list of likely key words and phrases and then tick your CV off, point by point, against them. Add in any that you've missed, but do so in a way that preserves readability. Do not spam keywords for the sake of it as your CV will be rejected if you do.

Emphasise your achievements on your CV, rather than your responsibilities. Have you shown what you made happen? Have you linked this to the benefits achieved for the places you've worked, or projects you've been involved with? Finally, have you quantified those benefits simply, where possible? Everything you include should build up your credibility, until it causes a screaming crescendo of burning desire within the reviewer to get you in for interview.

Have a reality check. Remember, the primary objective of your CV and application is not to get you a job, it's to get you an interview. Are you begging for the wrong thing with yours? Do you look professional and enthusiastic, or just desperate? Write with the reader in mind, not yourself. Leave them wanting more, not less. You're trying to stimulate interest and instil a sense of curiosity about you. If they want to know more, they're going to have to get you in for interview.

Run an ABC check for acronyms, buzzwords and clichés. We all commonly use them because we believe they make us look smarter and it's generally more efficient to do so. That doesn't apply to your CV. They're only more efficient if others are also in the know and you cannot assume this about the reader of your CV. If you intend to use an acronym to save space multiple times, make sure that you fully identify the acronym the first time you use it. Using acronyms without identifying them just risks alienating the reviewer.

Eliminate negativity. Is everything about your CV upbeat and positive or are some comments definite downers that will set the reviewer reaching for a large glass of whisky and a bottle of pills? If so, rephrase them into positives or cut them out altogether. Remember not to go over the top. Too much positivity can be a negative also. Yes, you're in a fight to the death, it's a competition and you should be as self-promoting as possible but do it without being boastful. Be enthusiastic and use strong, positive verbs but don't come across as though you've just managed to hoover up an entire kilo of nose candy in one go.

Run a 'so-what?' test on your CV. You 'had to liaise regularly with the marketing department.' So what? Why? Tell the reviewer about the reasons why, the problems and the outcomes.

- You're a Chelsea supporter. So what?
- You spend your time at weekends knitting woollen breasts for trainee midwives out of a thousand pairs of your granddad's old woollen pants. So what?
- Your hobby is shown as adding to your monstrous (in every way) collection of small porcelain figurines. So what?
- You really care about the rights of pensioners. So what?

Does any of this actually add to your prospects, or does it just add risk, if the reviewer is a Millwall-supporting, barren, minimalist with shares in Dignitas?

Is your age carefully listed as twenty three, right next to your date of birth? Who cares? What does it add to your CV? It's irrelevant, it's a waste of space and it distracts the reviewer from what they should be reading. Cut it out.

Ordinary interests are no better.

So you like watching the TV and walking? So does my dog.

If a word, sentence or paragraph does not add value to your application, cut it out. However, if it's really unusual and interesting shove it right in there, front and centre.

So you went trekking through Mongolia for a couple of months when you were only sixteen, you had to eat beaver liver and you did voluntary work at an orphanage for four weeks whilst you were there? Wow! How much more does that say about you than, "I like to travel abroad and walk about a bit?"

Be wary of accidentally offending others and thereby alienating yourself in the eyes of the reviewer. For example, there are people who believe the term pensioner to be highly derogatory. Bias and prejudice are forbidden but then so is crime, and we do seem to have a built rather a lot of prisons.

Recognise reality for what it is, not what you'd like it to be.

Apply the 'WTF?' test. Put yourself in the mind of the reader and test every single statement on your CV. If you say you worked for Blankety-Blank Products Limited, does that mean anything to anyone other than you, the other twelve people who worked there and your Mum? Blankety Blank Products? WTF? Where were they? What did they do? What did you do for them? You can't assume the reader will just know, or deduce things. Be explicit. If they made blow-up rubber Doreens, with real hair, for the socially disadvantaged, put it down, put it in context and show how it's added value to your career and to your skillsets. Do not leave it to chance. Similarly, you did part time voluntary work for a charity shop? WTF? What did they do? What did you do?

Run a 'lie-detector' test. With a highlight pen, mark up anything that you feel is either dubious, intended to mislead or, in fact, a down right lie. Why are those statements there? Get your head straight until you feel comfortable about the statements you've made, even those which are a slight stretch. Ditch the lies completely and find another way to say the same thing. If you leave lies on your CV, you leave subconscious worries inside your head. That will make you nervous when you finally get that interview you've been chasing. Your lack of confidence will show through. You want to be walking into that room with your head held high, knowing that you are truly indestructible – bring it on. By cutting the lies, your confidence will improve dramatically and you'll carry less risk.

Look for the career gaps. Have you dealt with them openly and positively, or do they look like you've tried to squirrel them away, out of sight? There must be a reason for them, so deal with them confidently. Look for what you've learnt during that time and how you've benefited as a result.

> "Hey, I was just doing it wrong for six months and was unemployed as a result but I learned so much about myself, and the way the world does actually work, that now I'm a changed person with a whole new set of kick-ass skills. For example, now I can speak Cantonese."

You can't write those exact words but if you can convey the sentiments, people will admire your honesty, boldness and determination to find your way through. They'll recognise that you're better for your enforced break.

Try a 'guffaw' test on your CV. Will including a lengthy section on your interest in home surgery and the messy tale of your DIY appendectomy add to your credibility, or will it make the reviewer spit coffee over the desk and reach for their Twitter account? Are there any spectacularly appalling typos? What about phrases which unintentionally jump out for all the wrong reasons?

> "I was pleased to finally have a female manager so I could fill a hole and write about it on my CV."

> "I ride the tube every day before work."

> "I'm bilingual in three languages."

> "I'm adept at dealing with customers' conflicts that arouse."

Auto-correct is a terrible curse.

Don't forget the 'hurl' test. You clearly need to big yourself up, but in the cold light of day some statements can be utterly cringe-worthy.

> "I'm a lean mean marketing machine," might be true, but it won't get you through.

> "I'm a natural born leader." Says who?

> "I am truly excellent at …" Uh huh?

Keep your statements evidence-based and let the reviewer decide whether you're excellent or not. This is the time to be implicit, rather than explicit, about the fact that you are your own personal centre of excellence. In reality, you don't need to be excellent. If you are, fine, but you only need to tick more boxes, more strongly, than the other candidates, in order to be the one standing victoriously, watching the walking dead being fed into the shredder as they collectively hum 'Always look on the bright side of life'.

Spelling, grammar and punctuation checks are absolutely essential. Even if you've already run a check, do another final check on your finished CV. Ideally, if possible, get a friend to proofread it as well.

I'm not going to lie, proofreading is painful, especially when you've been at it solidly for days, you're surrounded by a mountain of dead take-away cartons, your clothing reeks from a whole plethora of bodily secretions and you're just impatient to get the damn thing done with.

Nevertheless, proofread it and proofread it and proofread it again, until you've wrestled it down to being the world's best bamfing CV ever. Show yourself to be the true professional that you are. Aren't you going to be loud, proud and on a cloud when you get to that interview?

The above proofreading tests can be modified and applied to application forms and covering letters but there are some additional checks to make, when planning to submit an application form.

Print out what you think may be a final copy and proofread the printed pages as this will often expose previously hidden errors quite effectively.

Check each and every box with a fresh eye. Do it slowly, box by box and with your mind fully on the task. Check the spelling, punctuation and grammar.

Check the 'name' boxes very specifically, as forms vary as to whether they ask for the family name or Christian name first. Trust me when I say that there is little worse than having an interviewer gleefully score the first point against you with, "Hello Mr. Jon, please take a seat."

Re-read the guidance notes, if any are provided. Make sure you've complied with specific instructions. Sometimes strict word limits are imposed or there's an instruction not to add additional sheets. There may be specific instructions on how to list your employment experience. Break these at your peril.

Check the current / past employment box. These may be separated and there may be specific instructions provided on what each should contain. If you don't have a current employer then make sure you've included the words 'not applicable', or something similar. If you currently have a non-career job or a part-time job, normally you should list it, but make its status clear. That helps to avoid the occasional brain-crash experienced by reviewers, when they ask themselves why a council soil-movement technician is applying for a senior research analyst's job.

Previous employment experience is normally required in reverse chronological order. Make sure you've listed yours correctly. If you're asked for your responsibilities in each job, make sure to provide them. Unless asked for, your achievements are probably best presented using the main 'tell us why you're suitable' box. Study the form to see whether they are mainly looking for flat facts only in this section, rather than supporting commentary.

Check the 'tell us why ...' box. Hopefully by now, this is the one area that you've absolutely done to death but have another check through. Have you hit all of the main requirement points solidly? Have you clearly explained why you're suitable? Have you explained (if asked) why you want this job? Is it all concise, focused, interesting and readable?

Check the 'your interests' section, or whatever the equivalent is on your form. Do your interests directly support requested experience or character traits? Test whether each and every item, word and paragraph adds to your application. If it doesn't, remove it because to leave it in is generally a risk.

For example, have you listed rock-climbing simply because you're passionate about it? Then consider losing it from your application. It's a good, solid interest but will the employer really want a key resource who engages in such a high-risk activity? Alternatively, have you shown that the determination, focus and courage required to climb are part of your make-up and that the organisation would benefit from having you on board? You have to explicitly state how you and the job might benefit from your experience.

Submitting your application

Your whole application, whatever it consists of, should now be finely tuned and ready for submission. There's one more final, final check to do.

Make absolutely certain that everything you've written is one hundred per cent consistent with your online presence. LinkedIn is clearly useful but it is quite easy to end up with information that jars, when your profile and CV are compared side by side.

So that's it. You've searched, you've found, you've applied.

Now, if you cup your hand to your ear and listen really carefully, you'll just about be able to sense the first stirrings of the horde. You're in the game and now you're the prey.

Nothing you can do will stop them. Will you be one of those left standing when the first cut is made and the list of interviewees is compiled? If you've done your job correctly so far, that answer will be a 'yes'.

It's time to prepare. Start your fitness programme now so that you're ready for when that invitation to attend an interview comes.

Key point summary 4 - Applications

Key Learning Points

- Simply understanding how the basic selection processes work, and adapting accordingly, can move your odds from 1 in 1,000 to 1 in 10.
- At the application stage, you are not trying to win that job, you're only trying to win a place at the next stage of the selection process.
- Your application may be assessed by a software robot, looking for specific keywords, prior to being reviewed by a person.
- These days, your application is more likely to prompt a profile test and / or an early-stage telephone or online video pre-interview.
- Employers feel that graduates lack real-world skills. Any such skills that you can present will score highly for you, in comparison to your peers.
- It is not enough to have certain skills; you have to state that you have them AND show how you've gained them and what benefits they bring.
- Experience gained informally with smaller employers can be just as valuable as experience gained on project work with a larger employer.
- Trim out the surplus words from your CV / application to focus attention on the important points you make about yourself. Less is more.
- Your chances of success increase if you apply for roles to which you are inherently more suited, in terms of your basic character.
- Submit your application as soon as you can; shortlists can sometimes be drawn up before the closing date. If you miss the deadline, forget it.
- Applications for jobs in the public sector need to be structured very differently to applications for jobs in the private sector.
- As a rough guide, CVs should be as short as possible and formatted to draw attention to a minimum number of key points. White space is king. Write as much as you can on application forms, white space is death.
- Paradoxically, recruiters look for stand-out candidates but commonly reject CVs and applications that stray from the conventional.
- Competency-based questions require more comprehensive answers which can be developed using a tool like the STAR technique.

Signposts

- The more you understand about how your application will be assessed, the better you'll be able to prepare your application.
- There are two primary criteria for interview selection, against which your application will be judged: do you tick all of the boxes on the person specification and how do you compare to other candidates?
- Your CV / application needs to survive three stages of assessment: the removal of the definite 'nos; grading into 'yes', 'no' or 'maybe' piles and the sifting of the 'yes' pile to select for inclusion on the shortlist.
- Understanding what the employer says they want, and what unstated 'extras' they also want, will help you to target your application better.

- Producing a fully-tailored CV / application can easily take a full day; make sure that you do it right and that your time-investment is justified.
- Even for cold-calling CVs, at the very least, tailor your CV towards the industry that you're looking to work within.
- Accept that everyone has weaknesses but few recognise and address them. Being honest in your application can win trust from the reviewer.
- It takes a lot of effort to consistently present an upbeat, positive attitude; it only takes one negative comment to tear all of that down.
- Doing background research on the organisation, the role and their people will enable you to better match your CV to their expectations.
- Employers prefer candidates who can show a real interest in the role, their company and the sector. Understand their commercial pressures.
- Employers judge candidates' potential by looking for previous experience of teamwork, leadership, proactivity and personal initiative.
- The format and presentation of your CV should remain conventional: use the structure of the content to draw attention to yourself instead.
- Your covering letter (if one is required) should set the scene for the reviewer and lead them forwards to your value-added attributes.

Actions

- Find out exactly what down-stream selection processes will be used to assess your application and be ready to face them, well in advance.
- To maximise your chances of selection for interview, use your application to appeal directly to the reviewer – make their job easier.
- Use a strong, bullet-pointed, summary introduction at the start of CVs and application forms, to really direct the interviewer's attention.
- Align your ambitions with what you calculate are those of the recruiting organisation in the medium and longer term.
- Craft your CV / application until you feel happy with it, then revisit it to ensure that it has all of the right keywords included.
- Ensure that your CV and application clearly convey your highly-positive work ethic as employers complain that candidates often lack this.
- Reassure employers by showing that you are adaptable, trustworthy and loyal and have a strong sense of personal responsibility.
- List off-topic personal achievements which can demonstrate your potential to achieve things in your chosen field of work.
- On your CV / application, show that you have previously made things happen such that, if you hadn't done something, nobody would have.
- When you want to use bullet points in a section, try to limit yourself to three. Any more risks diffusing the attention of the reviewer.
- Proofread everything you propose to submit to within an inch of its life.

Chapter 5 – Interviews: meeting the tiger

"There are no secrets to success, it's the result of preparation, hard work and learning from your mistakes." Colin Powell

So, the letter's arrived. You're on a direct path to a potential job and now your work really starts. You're excited but you feel that clench of fear deep within your gut. Do you really want this? Are you tough enough? Is it actually possible for you to win?

Yes, yes and yes are the answers.

If you don't truly believe that, if you don't feel it deep within your soul, go away and come back when you do. Doubt is like a dementor on steroids. It will render you defenceless, steal your soul and leave your body an empty husk.

Fear, however, is completely different. Don't get the two confused.

It's not only okay to be afraid, it's a positive advantage. Tighten your grip on this opportunity by learning to channel your fear. You can definitely win this.

How do I know? There are three very good reasons:

1) someone has to win it, why not you?
2) you've already shown that you're a great match to the job and
3) the recruiter has decided that you're a contender.

Rest assured, they're not just getting you in for cup of tea and a bit of a catch-up. If you don't screw up during the interview process and everyone else does, the job is yours. Now that's not a bad position to be in, is it?

Recognise your invitation for what it really is – proof that someone already thinks you're worthy of this job. So far, you've silently massacred perhaps a hundred other applicants, now it's time for some hand-to-hand combat.

Opening yourself up to the judgement of others can be scary, but feel the fear and do it anyway, to quote the late Susan Jeffers, author of a self-help book by that name. If you win through, not only can you move your career forward, you'll regularly bank a pay cheque, probably for years to come.

How good is that?

It's time to be optimistic. Let's kick some arse, as they say in the world's best high-quality, low-budget, East End gangster movies. Get your weapon out and polish it until people go weak at the knees and quake at the very sight of it. Plan to fire that big gun and take 'em down.

During this chapter, we'll step through the following key topics:

- your rules of engagement;
- understanding the various interview selection processes;
- preparing effectively for an interview;
- attending your interview(s) and
- what to do after the interview.

This chapter will show you how to:

- conduct further research, to a deeper level;
- develop great answers to the tough questions you'll be asked and
- rehearse, rehearse and rehearse until you're perfect.

It's possible to gain experience of almost all of the commonly used interview processes beforehand, so this chapter will show you how to approach:

- making a personal introduction at a group interview;
- answering questions at a 'normal' interview;
- responding thoroughly during competency-based interviews;
- taking part in team-based exercises;
- behaving during role-play exercises;
- speaking during open discussion sessions;
- handling task-based exercises;
- making formal presentations;
- giving impromptu presentations;
- surviving off the wall 'creativity' questions.

The rules of engagement

Let's start by looking at three rules of engagement that I strongly urge you to commit to, right now.

Rule number 1 –You can win, you will win.

Rule number 2 – From this moment, you are never not in an interview situation until you have received the job offer.

Rule number 3 –You will not turn this job down until after you have an offer, even if you want to when you are part way through the process.

Rule number one is fairly straightforward to get your head around but rule number two needs considerably more work than you might ever imagine.

Absolutely everything you do online, offline, at home, in college or at work now potentially affects your chances of success. Every conversation, email, text and instant message that you exchange with the potential employer should be thought of as being under scrutiny. Not only that, but any Facebook and Twitter posting you make might be picked up.

> "Just got news of an interview with GigaCorp. I think they're a bunch of jerks but I thought I'd go along for the interview practice and you never know what they might offer me."

Yep, that's all going to go well then, if your posting is spotted.

Each single, positive, professional thing you do from this point forward may not increase your chances of success very much but one isolated, sloppy, negative, unprofessional error can wipe you out in a heartbeat. That's just the way things are. Learn to relax, but think carefully before you write or speak.

This becomes even more essential later in the process. When you arrive at reception for an interview, behave as though it's already started. At the interview, even if someone says, "Enjoy your lunch, this is not part of the interview process," it is. Even if they say, "Drinks in the bar tonight, it's not part of the interview process," it is. Even if someone from the organisation is informally running you back to the station afterwards, treat the situation as though you're still in an interview.

Finally, when you're on that train home let out a long slow breath, relax, pick up your mobile and talk to a friend if you wish. Just remember – you're still in an interview.

Sounds nuts?

You have no idea who else is in the same carriage, listening to you. There could easily be an employee nearby, either on their way to a meeting or on their way back home. At first they might secretly smile with benevolent amusement but that can change when they hear you gloating that the interviewer missed how you'd previously been sacked for trying to drive a wooden stake through your boss's heart, whilst high on battery acid cocktails.

Realistically, the odds of a problem are small but do you really want to put in days and days of work, only to throw it all away with one unguarded comment? As I said before, a dose of paranoia will keep you alive considerably longer than might otherwise be the case.

By way of example, I once climbed into a taxi waiting to take me back to the station, not realising that the taxi driver was the husband of the woman I'd just met. The two of them regularly used this arrangement to gain an extra insight into the views of people attending meetings and interviews. I made it through okay, but I still wake up sweating at my close brush with the hand of fate.

Whilst such things are rare, I'm just trying to ram home the point that you should be on guard and thoroughly professional from the moment you walk through someone's door until the point you walk back through your own.

Bear in mind that it's common for interviewers to ask receptionists or secretaries what they thought of the prospective candidates that day.

> "Hi Sue, any of today's candidates stand out?"

> "Yeah, that creepy one with the weird tie told me that he'd gone commando for the day and asked me if I'd tried it."

> "Uh huh."

You might be the world's most charming flirt or chat-up artist. Fine. Save it for when you're not on a mission. Only James Bond gets to work and play at the same time. No one likes the prospect of working with a creep, or a smug bastard, for the next few years. They'll kill you in a trice, just to be safe.

I had interviewed four people for a post, and the final two were neck and neck, until Sue told me that one of them was one pair of trolleys short of a best-dressed interview competition.

The point is to be aware of the need to behave professionally and think clearly about what you're saying at all times. Whatever else you do, don't get hammered for random stupidity after all your hard work. I've put a lot of effort into getting you this far and I'm beginning to feel an emotional bond. I don't want to see you fail now. You're going all the way, like it or not.

Speaking of which, don't forget rule number three. Get an offer before you turn the job down, even if it begins to look like the job or the package sucks when you're only part way through the interview process. Whether you accept the offer or whether you don't, it will do your confidence a power of good.

Having an actual offer in your hand is the only time you'll be in control but don't get cocky, offers can be withdrawn.

You can bank a real offer if you want to do so, but if you are going to turn it down, make sure that you do so professionally. That involves putting your real feelings aside and choosing your response very carefully.

Why should you bother and how honest should you be?

> "Your staff are a bunch of jerks, your organisation is doomed to failure and you tried to touch my arse at the end of the interview. I'd rather attempt a DIY wax-job, with gaffer tape, in public, than work for a perv like you."

> "Your salary offer is pathetic, if not actually illegal. Frankly, I'm just not that desperate."

> "I note that fourteen previous employees have filed cases with an industrial tribunal in the last month alone. After not much thought I've decided to pass on the opportunity to join them."

That's all a bit too honest.

If you are absolutely certain you don't want to work there, regardless of your reasons, go with a completely neutral statement to turn down their offer.

For example, "Regretfully, I've had an alternative offer," or perhaps, "Sadly I don't believe that it's the right job for me at this stage of my career."

Try and make your statement true but most definitely non-critical. If the recruiting organisation really are impressed by you, and can see your future potential, they might choose to make you a better offer. It would be a tragic waste if your rejection letter was so rude that it put them off the idea.

Likewise, it would be unfortunate if they advertise your dream job next year but your file has your old letter of abuse carefully stapled to the front with "Do not employ. Ever." stamped across it.

Never refuse a job offer purely as part of a strategy to lever more money or better terms. Such attempts at blackmail tend to be obvious and can backfire. Chapter six will take you through the finer points of legitimately negotiating the terms of any offer made to you.

In the meantime, I very much want you to stick with rule number three until you're either dead or you've received an offer. Committing to rule number three will maximise your opportunities, come what may:

- this job might well be better than nothing;
- they might unexpectedly offer you a more appealing job or
- you may be able to use this offer to negotiate better terms elsewhere.

Moving on, you've got an interview coming up and you've committed to the three rules of engagement. Now what?

Interview selection processes

It's very important to understand how the organisation is going to be running the interview process. Is there just one face-to-face interview at the potential employer's office to get through, and then the decision will be made?

If so, the next few days or weeks of your life are easier to predict and manage, but what will be involved? Will it be one person or several, facing you at the interview? Will one of them be your boss, if you're successful? Where do the others fit in? Will it be a straightforward question and answer session? How many people will they interview? Where are you in the running order? How long will it take them to make the decision? What's the expected start date?

You may or may not be able to get solid answers to any or all of these questions in advance of the actual interview, but the more you understand what you'll have to face and how the decisions will be made, the better prepared you can be.

The single interview is a very simple one-step process, but it is becoming rarer due to its lack of resilience as a recruitment tool.

When reviewed after twelve months, it used to be that less than half of all recruitment exercises could be judged as successful when the achievements of the candidate were matched against the initial recruitment objectives. Some employees would leave, some would be let go and many of those retained would stay, but underachieve.

That, bear in mind, was the case where a systematic and professional selection process was being applied. For those employers running sloppy and unstructured recruitment processes, the situation was usually much worse.

The cost in financial, productivity and lost opportunity terms was simply humungous for the organisation and sometimes fatal. It was argued that using a prospective employee's star sign as the primary decision-making tool might offer a better success rate.

As a consequence, selection processes have only tended to become more complex in recent years, as employers seek to improve their recruitment success rate. A great deal more attention is now devoted to understanding more about your capabilities, how suited you might be to the role and how well you might fit in with existing employees and the organisation's culture.

Consequently, employers now aim to spend much more time with candidates via multi-stage assessment processes. If you turn up to an interview not knowing what to expect, you are likely to be quite badly wounded in fairly short order.

On the plus side, you can now do a lot of 'fit-analysis' yourself, before you get anywhere near the interview room.

Armed with a deeper understanding, you can work out how to show that you do in fact match the role very well. That should put you right up there with the leading group of candidates, if not at the head of the bunch, depending on how much work the others have also undertaken in preparation.

Interestingly, despite the application of many additional assessment stages and techniques, it's not at all certain that the average employer's success rate has improved by very much, since both sides have now upped their game.

If you know how the game is played and you're well prepared, you're in with a great chance. If you don't, you're a dead person walking, hence your fundamental need to find out what the entire recruitment process will involve.

So, having survived the application assessment processes thus far, the following might now be coming your way:

- a preliminary telephone interview;
- an online video interview;
- multiple interviews with different people;
- an interview with two or three interviewers;
- a more formal, full panel interview;
- an assessment centre day and
- in-depth profile testing.

Multiple interviews are common. That might involve several interviews on the same day or further interviews on different days. In the latter case, the pool of interviewees may or may not be steadily reduced, stage by stage.

Multiple interviews can be used to look at different aspects of your suitability, or a later interview can be used to validate the results of an earlier one, perhaps by someone more senior.

Knowing what to expect will ensure that you are psychologically prepared and more confident.

Telephone interviews are possible. Likely even. They are now commonly used to cull numbers to a more manageable group-size, prior to real-world interviews. You should be told in advance if such an interview is to take place, so be prepared. Fully. Treat them as though they were full interviews.

Ideally, you'll receive an email inviting you to suggest a time for a telephone interview and a number for the recruiter to call you on. If the organisation is professional, they may include details of the structure and format of the interview. Take the time to prepare both physically and mentally for the call.

The worst case is where you get a call out of the blue and come under pressure to do a 'quick chat' there and then. This could be a deliberate ploy to try and get a more realistic view of you as a person and how you cope with the unexpected. It is more likely to be because it's a sloppy, unprofessional, low-budget recruitment agency in a hurry. Either way, your opportunity is a real one so you need to cope and the best way of coping is to be prepared.

If you do get an unexpected call and it really is a bad time, don't be afraid to say so and ask if it's possible to re-schedule. Any professional interviewer will want you to be in a fit state to give of your best.

We touched on some points about having answers to common questions well prepared in Chapter 2. This is vital, just in case of that unexpected call.

For the quick chat type of interview, the objective will be identify, at a fairly basic level, whether you're a serious candidate with a rational chance of doing the job. The interviewer will be likely to cover:

- why you applied;
- what you like about the organisation;
- why you feel you're suited;
- what you're like as a person;
- your longer term ambitions and
- a quick summary of your qualifications and experience to date.

The recruiter may use a check list of basic traits to tick or cross, such as:

- whether you can speak effectively;
- whether you can structure your thoughts clearly;
- how you respond to mild pressure;
- how you talk to people;
- your general attitude toward the job in particular and
- your work in general.

I once knew an individual who was extremely bright but a question such as, "Hi mate, how's the weather doing?" would leave him speechless for a full fifteen seconds, until he could muster, "It's alright." As there was a hurricane blowing through earlier, I was left wondering whether the storm had in fact abated and he just loved wearing that wet suit to come into work.

There are some environments, research perhaps, where such personality traits are acceptable. However, in some roles, line management for example, they would be disastrous.

Most commonly, a telephone interview is a first-cut attempt at gauging whether you fit the required personality profile for the role in question. Assuming that you do, the second objective will be to confirm the extent to which you match the person specification.

To those ends, it's vital to identify the three to five key 'must-haves' for the role and be very clear which aspects of your background show that you have them. For each 'must-have', imagine being asked, "Can you tell which part of your experience or which of your qualifications supports your application, in this respect?" Construct and rehearse a tightly focused, summary statement for each.

A formal, fully in-depth, interview is rarer at this stage but would encompass a detailed look at your CV, qualifications and experience to date. You would need to be as prepared as you would be for a face-to-face interview.

When the call takes place, if you don't know already, find out how long it's expected to take and some information about the selection process or judgement criteria they'll use. That will help you to judge how to pitch your answers. If it is literally going to be ten minutes max, you won't want to be wasting time banging on relentlessly about one narrow topic. If it's going to be a full half hour plus, you'll want to know, so that you can give comprehensive answers. Either way, be precise and concise, don't ramble.

If you possibly can, around and after the pleasantries at the outset of the call, try to establish a rapport with the interviewer. It might not be possible but try, as you have nothing to lose. A great question to ask is something along the lines of, "Do you have a lot of these to do today?" It's a nice general and inoffensive ice-breaker type of question but an exchange on the subject might uncover exactly how many people you're up against and where in the call list you are: gold dust.

If you can have even a brief exchange with the interviewer and they warm to you, they might just cut you some slack later. Where you come up short with an answer to a question, they may well give you a hint to develop it further.

Okay, they might do this for everyone anyway but you can be sure that, if you get off on the wrong foot and they hate your guts from the outset, they'll die before they give you any help whatsoever. The more they think you are a credible, pleasant candidate, the more willing they'll be to help you.

If you're invited to ask questions at the end, a great one to go in with is, "What's your organisation like to work for? What's been good and what's been more challenging to experience?" Bear in mind that if the interviewer is a recruitment consultant you won't be able to use this question.

At the end of the call, be sure to ask when a decision will be made, how they'll come back to you and what the next stage in the process will be.

You can try asking whether there have been any points covered that give them cause for concern and that might reduce your chance of being put forward. You don't want to be too pushy on this, especially if it doesn't feel quite right, but if you don't ask, you don't get. It's worth a shot as you may get another chance to bolster a weak answer you gave earlier in the conversation.

Don't ask for feedback at this stage as it's highly unlikely the interviewer would be able, or even willing, to provide it. Other candidates are still in the running and a comparison needs them all to have been completed. There is also a danger of coming across as either narcissistic or insecure, depending upon your tone.

Apart from obviously trying to establish yourself as entirely credible for the role, aim to build up a positive impression in the mind of the interviewer. You can do this in several ways, some of them quite subtle.

- When the call starts, smile. A lot. It sounds mad, but it comes across in your voice.
- Make sure that your enthusiasm comes across, even if you're nervous.
- Either stand up or, if that feels too weird, at least sit upright in a good chair. It helps your breathing and ups the depth and authority of your voice.
- Be professional and speak appropriately. You can't help your accent, nor should you, but starting the call with, "Whaddup bitch," or launching into, "Mate, I am so up for this," or ending with, "Laters dude," will get you flagged as someone who is unable to exercise good judgement in a professional environment. A tit, in other words. This behaviour, glib comments and offensive humour are the equivalent of turning up to an interview stripped to the waist and showing off your redneck tats.
- Consciously decide that you 'like' the interviewer and really feel it. Another weird thing to do, but it's something else that comes across in your voice and can make a startling difference to your prospects. If they like you in return, you have a chance of being put through. If they hate you, you have zero chance. Do what you can. In the same vein, use their name occasionally, and definitely when winding up the call and thanking them. People like to be noticed.
- Make sure that you speak clearly and precisely. There is no point in stressing your killer advantages if the interviewer is struggling to hear you, or just can't figure out your meaning on a certain answer. If the line is bad, ask them to re-make the call. Pay attention to your diction. Not pronouncing words fully and running them into each other detracts from your message. Enunciate clearly and deliver defined sentences. Both of these help to present you as a clear-thinking individual, even if you're really in a complete mental panic.
- When answering, give an answer and stop. Hand it back to the interviewer, don't feel obliged to keep speaking to fill a void, as you'll inevitably fill it with rambling piffle. Sad, if all the interviewer was doing was turning the page of his notes for a moment.
- Do not swear during the course of the call, no matter how well you might be getting on, even if you're sliding nicely into a convivial, relationship-building, comfort zone. Why? Because it fucking jars. See? Even if they swear, don't do it. Slang is also a big no-no.
- Speak at a similar rate to the interviewer. It helps put you both on the same wavelength. At all costs, don't mimic their accent.
- Consciously don't 'um' and 'er'. Silently take the time you need to think instead. Although a few seconds of silence seems like a life-time, it isn't. You're better off delivering what you really want to say confidently, after a moment's thought. The interviewer will respect you for having presence of mind and mark you up accordingly.
- Avoid the word 'like', like. Phrases such as " … and I was, like, …" get very noticeable very quickly, and not in a good way.
- If you know you had real difficulty with an answer, forget about it and move on. Concentrate on your wins, not your losses.

- Try and stay away from politics, religion and currently controversial subjects unless the interviewer specifically raises one of them. If you have to answer, give a considered, balanced, non-zealous, response.
- Have some questions to hand for the end. Alternatively, don't be afraid to say that your points were in fact covered during the talk. Keep things brief and you'll be thanked.
- At the end, make it very clear that you've enjoyed the chance to talk about the opportunity, that you like the sound of the job and that you really would like to go through to the next stage. Do this even if you're not sure.
- After the call make detailed notes. This is absolutely vital. What went well? What went badly? Where do you think you scored? If you do get selected for a face-to-face interview, what might they bring up again from this conversation? What did you learn about the opportunity and their organisation? If you could do the whole thing again, what changes would you make to your answers? Fill as much space as you can whilst it's all still fresh in your mind. Keep the notes for future reference.

A video-call interview, using something like Skype, is another possibility for an early-stage selection process which might be used as a quick and dirty method to cull no-hopers.

I personally suspect that this will grow rapidly in popularity since it's a fast and low-cost method of taking a much closer look at candidates. The interviewer is able to read body language, general behaviour, expressions and stress levels, just as in a normal interview.

In addition to everything covered previously for telephone interviews, there are some additional factors that you'll need to proactively manage if you're going to make the video-call work for you. Again, it's preparation, preparation and preparation that will get you through and cut the opposition down.

Body language is the really crucial extra factor that you need to work hard at controlling. Try and look into the camera as often as possible, as though you were trying to make eye contact. It cuts the risk of you looking shifty. Move the video window you're watching to be as close to the webcam as possible.

Try and sit as still as you can. Swaying from side to side or waving your hands in Russell Brand fashion, especially on a low bandwidth connection, will leave the interviewer feeling seasick. Sitting still demonstrates self-control, even if you don't have any, and looks more professional.

Try and keep a separate window open, showing your side of the call, to ensure your head and shoulders are framed correctly and you don't look like you're peering over the edge of a parapet.

Sitting too close to the camera will come across as scary and threatening. Sitting too far away, so that you're a pin-prick in the distance, makes it hard for the interviewer to read your facial expressions. A head and shoulders shot is perfect. Oh, and don't wear a hat, especially not a German WWII helmet.

Bear in mind that you'll need to control the visual space behind you during the call. The interviewer spotting your completely naked partner wandering across-screen on the way back from a shower might cause amusement but it will be distracting and unprofessional.

Be aware of what is on your walls and in the room. A poster declaring your belief that Adolf Hitler simply had a bad press may give the wrong impression. A bong bubbling proudly away in the corner will make the interviewer wonder about your reliability. A huge pile of traffic cones, road-signs and street nameplates will have him writing to his ten thousand fellow employees, advising them to lock their offices if they employ you.

Dress appropriately, jim-jams won't cut it. Neither will an Ed Hardy tee shirt. No-one will expect you to wear a three piece whistle or a ball-gown, so go with smart-casual. Even though you do have human rights, I suggest that not dressing like Grayson Perry, or not thrusting a full cleavage at the screen, will considerably up your chances of selection.

In terms of appearance, being unwashed, unshaven or having an unruly mop of mad hair will make you look disorganised. Likewise, black eye-sockets with sunken eyes and veins looking like a map of the underground suggests an inability to organise and prepare properly, even if you do obviously have a Bellatrix Lestrange fetish and not a hangover.

Although group conversations are possible, it's most likely that a telephone or Skype interview will be a one-to-one affair.

Several interviewers might be present when it comes to a face-to-face interview. Each will have a different set of criteria to assess you against.

Two interviewers is a common and fairly comfortable number to face simultaneously. One is quite likely to be your future line-manager or departmental head and the other could well be from the HR department.

If, beforehand, you know who is attending and what the interest of each person is, you can prepare so that you can serve both masters. You should find that each person has a defined set of questions that each candidate will be asked to answer, so that duplication of effort can be avoided.

Full panel interviews are a less common, somewhat more daunting, variation on the theme and you may have to face up to seven interviewers simultaneously. Each is likely to have a different area of interest but it is possible that some of them will hardly speak at all. Such interviews tend to be the preserve of very large organisations or, more commonly, government and public sector organisations.

It's normal to be nervous and they'll expect you to be so, but they'll usually work to quickly put you at your ease. They'll want you to show the best of yourself as it's of no use to systematically kick to death every candidate that walks through their door.

As always, preparation is the key. Don't allow yourself to be fazed. Make good use of eye-contact with whoever you happen to be speaking to at any point in the proceedings. As you deliver your answers, scan the group. Be inclusive, not exclusive. Smile at appropriate times. If you can do that, you're half way to being a wow already.

Being asked to give a presentation at some point through a course of interviews is a strong possibility, since personal communication skills are increasingly important. You'll be glad to know that the duration should be short (five to ten minutes, perhaps) and you'll almost always be given the topic prior to attending the interview. On the plus side, you have time to prepare. On the minus side, you have more time to worry about it and sweat, if you're that way inclined.

Assessment centre interviews are often used for graduate recruitment. These are run as group interviews, so that the candidates' full range of capabilities can be more deeply assessed. An assessment centre day (or more) is likely to involve some or all of the following:

- making a personal introduction to the group;
- a 'normal' interview;
- a competency-based interview;
- taking part in team-based scenario exercises;
- role-play exercises;
- a topic-specific open-discussion session;
- an individual task-based exercise;
- making a formal presentation to the group;
- a short impromptu presentation and
- handling lateral-thinking or creativity-assessment questions.

At the end of the day, such an exercise is looking to achieve the same result as a straightforward interview would – namely, roles are vacant and they need filling with the most capable people. Assessment centres simply enable a deeper look at your suitability in the context of a 'team' environment.

It's vitally important that you understand the odds before you attend an assessment centre interview as there are usually multiple places on offer. Group sizes may typically vary from between ten and twenty people, with between five and ten places on offer. You could be wrestling with odds of between fifty-fifty and one-in-four but, so long as you know, you can manage them.

When an invitation to an assessment centre arrives, the above list of what you may face might get you out searching the supermarket shelves for old-style razor blades. My simple advice at that point would be to stop being so self-obsessed. It's not as though you're going to be water-boarded as part of the interview process. Yes, you will be pushed out of your comfort zone but so will everyone else and such events are not only fantastic experience for you, they can be a great deal of fun.

Just think about it. Ninety five per cent of attendees are likely to be bricking themselves in the same way as you. Accept your nervousness, channel the fear and push on, regardless. You'll gain respect and your odds will improve markedly.

Back on the premise of 'people believe what you tell them', if you show up looking as though you're prepared to roll your sleeves up and pitch in, even at the risk of making a tit of yourself, you're already well ahead of the tail-end Charlies and one step nearer making the cut. Just think of it in the same way as you would a drunken night out with friends, where there's a game of charades somewhere down the line. It's something to be enjoyed.

What about those super-confident types that you will undoubtedly feel inferior to? Ninety per cent of those will be taken out the back and whacked with a shovel. It won't be because they are intensely despised by normal human beings, it will be because such people are typically blind to the needs of others and therefore don't make good team-players. They're not tomorrow's leaders, they're tomorrow's let's-piss-everyone-in-the-department-off merchants. They're not tomorrow's earth-movers, they're tomorrow's self-centred, narcissistic, what's-my-fastest-way-up-the-greasy-pole merchants.

As you assess each, put most them in the 'walking dead' pile. Trust me, I've known a candidate produce a bayonet in the middle of a group discussion, just so that he could make the maximum impression (which he did), only to find that one of the assessors plunged it between his shoulder blades later.

Bear in mind that the techniques commonly used at assessment centre style interviews can all be used during the course of a more straightforward and traditional style of individual interview, although they may be adapted slightly.

Profile testing is now also more common. The depth of this will ultimately be dependent upon the amount of investment that an organisation is planning to spend on the successful candidates. It can include:

- intelligence testing;
- psychometric profiling;
- specific skill assessment;
- personal commitment assessment;
- medical assessment and
- fitness testing.

It used to be very expensive to structure such tests for one-off recruitment exercises, but off-the-shelf packages are now available. Even smaller SMEs can obtain and apply them at low cost. That does mean that you too can now research and practise such tests beforehand.

'Inbox exercises' are commonly used to assess a candidate's critical reasoning abilities and potential organisational, decision-making and managerial abilities. These are usually task-based exercises, whereby a pile of unstructured information is provided and the candidate has perhaps an hour to review it, propose some actions and then prepare a feedback session.

Such exercises can be structured to directly relate to recent challenges that a department or organisation has faced. Your feedback may be to an individual interviewer or perhaps to a departmental group. There aren't necessarily any right or wrong answers, provided that you can justify the conclusions that you reach. However, bias on the part of an interviewer can be a major problem if they are only looking for thinking which matches their own. Finding yourself in a diametrically-opposed position is not necessarily fatal, provided that you can show an ability to see others' points of view.

> "You're completely wrong."

These are not words to throw at the interviewer but don't be afraid to (politely) stick to your guns, if you can justify doing so.

As with a lot of tests, psychometric testing included, there is no ideal template that you should aim to fit. Interpretation of the results is most effective when used to facilitate a deeper exploration of some aspects of a candidate's make-up.

In terms of general trends for the near future, the following are quite likely:

- face-to-face interviews will be reserved for the later stages of any recruitment process because they're time-consuming and costly;
- face-to-face interview sessions will be fewer but longer. An interview will involve more stages and will intensively assess a wider range of skills than previously;
- team, communication, interpersonal and managerial skills will become paramount, regardless of field;
- pre-interview online testing will grow as those wider skills take centre stage and may include online 'games' and scenario-type exercises;
- telephone and Skype interviews will ultimately replace what used to be called the 'first interview' and
- online social media tools mean that your whole life, working history and track record will become almost permanently visible to anyone who wants access to it. (You've been warned.)

With all that in mind, let's move forward.

Preparation

Preparation is always key. I would strongly argue that the job is won or lost before you ever set foot in the interview room. If you're thoroughly prepared, you can not only handle anything they throw at you, you can return your own salvo, showing why you're the best choice. You may be outnumbered but you'll never be outgunned if you're prepared to put in the front-end effort.

To prepare, there are a number of steps to go through:

- clearly understand the remainder of the selection process;
- take your research to the next stage;
- develop great answers to the questions you'll be asked and
- rehearse, rehearse and rehearse.

More research in preparation for the interview, whatever form that might take, is essential. Your previous research, conducted before submitting your application, was undoubtedly limited by the need to balance time available with the need to actually submit your application by the deadline.

All of that research was very useful but it's done its job and now needs re-focusing. It can be relegated to just sit alongside information from the web, press reports, the organisation's website, social media sites, trade magazines, etc. It's still valuable but it's important to re-define your objectives, get new material together and re-compile the existing material.

If nothing else, your objective has changed from trying to win an interview to trying to win that second interview, or whatever else is next in the overall selection process. Your objectives now change to:

- become thoroughly familiar with what the organisation does, what your role will involve and where your prospective department adds value;
- understand the main opportunities and challenges that the organisation faces and what initiatives are in place to address them;
- determine what might make you a considerably better choice for the role than any of the other applicants.

You might have noticed that, from your point of view, the juiciest objective is third on the list. It's only with a good understanding of the organisation that you can truly identify which will be the best buttons to press during interviews.

Staying with the third objective for a moment, three elements can drive your push to be victorious:

- you need to meet the person specification in terms of qualifications, experience and fit. If you didn't already meet those you presumably wouldn't now be the proud holder of an invitation to an interview;
- what extra can you bring to the party? Can you show more potential? Do you have additional 'business' experiences or capabilities that add unexpected but very beneficial value to your application?
- can you find an edge over the other candidates? A secret weapon, if you will. Can you arrange to hide a handgun behind your back for when your peers show up to what they believe will only be a knife-fight?

It's only by plugging in information from your focused research that you can hope to address these three elements successfully.

> "I have experienced all aspects of light bulb manufacture and took part in a project which cut production wastage by 38% and overall costs by 23%."

> "Wow. It's just a crying shame we don't make light-bulbs here. We're looking for people to work on wind turbine fabrication and assembly. NEXT."

There was great experience on offer, it just wasn't aimed at the target. The shot risked being entirely wasted or, at best, scored low on points.

> "I have very strong experience in problem analysis, solution identification and change management in a manufacturing environment. During my work experience, I worked on a project which successfully cut production wastage by 38% and overall costs by 23%."

Same job, different words. With the latter statement, you've put your generic skills across and shown how valuable they can be to the recruiting organisation, not just to light bulb manufacturers.

Research is key. Know what the organisation does, what you'll be doing and what the organisation needs for it to be successful. Then tailor the presentation of your attributes accordingly.

As a starting point, your invitation letter may well include further information that could provide additional research directions for you. But what can you do about finding an edge over the other candidates?

If your Dad was the interviewer's boss? What if your Mum owned a large chunk of shares in the organisation? Do you think that might influence your chances of success? It might. It might not, if anyone had any sense at all.

The vast majority of us will never be in that situation, but imagine if you already knew your interviewer, before you went into the room. Would that make a difference?

If everyone is professional, it wouldn't get you the job but it would probably ensure that you at least got a fair hearing. That's not something everyone can rely on. Interviewers are already biased before they even meet the candidates. They've already scored and ranked them, so how could they not be influenced by that?

If you are one of the lower-ranked candidates invited to an interview, all is certainly not lost. You will just have to fight that bit harder. That's where learning to present your wider capabilities and added-value will score for you.

But what if you could start to level off that disadvantage before you even entered the room? Or, what if you could further cement in the advantage you already have, if you're at the head of the list? What might get the interviewer to feel even more kindly disposed towards you?

Imagine if you knew something about the interviewer's job and what their biggest problems were. Imagine if you knew the one key thing that they were really stressed about and the other candidates didn't. Imagine if you had mutual acquaintances, or you'd both worked for the same organisation previously, or if you both did the same degree, or went to the same university or both undertook a similar project. Imagine if the interviewer used to be friends with one of your tutors. Maybe you've both supported the same charity by doing fun-runs. Perhaps you both support the same team in whatever sport interests you. Perhaps you've both holidayed in the same place.

Sounds unlikely? Sounds like it's all just wishful thinking? Today, with access to social media and some deep research on your part, it would be more surprising if you couldn't find something in common with the person you'll be meeting, even if they are a thousand years old, dry as a snake's throat in the Namibian desert and *the* world expert in the design of narrow-gauge knitting needles. With a supposed maximum of six degrees of separation between you and the Prime Minister, a line of contact will be shorter than you think.

Dig deep, you need some information. Any information. It will help.

If you think about it, you're attempting to play a variation of the 'school tie' card. You'll always read articles suggesting that you need to have attended the right school or university in order to win some jobs. That problem is not as prevalent as is often suggested, but the simple fact is that people will tend to stick with the familiar, and with known quantities, if they can.

This is now your opportunity to play a trump card. If you can find something in common with the interviewer, you're creating a new clique, putting yourself and the interviewer firmly in it and excluding the other candidates, regardless of what school they attended.

It's a neat trick, if you can pull it off. Sadly, often you may not know exactly who will interview you, or you just may not be able to find anything useable out about them beforehand but every so often you might. Be aware of the possibilities to subtly influence recruiting decisions in your favour.

What else might you do, in terms of deeper research?

Build some bridges. Make contact with someone at the organisation beforehand. Ideally, it would be great to exchange even just a few words with the person who will be conducting your interview. As a minimum, it can be an ice-breaker for you, helping you to de-stress by realising that the people you'll be meeting are human after all.

Furthermore, it can be a wonderful opportunity to gather a few small titbits of information that might just give you an edge to work with. You might hear those magic words, "The department needs the recruit to be really strong on …". There you go, inside information, straight from the source.

Finally, if you can hit your stride, you can start to bond with the interviewer. Any positive vibes you can induce might just swing it for you, when there's only two of you left standing.

What can you ring up about? Any area of ambiguity is useful as you can legitimately ring for clarification without sounding creepy or desperate. You could possibly ask if you need to prepare anything specific beforehand, depending upon what information you've been given in the invitation.

You may be unclear exactly where to go for the interview or who you should ask for when you arrive. Use that as a starter, if necessary.

It's also extremely useful to find out whether decisions will be made on the day, or later, and how quickly you're likely to find out the result.

The real key to success with making preliminary contact is to be direct, specific and confident. Have a checklist of points in front of you when you call and make notes on everything. Any new information is highly valuable to you, no matter how small a nugget, because then it's something you possess that the other members of the horde don't. Guard it jealously. Calculate how to use it to optimum effect.

When it comes down to it, you just may not be able to find a good enough reason to make contact. It may not be possible to speak to someone you will actually meet on the day. If that's the case, don't worry, you're no worse off than you were and no worse off than the other interviewees.

Bear in mind that this approach can be a double-edged sword. If you make a balls of it, you risk being worse off than you would have been if you hadn't bothered. Stay safe, keep things neutral and listen carefully to the reactions you get. If your call is clearly unwelcome, don't push it. You can always ask if there's a more convenient time to call back.

Try not to get too stressed about your call. At the end of the day, the recruiting organisation want the best person they can get for the role. They'll go a long way and do anything that will help achieve that result. They actually want you to succeed and should be more than happy to provide any extra information that you need, provided that your demands aren't unfair or unreasonable.

Whatever you do, keep your conversation relevant, to the point and short. Do not ramble. If you are really lucky, the person you reach may be a very friendly but hopelessly sloppy, untrained and thoroughly unprofessional interviewer who will do the rambling for you, with only minor prompts. If so, suck them dry for every nugget of information you can leech out of them.

Make encouraging noises throughout. At the end, thank them profusely and say that you're really looking forward to meeting them.

Anything not to talk about? Yep. It's a very bad idea to ring up, explain that your heavily-ulcerated legs mean you can't stand up, a sky-diving injury to your back means you can't sit down and chronic tennis elbow means you can't hold a telephone, but then enquire if any of that will affect your suitability.

"Not until now," will be the unspoken response.

Think. Only ever draw attention to the positives about yourself, never the negatives. Speaking of which, do remember to Google yourself and plan to handle anything that might ricochet at the interview.

Develop great answers to the questions you'll face.

But what questions will they ask you at the interview? Specifically.

If you knew every question coming up you could gain a substantial advantage by constructing responses in advance and practising their delivery until you could do so perfectly.

Whilst you're not going to be given a list beforehand, you can make a pretty fair stab at guessing the questions likely to come up. Depending upon the selection process chosen by the employer, you may have to face any or all of:

- standard questions targeting something specific about you;
- competency-based questions, which focus on situations you've faced previously and how you dealt with them;
- scenario questions, which present hypothetical situations to see how you would approach them and
- creativity-related questions, which aim to place you in a completely unfamiliar situation to see what you come up with.

The style of questions under each category is distinct and you will need to identify them on the fly and deal with them accordingly. You are very unlikely to be told, "Okay brace yourself, here comes a competency-based question."

Before you attend the interview you need to become thoroughly familiar with each type of question and be well-rehearsed in the delivery of your tailored responses.

Take the following main steps.

1) Identify stretching questions under each category.
2) Learn simple processes to deal with them.
3) Develop targeted answers.
4) Internalise those answers.
5) Practise delivering your answers.

We covered dealing with competency-based questions in the last chapter. These are sometimes referred to as behavioural questions but, confusingly, the same term is often applied when referring to scenario questions.

Rather than use the term 'behavioural question' as a catch-all, I think it's useful to separate such questions into competency and scenario categories, as it will help you to deliver better quality answers. Competency-based questions typically look backwards at real situations you've been in, whereas scenario-type questions look forward at fictitious ones you haven't yet experienced.

The STAR technique, which we covered in Chapter 4, conveniently provides you with a simple but solid process to comprehensively address questions from both categories. If you're not already thoroughly familiar with the STAR technique, now is the time to take it fully on board.

What about standard questions? In fact, what is a standard question?

This is really a catch-all term for questions which typically target something specific about you. They are theoretically easier to handle than competency or scenario questions, but therein lies the trap.

It's too easy not to provide a comprehensive answer, especially if you're slightly nervous or your mind goes blank. Perversely, it's also all too easy to nervously ramble on forever, spewing forth inconsequential piffle.

There isn't one defined process to use when answering standard questions. For many it may be possible to use the STAR technique but there are always three broad guidelines to follow, which will help you a lot.

- Follow the questioner's lead.
- Be positive throughout.
- Be succinct.

Firstly, follow the questioner's lead. Be aware of whether questions are 'closed' or 'open'. Closed questions are designed to elicit a very specific answer.

"What's your name?" clearly leaves only one possible answer.

Likewise, "Were you, or were you not, sacked?" leaves very little wiggle room.

Some questions can be unintentionally closed. For example, "Are you well?" That's a closed question but a 'yes' or 'no' response would seem abrupt or even rude. It's conventional to expand your answer to such a question as though it were not so closed, and thereby soften the response. No one will ever criticise your answer with, "Hey, asshole? That was a closed question. Duh."

In interviews, closed questions are normally used to clarify a specific point and you'll generally find most questions are open, giving you more scope to deliver a full response. "How are you today?" is an open version of the same question, which offers you the opportunity to provide that fuller response.

Even though there may be scope to work in a longer answer to a closed question, you should consider whether it's wise to do this. The 'are you well' question is probably being used, perhaps even subconsciously, as a means of sending the sub-text of 'we're all busy people so let's crack through the pleasantries'. If you then bang on for minutes, rather than taking the hint, you're inevitably going to induce stress and annoyance, harming your chances of selection. Be aware.

Closed questions are often used at the end point of a line of enquiry. To pin you down, they may be the result of frustration. If you fudge around something, like the sacking question earlier, it makes it obvious that you're trying to dodge a bullet and it will count heavily against you. If you end up facing an unpleasant closed question like that, face it directly, earn the respect for having done so and then try to move forward.

Secondly, be positive. Ideally, nothing negative should come out of your mouth during the entire interview. Negative responses inevitably put a downer on the proceedings and cast you in a negative light. Things can only go badly from there.

> "How are you today?"

> "Terrible. I was up nearly all night with diarrhoea and then slept through the alarm. I stubbed my toe, forgot my umbrella, missed the bus and got soaked in the rain. Just outside I dropped all my papers in a puddle, tripped over on the way in and now I feel nervous as hell. Thanks for asking though."

> "Oka-a-y. Hold on a minute there sport whilst I just go and type up your rejection letter."

Basically, no one cares about your problems. You're both there to do a job. At all times, give responses that bathe you in a positive light. It's expected of you, even if you are dripping when you arrive. Even if you've been mugged on the way there. Even if you end up being delivered in an ambulance.

> "How are you?"

> "Great thanks, glad to be here. How about you?"

> "Yes, thank you. Erm … you're a little wet. And … you're bleeding."

> "Oh, it's nothing, I just got caught in a shower, tripped up and fell under a bus. It's only my left arm that's a problem. Can I leave my coat somewhere to dry?"

It's got to get you off to a better start than wailing at the gods would.

Thirdly, be succinct. Say what you need to say and stop. Answer the question as precisely as you can and then, if you're confident you've covered all the ground, shut up. Less is more. Hand it back to the interviewer.

Do not feel obliged to fill silences. If they stare at you, smile and wait. If, after ten minutes, you find you're still delivering your response to the opening 'how are you today' question, you can rest assured that, when they've revived the interviewer, your application will be put on the 'over my dead body' pile.

Those three basic guidelines should keep you on track for most of the standard questions you'll ever face and can certainly help with your delivery of answers to competency and scenario questions as well.

So, where do you get the questions from, in advance?

In Appendix A, there's a selection of questions to get you started. However, do tailor them more specifically to your own situation, if you can. To help you do that and to help generate further, more targeted questions, start with the information you have that is specifically relevant to this position, namely: the brief; your research and your tailored CV / application.

Questions you'll face are likely to be focused on the following broad topics.

- **Suitability** – your background, qualifications, career to date and career expectations.
- **Experience** – your work experience and any other relevant experience gained from your outside interests and activities.
- **Competence** – your capabilities with respect to role responsibilities, planning, resource management, leadership, team-work, interpersonal relationships and communication.
- **Potential** – your character, general attitude, motivation, achievements, level of initiative and fit with the organisation.

Draw up lists of standard questions that you think you might be asked under each heading. Aim for at least ten questions under each. If you have more, prioritise those which you think are hardest to respond to. Make sure that your list covers the full scope of requirements listed in the job description and person specification. If you need to, increase the numbers.

Separately, identify the core competences required for the role and draw up ten competency-based questions for yourself. Refer back to Chapter 4 so that you are clear on the format of a competency-based question. "Tell me about a time / situation when … ," is a good start for such a question.

Then, using the brief and your research, draw up ten scenario-type questions that consider issues you might face when working in the advertised role. "What would you do in a situation where … ," will get you going. Be as inventive and challenging as you like. Just make them relevant to the job.

What you need now are excellent answers to all of those questions, but what makes for such answers? Why might one answer be better than another? What would make your answer stand above the next candidate's answer to the same question?

Let's spend a few minutes on this, because if you spend all of your time generating merely average answers, you're less likely to win through. That's because you'd be relying on every other candidate being a wild-eyed power junky, demonstrably insane or eight months and twenty five days pregnant.

First and foremost, with all of your answers, focus on the needs of the job, the organisation and the interviewer. Your needs are rarely relevant.

Every single answer has to relate in some way to what you can do for them.

> "So tell me, what do you want from this job?"

> "I'm not sure, what's in it for me?"

If you hear those words coming out of your mouth, they'll be your last. If the interviewer even suspects they're behind an answer you give, you'll be on a feet-first trip back to the boonies in a box.

> "I really want the satisfaction of knowing that I achieved all of my tasked objectives and helped the whole department move forward. That way I can be sure of building my career on solid achievements that have delivered real benefits for my employer."

Better. Not only are you focusing on their needs, you're showing that you're ambitious, and have a clear understanding of whose priorities come first.

The second thing to bear in mind is that you should answer the question that is asked, not the one you wish had been asked. If you fail to cover the ground fully you'll lose marks, no matter how much extra (unasked for) information you provide.

Thirdly, aim to be as informative as possible about any previous work or projects. Set the context clearly (where you worked, what you did and in what circumstances). Be explicit about achievements and quantify things simply.

Don't try and blind the interviewer with science, or baffle them with endless numbers, as you don't get marks for being geeky, opaque or elitist. Put things into terms everyone can understand and link your achievements to the benefits attained by the department or organisation.

Fourthly, use your best information only. Don't drag in everything you ever did on a previous project or job. Distil out the salient parts and discard the rest. To repeat a point from earlier, if you reel off a list of ten things, the interviewer may remember only the last three, undoubtedly the least important ones.

Fifthly, focus on situations where you've added extra value in the past, or where you might do so in the future. For example, if you're applying to a French organisation, even though you might be UK based and a second language is not a requirement, if you're fluent in French you obviously have more potential long-term value than the next person.

Likewise, even if you will be the most junior member of a large department, if you've already undertaken some workplace-related training and had some basic experience, you potentially add more value than candidates who haven't.

Consciously look for your added value, relative to every question. You won't get chance to show your added value every time. It might only be one question in ten, but be on the lookout for those opportunities.

Lastly, the 'don'ts'. Whilst you shouldn't hide your light under a bushel (whatever one of those is), don't come across as a know-all. Big yourself up, but don't exaggerate and don't lie. Don't be afraid to tell the whole story, but don't ramble.

Oh, one final point – for the love of God, make it interesting.

Okay, you can generate questions and you've got an idea what content to use to press the right buttons. How do you go about creating the answers?

Obviously, you can write (or type) them out but you need to be able to remember them later. Under stress, you don't want to forget the key points that you've carefully crafted.

Also obviously, you could then memorise those answers. However, ideally you need to deliver them naturally in an interview. You don't want to sound like a robot serving up pre-recorded sound bites.

More importantly, bear in mind that the questions actually asked may be similar to the ones you've worked on but there'll be variations. You'll need to adapt your memorised responses on the fly. However, you don't want to be jumping all over the place with disjointed responses which make you sound like the auditory equivalent of a mad person's patchwork quilt.

Tricky.

When a ball is thrown to you, you don't need to work through the slow, tedious and frankly mind-numbing process of figuring out the ball's speed, trajectory, location relative to you, position at which you can catch it, which hand you're going to use and how you should relocate your body in space for best effect. You just catch the ball instinctively.

How does that happen? Your apparently instinctive response is the result of preparation, rehearsal and experience. You've internalised the mental processes involved and you've got a vast data bank of historic information and situations to back that up with. Your mind is free to think about what you're going to do with the ball when you've got it; it's not tied up with getting it. You're at least one step ahead of the game. The more you've practised, the further ahead you'll be.

When you attend an interview and you're given a simple question like, "Tell me about yourself," your response will be like road-kill compared to fillet steak, without preparation and rehearsal. At best you'll be slow and give a disjointed response. At worst, your mind will seize and then you'll fall apart in excruciating panic.

If you're thoroughly prepared, your subconscious can automatically deliver a response whilst your conscious mind is free to figure out the angles, read feedback signals from the interviewer and calculate how best to influence the odds in your favour.

So your challenge then, is to fully internalise your stock answer beforehand, so that your subconscious can naturally mix and match smooth responses to the interviewer's questions, whilst you remain perfectly clear-headed.

You wish, huh? Trust me, it can be done, it's a learned thing. What works for me and many others is the following. It's called the **Spotlight Process**.

- See the full scope of the question and note down the key points you need to make.

- Hand-write an answer to each question. Write the words out, using a pen, in the way that you would naturally speak them when answering a question. Do not try and force the words into a normal written structure. Don't spend a long time crossing out and changing things. Think briefly, write out what comes. Move along at a moderate pace.

- After doing every question in this way, go back to each question in turn and improve your answer. Completely re-write out your modified answers so they are clear and easy to read. Make sure that you hit all the key points. Remove all rambling, duplication and unnecessary information but ensure that it's still written in the way that you would naturally speak.

- When you've finished, stand up, or sit up straight, read out a question and then speak your answer out loud to the room, imagining an interviewer. Yes, you'll feel embarrassed, but it's nothing to how you'll feel if you face the interview without preparing properly. Do this for each question in turn.

- When you've finished, go back to the top of the list, read out each question in turn, then put your notes face down and speak the answer. If you stop or get jammed up for a moment, don't look at your answer sheet. Keep going until you've got past the problem and finished answering the whole question. Only afterwards, go back and check how you did.

- Immediately repeat any question where you had a significant hesitation when delivering your answer. Don't get hung up on using the exact same words that you have written down. You're not learning the lines in a play. Learn to feel comfortable with the fact that your words may vary but you're still delivering all of the key points. If you learn to trust your instincts, your subconscious will handle the delivery well.

That process enables you to do three things:

1) systematically ensure that you cover the ground you need to;
2) fully internalise your responses and
3) deliver them naturally when you're asked to do so.

It's called the **Spotlight Process** because when the interviewer turns the spotlight onto you, you can be confident of being able to keep your head.

I recommend writing, rather than typing, your responses because it assists in taking the information on board at a deeper level. The more embedded your answers, the more easily you will deliver your responses at the interview. Using this method will help ensure that you sound entirely natural, even though you may have rehearsed a hundred times by then. That's because you're starting from the way that you naturally speak, you're not just memorising tracts of text.

By all means, subsequently type out your handwritten sheets so that you've got them safely captured for future reference. Whenever you practise your answers, do so without reading your notes. Only use them for checking.

The above works equally well with developing answers to competency-based and scenario-type questions and you can practise them in the same way.

Rehearse, rehearse and rehearse. Congratulations. You've got all of the basic tools built, tailored, sharpened and lined up in your armoury. You're almost ready for the hand-to-hand combat, but first it's time to make sure that you're proficient in using them. It's also time to start limbering up and polishing your secret weapon.

Let's work through some practice and rehearsal for each of the following:

1) making a personal introduction to a group;
2) attending a 'normal' interview;
3) experiencing a competency-based or scenario interview;
4) taking part in team-based situational exercises;
5) undergoing role-play exercises;
6) taking part in a topic-specific open-discussion session;
7) conducting an individual task-based exercise;
8) making a formal presentation to a group;
9) making a short impromptu presentation and
10) handling lateral-thinking or creativity-assessment questions.

Before we do, remember that your primary objective, assuming your content is good, is to internalise your responses, behaviours and actions until they're second nature. When you've practised and are fully confident in each area, you'll still get that adrenalin rush when the time comes, but you'll be able to stay in control, do an excellent job and lay waste to the remainder of the horde.

My suggestion is to work through all of the above, even if you doubt you'll face some of them at this next interview. It will not only develop your capabilities, it will strongly build your confidence. You'll be slicker than the well-oiled slide on a new Glock.

One of the absolute keys to success is to realise, at a fundamental level, that you can never know everything and you can't predict every eventuality. No one can. What you can do is be absolutely sure that you can handle whatever comes at you because you know the process to deal with it and you've practised.

Let's get right in there. In this first topic, we'll cover a lot of things that will also be useful in the later ones, so have patience. It's perhaps the biggest, hairiest and scariest task of them all at an interview.

1) Making a personal introduction to a group of peers and interviewers

This scares most people, me included. I remember hearing Michael Caine being interviewed on Desert Island Discs about his early years, appearing in repertory theatre. He told how there was always a bucket in the wings and it was common for actors and actresses to throw up in it before going on. They'd do that night after night. One minute of personal intro at a one-off interview doesn't seem quite so hard, in comparison.

What the hell, YOLO. Feel the fear, do it anyway (thank you Susan Jeffers). Even if you're terrified, there's no reason why you can't make enough of a job of this to keep yourself above the cut-line, if you prepare well beforehand.

What are they going to ask of you? It's common to do a round-the-table, one-by-one intro and it's particularly stressful to sit in line knowing that your turn is getting ever closer.

You may or may not be asked to stand and / or go to the front to speak. Your allotted time can vary from a few seconds up to perhaps a couple of minutes.

This is most likely to be a request for a short off-the-cuff intro. Occasionally you might be asked beforehand to prepare a speech to a given outline. Either way, there's no reason why you can't prepare now.

Start with a worst-case situation of needing to speak for three or four minutes. Think of it as a 'tell us about yourself' question and use the Spotlight Process you learned earlier to generate your content and rehearse with.

Think about the main title blocks you might use if you were writing more formally. These might be any, or all of:

- name;
- why you're here today / what you're applying for;
- your background;
- your education and
- your experience.

You might work in a 'claim to fame', a personal ambition or something about an interesting personal interest. The latter points can be used to show that you're human, hint at some of your potential and add some interest.

Note that word 'interest'. You and the interviewer are going to be sitting through the dullest collection of excruciating speeches you've ever heard in your life. You may not notice that, because of your adrenalin rush, but the interviewer will.

So, base line number one is to make damn sure you cover the basic ground adequately and competently, even if you are noticeably nervous. Keep it short, sharp and focused. Make your points in a clearly delineated fashion. In other words, don't cock it up. That alone can get you through.

Base line number two to reach, if you possibly can, is to add in a nugget of something that is interesting. Something that marks you out. Something that piques interest just a little. Something that makes the interviewer smile, pay attention and want to know more later. Again, keep it short, sharp, focused.

You're unlikely to have to go for base line number three. That's where you're asked to specifically include something about what makes you suitable for recruitment, or even worse, something about what makes you better than the others. It tends to be divisive and sets the wrong mood for a session that's aiming to leave people more settled after it, than before, so it's rarely used.

Having said that, work it in to your preparation in case you need it. It may be useful for the 'tell me about yourself' question at standard interviews anyway.

So, write out your speech in clearly delineated paragraphs, each being a building block towards a full three or four minute 'off-the-cuff' (LOL) speech.

Practise saying it aloud as often as you can stand it. Try delivering different versions and time yourself to see if you can do a thirty-second version, a one minute version and so on.

Get used to mixing and matching your internalised blocks of subject material so that you can comfortably handle variations on the theme. Deliver the blocks in different orders, to see what feels best.

Get to the stage where you're sure of your material and know that you can guarantee to deliver what's required, even if you'll have to face the interview standing in front of a whole wall of Andrex, whilst holding a bucket and clutching rehydration tablets.

From there, we can move on and tackle 'that which must not be named'.

"What? You mean the nerves?"

Gasp.

The only people not nervous are either absent, over-confident or dead. If you see the news, or listen to people being caned on the Today programme on Radio 4, and concentrate on the person, rather than what they're saying, you'll be amazed how often you'll realise that the poor sod on the receiving end is terrified and showing signs of extreme stress. Yet they still get through it and deliver the points they wanted to make.

The biggest problem is usually a quivering voice. If you were there you'd often see hands shaking about with a palsy of biblical proportions, or knees knocking together with a resonant frequency that threatens to destroy the building.

Often you won't notice because you're focused on the content of what they're saying. It's only when something draws your attention to it, as I just did, that you become aware of their nervousness. That's great news for you because, no matter how bad you feel, ninety nine per cent of people will probably not spot your nerves if you don't draw attention to them.

Never ever tell people that you're nervous. Trained interviewers will spot it fairly easily anyway but they won't attach any importance to it because it's normal and they'll have forgotten about it within ten seconds of you finishing. Do your bit, feel nervous, forget about it. It's normal, so what?

Some people are lucky and naturally don't show physical signs, even if they have got more adrenalin on board than a soldier going over the top at the Somme. They're perhaps the hurlers. Others don't show many signs because they've learned to literally act a part, despite the adrenalin. That can be you.

There are quite a few things you can do in preparation that will substantially help you when the time comes to speak for real.

- As you rehearse, say your introduction out loud.
- Practise delivering it to friends, if possible.
- Record your voice and video your delivery.

There is one thing that really helps to settle your voice specifically and your nerves generally. It's pathetically simple but I can't stress its efficacy enough. It's this.

Every single day, read pages from a book out loud. Twice a day if possible.

Is that it? Yep. But there's a bit of work to do with it.

Let's get serious. Find a book with a section of text that you feel comfortable to read aloud. Now, think of Winston Churchill delivering his 'fight them on the beaches' speech to the House of Commons on the 4th of June, 1940.

Stand up, put your your shoulders back, lift your chin and take the deepest of deep breaths. Imagine you're reading an important address to the entire nation. Show gravity and hold the book accordingly. Look the nation in the eye. Pause.

Now, read out loud.

Do it sentence by sentence, paragraph by paragraph, slowly. Enunciate every word cleanly. Don't chop the ends of your words or roll them together. Make it sound like you're reading the most interesting story the world has ever known.

Let your voice rise and fall according to the content of the text. Don't shout. Project your voice. Feel the appropriate emotions dictated by the story and pump them out with a force to make grown men weep and mothers draw their young closer.

Get comfortable with the sound of your voice. Be aware of your feelings. Smile where you can. Learn to detach your mind and see yourself performing. Become aware of your surroundings. Let the details register on your mind.

There you go. It does take practice but, for interviews, you can make a substantial difference to your performance within a week. It will really help you to learn how to control your breathing, your projection and your voice and thereby it will help you to curb those fear-driven adrenalin surges.

If you persist, although it might take months or years of practice to become truly proficient, your skill will continue to develop. It's a skill that will stand you in good stead for the rest of your life, even if you have absolutely no intention of delivering any form of speech anywhere, ever.

You'll be delighted at how comfortably and easily you subsequently handle your fear and your emotions, when you're suddenly put on the spot at odd times during your future career. That skill is worth a fortune in interviews.

If you look the part and if you sound the part, you are the part. People will trust you.

If you really want to get over your nerves and perform the very best that you can, with whatever other skills you have under your belt, learn to read aloud.

Some additional things can support your work in this area.

- If you have access to children, read aloud to them regularly.
- Consider joining a debating society.
- Try auditioning for am-dram productions.
- If you have a special interest, try teaching others.

2) Attending a 'normal' interview. This suddenly seems a bit less stressful and dramatic in comparison, doesn't it? All of your work on delivering personal introductions will help you cope with standard interview questions. That's especially true for handling the very open 'tell us about yourself' question and that other on-the-spot, wind-up special: the 'why should we pick you?' question.

You've already created a number of standard interview questions that you might be asked and you've developed answers using the Spotlight Process. You've hopefully already rehearsed them as part of that development process. Now it's time to do so again. Practise makes perfect, hashtag cliché.

This time, step up your rehearsal to the next level by immersing yourself in a mock interview situation. You can do so mentally, that's half of the battle, but you can also do so physically. This can all be quite stressful in itself (that's the point) so I recommend doing this at least two or three times.

If you do so, by the time you attend the interview you'll pretty much know what to expect and how you'll feel. You'll be more confident, despite the expected nerves and you'll be able to answer questions a great deal more competently.

The Gold Standard for rehearsal is to undertake a mock interview as a full-blown role-play exercise. Normally the best way of doing this is to use an experienced trainer but that can be expensive and you'll be very limited in the number of times you can afford to go through the exercise.

Let's look at a way you can do this for yourself, as often as you like, for free. Actually, when I say free, that's not entirely true. You ideally need the help of a friend so it might cost you a couple of drinks.

Firstly, get your setting right. Any small table with a pair of chairs, one either side, will do. The location and decoration are not that important so long as you can be fairly sure of remaining undisturbed for around half an hour or so.

Provide your, hopefully willing, friend with a one page briefing sheet, which summarises the organisation, the role and the type of person required. Also provide a list of interview questions. Leave some space in between, for your friend to take notes about your answers as they interview you. Lastly, instruct them on the format and rules of the interview.

Your interviewer should aim to put you at ease but stay professionally focused on conducting a formal interview and evaluation. Ideally, you would both be dressed more formally than normal for this.

From the moment the interview begins, you should both remain in character for as long as it takes. The interview starts when you knock on the door to the interview room and it ends after the interviewer has shaken hands and you've walked out of the door and closed it behind you.

Under no circumstances pause the interview part way through. If you seize up, bad luck, work through it. If you both get the giggles, ignore it and push on. Once you're both in character (it takes a small amount of practice), you'll find staying there very easy. Then things get intense.

Never give facetious or jokey answers. At all times be mentally right inside a real interview and deliver the answers you would give as though you were fighting for your life.

In fact, you are fighting for your life. Do you want a life with a successful and well-paid career, or do you want a life with a stream of disjointed jobs, such that you'll hardly be able to afford to get out of bed and piss for what they'll be paying you? If it's the former – fight for it. Right here, right now.

The interviewer has a script of questions so they won't have a problem. You need to make sure that they are strong enough to stay in character, even if you're reduced to desperately muttering the words, "Hold on, can we start all this again?" The answer is no, pick it up from where you are.

If you want to start again, finish this interview session first, review it, then do another complete session. Recovering from a brain-freeze is all part of the learning process. Better you do it now than in the real interview.

After the end of the interview, sit down with your friend and jointly review where you did well and where you did poorly. You need to recognise the latter and focus on how you can improve your delivery of those particular answers. If the answers themselves are poor, re-work them.

Your only disadvantage is that a professional trainer would be able to give you more structured feedback than your friend can. However, this is more than outweighed by being able to run repeat sessions, perhaps on different days. Always keep an open mind and accept that you're not perfect and that there's always scope for improvement.

The key to success is not to take criticism personally. Make sure that your friend doesn't hold back. Equally, they shouldn't brutally nail you to a cross over small errors. They need to tell you, honestly but factually, what they think worked and what didn't. Out of that, build a simple improvement plan.

You'll find that some people are better than others at this, so don't be afraid to try a few friends – it's all practice. Try and do the same for them. See how it feels to sit on the other side of the table and be the quiz master. Look at how people behave when the spotlight is on them. Register the negatives and resolve not to show them yourself, when your time comes.

The above is the best way to approach role-play interviews but there are variations around the theme that also work well if you're struggling to get such a session set up.

You can try a video call on Skype and use that to run the same style of role-play interview. It's not so good but is still highly worthwhile experience.

Alternatively, if you're stuck finding someone to help at short notice and assuming you don't have your own blow-up rubber Doreen (or Donald) handy, stuff a pillow inside a sweater and sit it in the seat opposite. Go through all of the same motions but read the questions out loud to yourself before putting the sheet down to answer. Speak directly to the dummy but see the interviewer as a real person in your mind.

You can step things up to yet another level if you wish.

- Use a meeting room, if you have easy access to one.
- Dress fully for the occasion, if you possibly can.
- Video your interviews to find areas for improvement.

In case you've forgotten them, go back and re-read the guidance points we looked at earlier, when we looked at telephone and Skype interviews. See whether you've committed any sins in your interview practice and, if so, take the steps necessary to clean up your act.

3) Competency-based / scenario-type interviews. Rehearsing for these is slightly tougher because you have very little chance of predicting the actual questions that will come up. This is unlike standard interview questions, where you will undoubtedly have covered many of the exact questions that will arise, if you've been thorough in your preparation.

The competency questions you've generated will at least sit in the same broad territory as the real ones, when you consider the categories of personal characteristics you'll be assessed against. Remind yourself of these by going back to Chapter 4 and looking at the section covering online application forms and the STAR technique.

Your way around this problem is the same one you might use with exams. Practise as many examples as you can so that, in a real situation, you've got the process for handling any question off pat.

You can use exactly the same role-playing exercise approach as before, to help you practise competency-based and scenario-style questions.

I would suggest that you structure the practice interview question sheet so that it starts and finishes with a few standard questions but slide four competency and four scenario questions into the middle of the proceedings.

If you want to push yourself a bit harder, get your friend to generate one or two more of each so that you haven't had chance to practise your responses. You'll have to take them on the fly, as you would in reality.

Every time you re-run this mock interview, use new competency-based and scenario-type questions in the middle, instead of the ones you've already practised. Ultimately, aim to do as many as you can so the process becomes deeply embedded in your psyche. Practise and you'll learn to handle them comfortably. Mixing and matching the answers you've rehearsed previously will become second nature.

In particular, get used to spotting them when they crop up buried in the middle of a bunch of standard questions. Having said that, don't be afraid to use the STAR technique to cover some of the standard questions as well, if that helps you give a more structured response. It's a good way to spoon-feed the interviewer opportunities to give you full marks on suitable standard questions because you can be sure your answers completely rock.

Get used to thinking for a few seconds before you engage your mouth. Get your STAR clearly in mind before you start so that you know the whole story for the particular answer you're about to deliver. Know when you're going to finish so that you don't ramble or end up having to plaster forgotten bits on top of your answer.

With practice, your start-up thinking time will reduce. It's better to be a slow starter on a question but then give an excellent answer, than it is to be a quick starter but stammer your way uncertainly through the middle and arrive at an inconclusive end, with a poor punch-line sellotaped over it.

Stress can make it hard to think on your feet. If you're comfortable in handling these types of questions, you'll be less stressed and more able. You'll appear much more confident, competent and professional as a result.

It's essential to provide your helper with a score sheet for each of the particular questions you're going to use in the session. At the simplest level, your friend can tick off an S, a T, an A and an R as you work through your answer. You can also add a box for them to make quick notes in.

After the session, you'll be able to check back on what you missed or handled poorly. You should still be able to remember the answers you gave, if you run a feedback session promptly. If that proves to be problematic, you can always video the session for subsequent playback. The latter does tend to be time-consuming but is useful to do at least once or twice so that you can see how you look to others.

4) Team-based situational exercises. These are commonly used during group assessment days and are hard to prepare for as it's impossible to predict what will come up. Preparation is centred on understanding the format and remembering what to aim for. They can be a lot of fun to take part in.

You'll probably be in a group of up to six, tasked with deciding what to do about a particular problem. You'll be given a short brief and told you need to make a presentation in, say, one hour, outlining what actions your group proposes which would save the day or solve the problem.

It's usually pretty obvious what the possible solutions are but it's the team aspect that will become the major stumbling block, since there's normally more than one viable solution. Unsurprisingly, different people will have different views on which is best. They may refuse to be swayed by others' arguments as they remember that selection is a competitive process. Many people fail to appreciate the team-based nature of the exercise.

In the real world, time would pass and people would take a break to consider their positions. In this interview world, there's an absolute deadline and so the dead-lock has to be broken.

The result is pressure and stress as team members become frustrated and utterly convinced that half of their number must be a new sub-species of particularly dense bog dwellers. Slugfests often ensue.

Observers will watch from the sides and take notes about individuals, whilst trying very hard not to explode with laughter, chuck in a bucket of water or grab a Taser and ring for an ambulance.

Discussions sometimes start politely and democratically enough. Progress is often slow until the last fifteen minutes, when it suddenly becomes apparent that everybody is up shit-creek against the clock. Anarchy often results and one person, or a small group, will then attempt to seize control and railroad decisions through.

It is possible for the whole group to remain stable if someone has the presence of mind and strength of character to pull the group together.

Either way, decisions will get made rapidly, sometimes against stiff opposition, and a sub-optimal presentation may be literally thrown together in one minute.

The potential for argument throughout is mind-blowingly huge.

All of the group members are in competition for a limited number of places. Individuals feel the pressure of needing to be seen to be making a valuable contribution. Some of them will feel driven to be acknowledged as the one making the best contribution. Others feel that they should lead the group. Still others will think that being the one to make the final presentation will get them chosen. A small proportion of people will go in, certain that being openly ruthless will get them through.

Try watching Alan Sugar's The Apprentice if you want to see the full range of behaviours that people under competitive stress will exhibit. From malevolence, meltdown and megalomania to bravado, betrayal and back-stabbing – it's all in there.

Regardless of all that, group members have different backgrounds, belief systems and personalities. That alone will cause a divisive mix of strongly held opinions over issues as simple as whether to put the milk in first, or not.

Sometimes a group member becomes convinced that there is 'a right answer' and the group simply must deliver it, if anyone at all is to stand a chance of selection. They exhibit a frenzied mania, as they attempt to knock the whole group into line.

Occasionally a group member will divorce themselves from the situation and tut-tut from the side-lines, trying to make it clear to the interviewers that they alone have the real answer and everyone else is a Neanderthal.

In a heartbeat, group members can lose the plot completely. It's truly spectacular to see emotions explode and watch one poor bastard get the pasting of their life as everyone else blames them for the lack of progress.

Vast numbers of PhD theses have been written around this very subject.

It's all great material for the interviewers and shines a searing spotlight onto a candidate's true potential. Or lack of it.

So, how should you behave?

Start by keeping in mind that it's not a straightforward pass or fail situation. A bit like psychometric testing, the exercise is designed to give the interviewer the ability to probe your capabilities, strengths and weaknesses more deeply.

The key is to follow positive behaviours which help move the whole group forwards. When the yelling has started and you're surreptitiously holding up a notebook to keep the spittle off your clothes, it's difficult to keep this in mind. At all costs, avoid behaviours which are self-serving.

The easy way to keep your behaviour channelled is to think about what role you should play at each stage of the proceedings. The group can morph from a congregation of saints to a band of blood-crazed killers and back again. Keep a clear head and change your behaviour to suit the situation.

At each stage, choose to task yourself with something that supports the objective. Think of it this way: it's the group that is tasked with achieving a result, not you and certainly not the maniac with the flared nostrils sitting across from you. It's a group thing.

You'll personally score marks for encouraging progress and supporting the development of a better quality output FROM THE GROUP. You'll lose marks for hindering progress and reducing the quality of the output FROM THE GROUP.

Group.

Group, group, group.

Think group.

At the start, what can you do to help the group move forward? It's possible someone will kick straight off with a power-grab.

> "Okay, let's choose some roles so we can all be effective. I'm happy to do the presentation at the end, who wants to take notes and keep us on track?"

That's a slick hijack, but hopefully not slick enough to get past you.

> "Maybe, but how about we all contribute our first thoughts and then later we can see who's best suited for which role?"

That way, you've stopped the group being railroaded, confidently asserted yourself and presented a solution which is potentially better for the whole group.

Don't get suckered. Making decisions quickly is good. Making dubious decisions quickly most definitely leads to a sub-optimal performance.

In the discussion phase, what knowledge, experience or ideas can you individually contribute to the group's discussion?

In the middle, disagreements will abound. What can you do to unblock the situation and get the group moving forward again?

At the decision stage, someone will be getting a kicking or there'll be a gigantic slugfest as frustration boils over. What can you do to help the group stop wasting time and begin engaging in more positive activity?

Near the end, someone has to stand up and present the proposals. Who's the best to do that? How can you make sure that they get that job, rather than the opportunistic, loud-mouthed bully?

Whatever the result from the exercise, you can score highly by rising above the carnage and staying focused on the objective. Because you're in a competitive situation, your instincts will make you want to directly challenge the thrusting individuals who are keen to grab power and attention. Don't worry about them. Stay confident.

The self-servers, who are more focused on their own objectives, rather than the objective of the exercise, will steadily lose marks relative to the team-oriented contributors. Concentrate on steering the group back onto the path, regardless of who 'leads'.

There are various sins that you can hopefully avoid committing.

The very worst thing you can do is stand in the middle of the group and doggedly insist that you know best.

> "I'm right and you're all wrong."

Uh-huh.

Such an attitude causes the timid to give up, the majority to clam up and the feisty to start the punch-up. The group's objective-achieving capacity will drop to zero, along with the career hopes of the person causing it.

Next up is attempting to impose yourself as 'leader', on the grounds that it's a competition and the organisers are looking for the strong. Well, there's strong and there's strong. Natural leaders who float to the top are buoyed up by a groundswell of popular support because they're repeatedly saying and doing things which are moving the group towards the objective. People who stab and bully their way in are not natural leaders. Such people tend to impose their will on others so the group will only do well so long as that 'leader' always chooses correctly. They'll get marked down.

That error is closely followed by the one of forcibly making the final presentation, when it's clear that you're by no means the most capable speaker. Be relaxed about who makes the final presentation. If they're good, that person may well gain some marks but you can match them if you're the one to put them forward because you've recognised their talent.

Another major sin is failing to toe the line once the group has made a collective decision. By all means put your case vigorously but once the decision is made, accept it and do your very best to implement it. Undermining the rest of the group, whilst they try to implement it, on the grounds that you know best, will get you marked down quite severely.

Criticising another team member, particularly ridiculing them, is the equivalent of painting yourself with honey and waiting for the ants to come. Their willingness to contribute will certainly be choked off, along with your hopes.

So in short, you're in a group. If you help the group, you help yourself.

So what if some person does end up 'leading' by railroading decisions, writing the presentation and delivering it? Firstly, there are usually several places on offer anyway and secondly, would you really want that sort of person running amok inside your organisation? Neither will the interviewers.

Whilst you watch some of your peers commit career suicide, concentrate on three positive behaviours that many of your peers will forget on the day.

- Watch the time. Have in mind the latest point by which decisions should have been made and construction of the presentation started. Be the one to keep the group on track.
- Strive to be inclusive. Everyone has something to offer, even the maniacs, otherwise they wouldn't be there. If you make your job figuring out what that is, and then help it to see the light of day, you're on your way. Not only will you score highly, you'll be showing real leadership potential.

- Keep the objective front and centre in your mind. Help the group to stay focused on it.

5) Role-play exercises. Now, these you can rehearse. Hopefully, you've already been doing so when practising mock interviews.

If it's used on the day, a role-play exercise will often be a one-to-one affair. You'll be given a brief which outlines a problem and you'll be told to meet with someone to try and achieve a specific objective. If you'll be meeting with one of your peers, they'll be given a brief which outlines the same problem but from their point of view. Their objective will be different to yours.

The result will be conflict and the problem may well be irresolvable at the meeting, so the exercise will ultimately be time-limited. There's probably no right answer, only correct and incorrect behaviours, and the monitoring interviewer will score you accordingly.

You'll be expected to think logically and present a strong argument, whilst listening and taking account of another's point of view.

Some people find their biggest challenge is in thinking their way into the role and behaving accordingly. This becomes much easier with even a small amount of practice and you'll find the self-consciousness falls away quickly.

To practise, find a friend willing to help you by taking part in some mock exercises. Draw up a number of exercises and for each, create two briefs and a score sheet.

An example exercise is provided in Appendix A. You can trawl the web for more but once you understand the format, you'll be able to draw up some of your own fairly easily.

Your helper won't be able to mark up a score sheet for you, until after you've stopped the exercise, so make scoring a quick and simple process. Give marks out of ten against the following categories:

- reasoning skills;
- persuasive skills;
- listening skills;
- assertiveness;
- decisiveness.

Make short bullet point notes on what went well, any criticisms and suggestions for improvement.

Here are some simple guidelines which will help you stay on track.

- Make sure that you have enough time to digest the brief and understand the objective before you start.
- If you can, make a quick plan for the lines of discussion you want to follow, specific questions to ask and perhaps, any fall-back positions.
- Stay in character from start to finish but remember, it's not your acting performance that you'll be marked for, it's the content of what you say and your modus operandi in steering toward the objective.

- Feel free to feel and use emotion, but stay in control. Be forceful if necessary but don't shout, swear, threaten or ridicule others.
- Ask questions but listen and watch more than you speak.
- Don't be afraid to take a few seconds to gather your thoughts and re-focus your position now and then.
- Silence can be a massively effective weapon to deploy.
- Avoid wild off-topic statements aimed at throwing the other person off. Lobbing in, "I know you're a card-carrying member of the Communist Party because your partner told me when I slept with them the other night, and by the way they're leaving you for me," is pointless. Only ad-lib within the obvious confines and context of the situation.
- Call a halt when one of you reaches your objective, you're at a deadlock or you find yourselves stuck in a looping series of arguments.

To improve your prospects, here are some positive behaviours which help.

- Start the role-play meeting by clarifying why you're both there and the scope of what you're going to talk about. Sometimes that will immediately expose the difference in the participants' objectives.
- If you think you also know the objective of the other person, summarise both positions and then explore the situation for common ground.
- Ask questions and listen carefully. Try to understand the other person's position, even if you can't agree with it. Be flexible.
- Use body-language to help. Pay attention, use eye contact, smile, nod, frown, lean forward, sit back, cross your arms or open them up as the conversation develops.
- As you go along, solve what's possible, not world hunger. Mentally divide any issues into those that you should be able to agree on there and then, and those that will have to be solved after the meeting.
- Remember the context of why you're there. For example, imagine you're meeting an upset customer. In the real world, you wouldn't normally bully them, batter them senseless with an argument they can never win or attempt to convince them it's all their own fault, so avoid doing so in this exercise.
- Try your best to achieve the objective but don't get stressed or angry if you can't. You might feel a roller-coaster of emotions when you're lost inside the exercise. React but stay level-headed. Never swear.
- Pick up on the other person's emotions and behaviour, react and adapt your own behaviour just as you would in the real world. If they're already angry at you, deliberately provoking them into a state of frenzied mania will cost you marks, even if you win the argument.
- Just before you plan to stop, summarise the updated situation and check that the other person agrees with it.
- Agree the terms under which you're finishing the meeting and what actions one, the other, or both of you might go away and take, as a result of the discussion.

At the end, you may or may not have achieved your original objective. It may not even have actually been possible to do so, depending upon the brief and the starting position of the other person. What matters is the quality of your ability to listen, adapt, handle knock-backs, keep a clear head, stay focused on your objective and keep moving towards it.

It's not possible to predict the topic of the actual role-play that will be used on the day but rehearsing like this will put you more at ease. Familiarity with the process will enable you to keep your head and score much more highly than if you were going in cold. Also, marking your helper's score-sheet will help you to understand how the interviewer works.

It can be very useful to video one or more of your sessions so that you can see what you look like and how you behave. You might be amazed at how deeply you can become immersed in role-play exercises and stepping back out of them can sometimes be a real shock.

Some larger organisations may decide to stage group role-playing exercises instead. Each member of a group will be allocated a specific role and given an individual brief and personal objective, as well as a group objective. There may or may not be a leader appointed. You'll probably be given time to prepare individually and then time to prepare as a group before the actual exercise begins.

The lines are obviously beginning to blur between whether this is a role-play exercise or a team-based situational exercise. The only way to sensibly prepare is to make yourself thoroughly aware of the issues surrounding both types of exercise and to rehearse individual role-plays, as above.

A group role-play exercise will be looking at your skills of team working, negotiation, time management and leadership as well as those individual skills mentioned earlier.

6) Topic-specific open-discussion sessions. Here, preparation is focused on understanding what you'll be walking into, making yourself aware of the dos and don'ts and trying to source some experience beforehand.

Group size can vary between four and a dozen or more people. Your group will be given a topic to discuss, which should have been chosen to ensure that everyone will be able to make at least some contribution. A chair person may or may not be designated and, if one is, they could be a group member or somebody from the interview panel. Observers will watch from the outside and score individual performances. The whole exercise will be time-limited.

The discussion will be to explore a particular topic. The achievement of a consensus may be a set objective. Bear in mind that the scorers will not be marking the discussion itself but the quality of the candidates' contributions.

At the end, someone might need to summarise the conclusions. Alternatively, each of you may be asked, in turn, for your summary and final views.

You'll undoubtedly feel some pressure to contribute positively and present yourself well. Afterwards, people often complain that they didn't get chance to properly air their views. The simple fact is that such discussions can be like trying to find space to run across both sides of the motorway in rush hour.

Getting your voice heard gets easier, once you've already done it once or twice. Wedging your point into a vigorous discussion, and being effective when you do it, is a question of timing, but also confidence. Any group-discussion practice you can get beforehand will help you to master the art.

To practise, get half a dozen of your friends together and ask someone strong to chair some discussion sessions. Set rules and time limits, but make sure to pick controversial topics. Alternatively, join a debating society.

At your actual interview, be proactive.

- Get in early, be assertive, make your own chances.
- Keep contributions: on-topic; confident; positive; enthusiastic; short.
- Ensure you're heard: speak firmly; speak clearly.

The earlier you get through the first barrier of saying something, the more often you'll subsequently contribute and the higher your standard of contribution will be. The later you leave it, the harder it will be.

Here are some behaviours to avoid.

- DO NOT SHOUT to interject.
- Only butt in when someone has finished (or almost finished) their point.
- Don't chop off a good line of discussion.
- Don't ramble on, quantity won't cut it.
- Don't persist with bigoted views, keep an open mind.
- Remember the overall picture, don't get bogged down in detail.

Those nine are the basics that will get you through with an average score. Now you need to think about lifting yourself further up the pecking order.

- Participate with insightful points, not just comments or nods.
- Open up a rich, previously unthought-of, line of discussion.
- Actually interact with others, encourage them, influence them.
- Use eye contact and body language to help engage with others and gain support.
- If you disagree with someone, say so and explain why.
- Concentrate your contributions around the strong members of the group and the points they make. Minimise time spent interacting with the weaker wall-flowers.
- Pose questions which stimulate strong responses.
- Unlock a going-nowhere discussion by making a quick summary of where things are and suggesting the positive lines to concentrate on.
- Keep your eye on the time and be ready to make a summary, if asked.

To help you keep your head if the spotlight jumps to you and you have to present a summary, try keeping scribbled notes of the latest key points every few minutes. A bullet point and a couple of words will do as an aide memoire. As things step forward, draw a line and note the latest points.

At the end you'll be left with the very latest position to hand if your brain freezes. You'll be able to capture the full scope of the latest position without forgetting anything and

165

you'll easily be able to remember both the starting point and the course that discussions have taken.

You might not need to make a summary, but you never know. Be armed.

It's not uncommon for discussion topics to be centred around a current affairs issue and / or for such topics to be used as part of a normal interview, so there's a last vital point on preparation.

From now on, catch the latest national and international news each day. Know the current major topics, what's happened recently and what's likely to happen next, in the opinion of experts and editorial bloggers.

This doesn't have to be a major mish. A few minutes a day on a major news site, like the BBC's, will enable you to scan headlines and articles and will give you relevant links for further digging. Radio news is also particularly easy to pick up, regularly and effortlessly, whilst you're doing something else.

Your objective is to be aware of what issues are current and to ensure that you've got enough general information mentally on board to be able to comment on them, to at least a basic level. Again, be armed, just in case.

7) Individual task-based exercises. This will aim to assess your capabilities of individual analysis, reasoning, decision making and communication. You're likely to be given:

- a lot of information to sift through and assess quickly;
- an objective to achieve or a response to deliver;
- a wind-up review session at which to present your findings.

There are various forms that this type of assessment can take. Commonly used is an in-tray, inbox or e-tray exercise, designed to provide a real-world scenario for you to work with. You're given an outline brief and provided with a mountain of letters, memos, emails, files and folders to work through.

Dumping you with information overload is intentional. The subject matter will normally be related to the type of job that you're after. Such an exercise will be a test of your ability to:

- keep an objective in mind;
- process information quickly;
- manage your time;
- identify problems;
- prioritise;
- decide a route forward;
- propose actions and
- express yourself tactfully in any responses that you're required to give.

Your requested response might be in the form of:

- a prioritised action list;
- an email or letter proposing your suggested actions;

- a response to a query or complaint;
- a plan delegating work to colleagues and so on.

Variations may involve:

- making a telephone call;
- meeting with your notional boss or
- feeding back to an employee group.

You'll have a deadline to work to and usually there'll be a review session with your interviewer, after you've completed the exercise.

Once you start, it's vital to read the brief thoroughly so that you understand what you need to achieve. Take note of deadlines and plan your time carefully. From there, amongst the pile of information you've been given, you'll need to separate out the urgent, important and relevant from the unimportant and irrelevant. That can be a challenge if there's a lot of information provided.

Once you've sorted all that out, you can identify the issues, weigh up your options for dealing with them and make some decisions. Throughout, you'll need to be sensitive to how your analysis and related decisions might be received.

For example, recommending that a major product be canned and another favoured may well have political, departmental and staffing ramifications. You'll need to be factual and practical but diplomatic. A blunt 'sack 'em all' statement might be succinct and the correct thing to do but it's never going to be easily received by anyone involved. If your response is likely to cause more problems than you'll be solving, you'll be marked down accordingly.

Remember that assessors want you to identify the essential key points, rather than over-analyse and become overwhelmed by detail.

As part of the exercise, there might be several emails or letters that require responses along the way. The assessor wants to see that you didn't get distracted by the strident demands and possibly misplaced hysteria of others.

For anything you put in writing, use an appropriate business style. The exercise is as much an assessment of your ability to communicate as well as to analyse. It can help to jot down an outline of what you're going to say, your key points and their order. Keep things concise and use bullet points. Write in good, clear, plain English. Save the eloquently crafted prose for your love letters.

There are a couple of additional risks to be aware of.

- You may not have sufficient time to read everything to give a completely informed response.
- You might end up spending a disproportionate amount of time on an issue, only to later find it's a minor topic in the overall scheme of things.

So, you need to learn to read and digest a lot of material quickly and you need to be practised in separating the urgent, from the important, from the irrelevant. But how can you do that without actually sitting such an exercise? Try this exercise, called **Take Five**, instead.

- Get a copy of a broadsheet newspaper and give yourself a maximum of five minutes to read it. Then give yourself five minutes to decide on the five most important stories from the point of view of what will have the biggest impact on your own future. Within that time, list the five in order of importance and draft an email to an imaginary colleague. Include a brief summary of each story and a separate paragraph explaining and justifying your chosen order.

Be ruthless with the time limits. If you haven't finished, just stop.

Have a break for a few minutes and clear your head. Now review what you've written.

- How does it read?
- Does your order or reasoning still make sense?
- How effective was your original scan?
- Did you miss any other significant stories?
- Did you miss any important points you could have made about a story?
- Is there anything you'd like to change about your email?
- How could you improve, if you had to do it all again?

If you wish, you can give yourself an arbitrary score out of ten to enable you see how your performance improves each time you try this exercise.

Obviously, you can run this exercise with different papers and / or on different days but you can also stretch yourself further, even with the same paper.

- Allowing yourself only five more minutes, draft another email about five different stories. Pick those you judge most economically important for the country. Remember to include summaries and your justification of the order of importance.

After reviewing your results, you could repeat the exercise using the same paper, but choosing other perspectives:

- political;
- religious;
- technological;
- medical;
- sporting and so on.

You can also try the same exercise using a major news website, such as the BBC's or CNN's.

Aim to stretch yourself with challenging topics that push you out of your comfort zone. You should find that the process of picking up information rapidly gets easier, the more often you try it.

Speed readers have a big advantage so that's your next area of preparation.

Trawl the web or find a suitable book that can teach you how to scan and speed read. Only a small amount of practice will lift your performance a long way and give you an edge over most of the people you'll be up against. Yet again, it's a skill that will stand you in good stead for all aspects of your life.

Try asking your local or university's career service if they run mock in-tray exercises. Some do and the experience will be invaluable.

If not, try looking online for in-tray or inbox exercises. You may find examples with limited access for free. Just make sure that they're appropriate for the stage of your present career development. You can buy access to in-tray / inbox exercises, but the same caveats apply. There's not too much point in you trying to decide the fate of BP in the aftermath of the gulf oil spill at this stage of your career, unless you're completing a business degree or MBA.

8) Formal presentation to a group. Preparation is again essential as it is very much a practice makes perfect situation. We're typically talking here about an invitation to make a presentation to an interview panel of a few people. Such formal presentations to a group of peers at an assessment day are rarer, if only because of the extra time involved for everyone to listen to everything.

There are two challenges. Firstly, structuring and preparing your presentation and secondly, standing up to deliver it. Let's take them in that order.

Make absolutely sure that you know how the interviewer will expect you to deliver your presentation. Are they expecting to see you use a power point presentation, a flip chart, printed hand-outs or just your voice?

If they want to see a power point presentation, can you bring it on a USB drive to save lugging a laptop or, even better, can you email it in advance? Whatever you do, take a backup solution with you on the day. Take a USB stick anyway. Take a spare as well, preferably a different make. Take hard copies in. If there's a power cut and you're the only one who brought in six printed copies of the slides for the interview panel to use instead, who's going to look like The One?

There are as many books and web pages devoted to presentations as there are for CVs. It's always worth getting some depth on this subject but the real basics pay the biggest dividends when preparing any presentation.

- It's essential to read, understand and follow the brief given to you.
- Know your audience and what they want to see.
- Your presentation must be firmly on-topic throughout.
- It must have a point or purpose and therefore a conclusion to it.
- Figure out what will make yours the best presentation.
- Keep the number of slides to a minimum. One per minute works well.
- Use page titles, three bullet points (ideally) and illustrative images.
- Avoid slabs of text and massive tables; use key-word summaries.
- Choose high-contrast fonts and point sizes for readability.
- Make it interesting: reach your audience on a human level.

There are three things to bear in mind when delivering your presentation.

- a) Do not under or over-run. Time your presentation beforehand.
- b) Use the titles, bullet points and images as prompts.
- c) Hold the audience's attention through clear navigation.

169

The last point is important if you're to avoid boring your audience. People switch off if they lose track of where you are in your discourse. Remembering to divide your presentation up in the following way helps:

- tell 'em what you're going to tell 'em;
- tell 'em;
- tell 'em what you told 'em.

This sets expectations for the content of your presentation but better, it also gives you an opportunity to pique their interest in the same way as trailers for news programmes do.

Point b) above will make a big difference to your perceived professionalism. Not using detailed notes and speaking freely about your slides, rather than reading them out, leaves you free to properly engage with your audience. You're free to make eye contact and draw on individuals' expressions and body language so that you can direct your own performance.

If that prospect fills you with horror, you are not alone. People list death as preferable to public speaking, when listing their worst fears. It's obviously rubbish though. I've never known anyone actually top themself on the run-up to giving a presentation. Victor Hugo, author of Les Misérables, noted that courage comes not from the absence of fear but from the mastery of it. Michael Caine and his bucket at the side of the stage might support that sentiment.

If my notes on point b) make you think that you could never be that relaxed, think again. It's a learned skill. That means that you can learn it too. Yes, some people are naturally more able to speak publically, but they risk being complacently over-confident.

All of that leaves space for you to make a better job of things, standing out from the dilatory droners and the overly confident, oratorical arseholes. So, how are you going to do that? Ooh, time for a bit of practice again.

- Read aloud every day, as earlier. It really does make a huge difference. It teaches you how to breathe properly when speaking. You'll get used to hearing your voice sound measured, even powerful.
- Use the Spotlight Process to internalise your presentation.
- Practise delivering your presentation to a friend or friends.
- Put your notes away and practise speaking, using the slides as prompts.
- Video your delivery. Identify bad habits and eliminate them.

All of that will enable you to speak naturally and confidently, even if you are slightly nervous. If your mind goes blank on a slide, skip it, jump back to it later and then move forward again. You'll be surprised at how slick you can get, after some practice.

Let's look at some things to help with nervousness.

The real trick is to look forward to having the opportunity to deliver your presentation. Imagine preparing well so that, on the day, it all runs smoothly. Think how good it will feel to get through this next stage of the process and come out a winner.

Visualising yourself doing well and imagining a positive outcome makes a substantial difference to both your confidence and your performance. Top level sports people use this technique all the time.

They imagine every detail of making a winning shot to the extent that, when the time comes, they're in the zone and it's automatic. They still go in with the nerves but they use the adrenalin to help them find an edge. They don't let it control them, they push on and push through it.

Try sitting alone quietly, close your eyes and then let your mind step through your presentation. Imagine facing the panel.

- 'See' every slide coming up, one by one.
- 'Hear' yourself speaking about each in turn, exactly as you would if you were doing it for real. Run through at the same pace you would use in reality – slowly.
- 'Feel' the rise and fall in tempo as you emphasise relevant content.
- Be aware of the positive body language in the faces of the audience, as they smile and nod approvingly at key points.

When you can do that, you will have one hundred per cent confidence in your ability to remember your lines and deliver them flawlessly. Crucially, you'll come across naturally, unlike if you learn your lines by rote, or if you just read them out from the slides or pieces of paper.

Something else to do is to practise smiling whenever you practise delivering your presentation. Plan to make eye contact and smile at the panel, right at the start. The people on the panel will smile back. Feel their warmth, their wish to see you do well. Think the words, "I really like you." Feel those words. Beam them over alongside that winning smile.

It's a hard interviewer that would blank you at that stage. If they do, there's one word that will save you and you should pull it up into your mind. That word is 'loser'. Increase your smile, think the words, "I still like you, even though you're a sad, insecure, loser," and then begin.

If you do sometimes suffer from the voice shakes, you will find that reading aloud and some practice sessions will both make a big difference over time. It's important not to overly dwell on your nerves when you start. Focus instead on the job you're doing. Once you get into the flow, your sensitivity to your own nervousness will fall away, as indeed will your nerves.

Try practising your breathing. Whoa, breathing? We all do it every day. How hard can it be? Actually, it's fiendishly difficult to do well.

Try this. Stand up, ready to speak your words. Study your natural breathing rhythm for a few moments. Breath out and then start reading something aloud. Your body is now calling for breath at exactly the same time as you've embarked on an action which requires you to breathe out further.

What's the result? The power of your delivery drops through the floor. You sound awful, even to yourself. In a real situation, you start to panic. Your stress levels rise. Adrenalin kicks in. The pounding starts in your chest. Your knees knock. You wonder if there's a bucket nearby.

Does that sound familiar?

Now, after calming down, take the deepest of deep breaths. Hold it for a brief moment and then start reading again.

Take it slowly. The power of your delivery increases. You feel stronger and you feed off that. When you reach the end of a sentence, pause. Breathe back in deeply and then continue. Get used to those pauses. Use them to breathe but also use them to emphasise your content. You sound stronger, even to yourself. God, you feel good now.

Practise that a lot and it will become second nature. It's really important to hear your own voice and get to the point where it sounds good to you. Once you feel that you can control the power of your delivery, just by controlling your breathing, you will be an unstoppable force.

Something else that can help is to try shouting. Not as in yelling, "Aaarrrgh! Pick me you bastards," but as in speaking as though the people are seated at the other end of a moderately long room.

Practise now. Stand up. Straighten up. Imagine you're facing a panel and in the normal voice you'd use to talk to a friend, say the words, "Hello, I'm here to talk about helping you to pick the best candidate." Now, take a deep breath and deliver the same thing, but this time several decibels louder. Rather than concentrating on your voice and shouting, think of projecting. Speak to a point ten metres distant. Focus there. Your body will automatically adjust.

The fact that you've chosen to speak to a distant point almost unconsciously forces you to take a deeper breath. Your delivery is thus more positive and confident. It is very hard to experience a shaking voice when you're bellowing fit to make a town crier crap themselves. With practice, you'll be able to pitch the volume so it's louder than normal, but not weirdly so.

Some years ago, I met a new colleague for the first time. He leapt around his desk, thrust his hand out, pumped mine and screamed "HELLO JON, GOOD TO MEET YOU. HOW ARE YOU?" People in the adjacent office block began to evacuate, in every way. The only thing that stopped me being pinned to the opposite wall was his mountaineer's death-grip on my hand.

Blimey, this is one powerful dude, I thought, as I bandaged my hand and mopped up the blood running from my ears. It took me a while to realise that he did this whenever he was nervous. It was a trick that he'd picked up to mask signs of his fear and to get through the first moments of meeting someone new. Despite his fear, he'd worked his way up to being a Finance Director with one of the UK's largest public companies, so the trick worked.

As part of 'shouting', it's important to speak in a measured way and to enunciate clearly. You need to sound in command, not as though you're hysterical and on the edge of losing it big time. Aim for cut glass, not mush.

Try consciously raising the volume of your speech. You'll be surprised at the effect. But remember to focus it. Be clear; be positive; be in command.

That's a step along the way but, in fact, what you really want to aim for is more power, not necessarily more volume. You sometimes meet people who don't raise their voice, but their words always cut through the thickest fog in a meeting with ease and clarity. That's power, not volume.

You can develop that power by pushing air from the bottom and sides of your lungs, not from the very top. When you take a deep breath in, fill your belly, as well as your chest. Then, when you speak, imagine squeezing from your floating ribs at the side, rather than from your belly, chest or throat. Lift your chin and stretch your neck very slightly. That will enable you to project your voice some distance without actually shouting.

Notice that some people naturally speak with an almost breathless delivery. I call it a 'breathey' voice. They're speaking from the very top of their lungs and there's absolutely no power there. In a crowd, they're swamped. You'll find that they've unconsciously learned to bodge around the problem by reaching for a higher pitch, so as to penetrate further. Unfortunately, there's still no power there and such voices can become very strident, as they try to shout, but effectively have nothing to shout with.

Speaking from the top of our lungs is something each and every one of us has probably experienced at some time. Often, as we lead our sedentary lives, we breathe using only the very top part of our lungs. If we experience momentary stress, perhaps being suddenly asked to speak, all we've got is a shallow breath to draw on. We sound weak and then we sound nervous to ourselves. As a result, we get more stressed and slip into an accelerating spiral of doom.

You can break that cycle. It just takes a small amount of work. Get into the habit of taking a very deep first breath before you begin. Hear the start of your first sentence and think, "Yep, it's coming out okay". Feed off that and then forget about it. Slip into the moment; the zone, if you like. Hear what you're delivering but concentrate on the impact it's making. Pick up on the facial expressions and subtle feedback from your audience. Now you're in control, learn to enjoy it.

Practising all of the above will help you to be thoroughly prepared to make a good job of delivering your presentation.

Communication skills are important but never lose sight of the fact that they alone will not get you a job. You'll get the job because of what you have to offer the role and the organisation. If your communication skills are passable, that's probably enough, unless public speaking is a central feature of the job. After that, anything's a bonus.

That's sometimes why highly confident public speakers fail. They're demonstrating one narrow skill in spades but are failing to show that they have anything else to back it up with. "Speaks really well but sadly does a crap job," is not something you ever want on one of your appraisals.

So, stop focusing on yourself, focus more on what you have to offer and what will make you a better bet than the next person. Grip your knife firmly, smile disarmingly and go for the jugular. Look for a weakness in your peers and capitalise on it by showing that it's one of your strengths. That way, you're never seen to be the attacker, you're ahead of the pack and the tiger gets the rest.

A last quick point. When you finish a presentation, do so professionally. Don't grab your notes and leg it, looking as though someone's just called last orders. Say something like, "That's it, thank you for listening. I'd be pleased to answer questions if you have any," or whatever is appropriate. Make eye contact with the panel, smile and leave with dignity, even if you do need to change your trolleys.

A lot of the above points will also stand you in excellent stead with most of the other interview topics we've covered in this chapter. They'll certainly help you with this next topic. It's one that gets most people wishing they'd remembered their bicycle clips.

9) Making a short impromptu presentation. Yep, that'll get the blood trotting around your system on the back of an adrenalin rush so strong it will make an Icelandic volcano look like a toddler's firework.

> "Please stand up and talk to the group for two minutes on the subject of ping pong balls."

Great.

That's in danger of being the longest and most excruciating two minutes of your life. What sort of a bloodless sadist dreamed that one up?

When I was younger, I'd have rather crawled for a mile, naked, over a minefield littered with angry scorpions, broken glass and used heroin needles, than stand up for that.

Since hiding will not be an option, how do you prepare for this type of question?

Firstly, everything we've covered so far on preparing to speak to a group applies. Keep practising that, whatever else you do.

Secondly, on separate pieces of paper, write down the most obscure topics you can think of and draw one out of a hat.

Thirdly, stand up and speak for two minutes on that subject.

This will no doubt feel weird, even if you're on your own. If you get stuck, don't stop and try to start from the beginning again, just roll with it. It's better to suffer now, on your own, and learn how to get yourself out of the black holes that your brain can drop you into, so you're ready if it happens on the day.

Get used to thinking on your feet. Get used to taking a few seconds at the front end, just to get your mind in gear. Get used to pausing now and then, for a few seconds, to mentally re-group.

When you're standing up in front of a group, pauses feel like they're going on forever. In reality, they're commonly very short. With the correct behaviour on your part, they can actually look controlled, classy and professional.

So, you can actually use up time, say nothing and yet appear staggeringly professional?

Yep. It just doesn't get better than that. Truly. Best trick ever.

Now what you need are some other techniques, to help your brain latch onto things you can talk about, when faced with something new and obscure.

Repeating the topic is always a great start – it sets the scene, it uses a few seconds and it buys you some thinking time.

Think systematically about the ping pong ball. What's it made of? Why? What's it used for? How? Who uses it? In what circumstances? What other uses could it have? (Think cats. Think raft. Think Thai bar girls. … Actually, perhaps not.) Where would it get used? Where wouldn't it work? (Space? Underwater?) How are they made? How would you clean them? Anybody famous ever play ping pong? Who wouldn't play ping pong? What does the Queen think about ping pong? Would she win and, if so, why?

Two minutes? There's a whole Master's thesis there. If you stay systematically in control, you can easily talk for much longer than two minutes.

So, that's your base line. You can speak for that time. You can score without falling apart. Even if you do seize up for quite a time, if you stay in control you'll still score for it.

If you get stuck part way through, try, "Gosh, my mind's gone completely blank. Help. Let me just think for a moment."

Smile. Tough it out.

"Okay, here we go again …"

Brilliant, you've stayed in control AND used up eight seconds AND got yourself moving forward again. Fill the gaps with piffle if you have to, just look like you're taking it in your stride.

Your next step is to make it interesting, if at all possible. Try and spice things up a bit now and then. The wild and wacky, the humorous, the strange but true, are all useful areas to draw on. Humour is particularly good for lightening the tone, if you can carry it off.

> "The Queen doesn't allow ping pong at Balmoral because, after a good lash-up the night before, the sound of the balls on the wooden floor plays hell with the Duke's migraines. The bouncing balls also whip the Corgis into a complete frenzy and the whole commotion makes it impossible for her to concentrate properly on the racing pages. She used to play a lot, and tried out at county level, but Prince Harry swallowed her ping pong ball in the middle of a championship game when he was a toddler and retrieving it was so traumatic that she stopped all serious competition work at that point."

There's always the possibility that the brief chuckles from the audience will use up a few more seconds. Better still, that sort of feedback will give you a lift.

Whatever you go with, don't swear, keep it clean and stay away from risqué or potentially offensive subjects. If in doubt with a topic, don't take the risk.

As you practise on other examples, build up a systematic idea-generation process for yourself that you can re-use time after time on any question that crops up.

As you move forward, try working on tighter, harsher subjects. For example, "Talk for two minutes on the inside of a ping pong ball."

Oh, goody.

Despite the opportunities for levity, take these practice sessions seriously. On the day, you'll need to make a reasonably professional job of things, not make an air-headed tit of yourself with two minutes of giggly fluff. Aim for Jack Dee, not Benny Hill.

Video your sessions and watch them back to hone your style and appearance. Get used to changing direction when you can see the end of a blind alley coming at you.

> "Gosh, how did I end up talking about the Queen in the middle of talking about ping pong balls? Okay, let's change tack. Ping pong balls are not made out of lead for several reasons."

Okay, that covers the lighter end of the impromptu speech spectrum. Unexpectedly, such things can end up being a lot of fun for everyone. Let's step you forward into the more serious end of things. You might be given a serious topic to work with and will need to adjust accordingly.

> "The American, British, French and Russian positions with respect to Syria were all influenced by the war with Iraq. Give us your views for the next two minutes."

Ooh, there's a barrel of laughs to be had. Not. Clearly we're in way different territory to the Queen's prowess with a number three-sized pimple bat.

Try your hat routine with a new bunch of topics in this same vein. Pick up a newspaper and pull topics out of that. Don't just pick ones that you know about. Pick some where you suspect you have almost no knowledge. Aim to get used to handling the unknown.

Clearly, any work you've put into staying up with current affairs might pay a few dividends at this point but don't worry if you're not familiar with the subject itself. Think around it. Look for parallels and start to carefully extrapolate.

Try using the **PREP model**.

It stands for Position, Reason, Examples, Position.

- As you begin, state your starting position on the subject.
- Explain why you think that and what justifies your position.
- Build a story around examples that support your case.
- Finish by re-stating your position or offering a proposition.

As an addition, consider weaving in alternative views or positions and why they may or may not have merit.

With practice, you'll find that with only a few seconds thought at the front end, you can build a quick outline structure in your mind that will carry you all the way through.

Aim for beginning, middle and end sections, with a few sub-headings under each. If you can't get all that done in time, start on the intro and drop the rest into place as you go.

With practice, it gets much easier. Don't be afraid to pause. Grab a heading, move forward with it. Know when to close off a line that you've exhausted. Don't draw things out to the death, as you risk losing the audience's interest.

Try for a beginning that grabs the audience's attention and aim for an end that ties things off cleanly. Build a middle that delivers your main points.

The key to it all is to learn how to think under pressure whilst staying calm.

Be brave and get a friend to pick out the random topics you've drawn up and get them to score you on them. Scary, but what the hell? Do you want the job, or not?

Now it's time to move into even darker territory with your practice. The final topic to cover is ... drum roll ... you.

> "In two minutes, could you please tell us why you think you'd be able to make an excellent job of things in this role?"

There's always the possibility you'll be asked variations around that theme.

Even if not, I have to say that the practice you'll get, with this type of question, will be great preparation for standard interview situations anyway. At the very least, you'll have mastered a process for handling questions that crop up unexpectedly and don't fit with your previously rehearsed ones.

Run your hat routine again with various questions linked to your suitability. Aim to keep pushing yourself out of your comfort zone. Aim for the worst, such that when something crops up on the day, you'll breathe a sigh of relief.

- "Please give us two minutes on why we should pick you and not the other five people you're sitting with in your group."
- Or, even worse, "In two minutes, please tell us five things that mean others might be a better bet than you, but finish with a strong justification for your selection anyway."

You'll never be asked anything that vile, but hey, it sure is good practice for thinking on your feet when you draw it out of the hat.

10) Creativity / lateral-thinking questions. This is another area that's tricky to prepare for because questions will again be impossible to predict. We're thinking here about offbeat and slightly wacky questions.

> "Why are the vast majority of manhole covers round?"

Microsoft apparently made this question famous by including it in their interviews, to test the creative abilities of interviewees.

Such questions are sometimes slipped in near the end of an interview and may well have more than one correct answer. Indeed, some of them may have no definitive correct answer at all, being literally impossible.

Notice that the one just above is an open question on a topic that you're unlikely to have any knowledge of and you'll therefore need to think laterally and adapt your previous experience.

In the stress of the moment, such questions commonly induce 'vacant brain syndrome'. You feel pressured to give quick positive answers but you have no idea where to start. It's therefore important not to rush yourself. If you relax, your brain will work much more effectively. Smile, acknowledge the challenge, take a deep breath and take your time.

If it's hard to get a handle on the question, try firstly identifying the broad lines by which you can break the issue down, before you later push into specifics.

For example, reasons might be categorised under the headings of practical, aesthetic or economic. The practicalities might be further sub-divided into manufacturing reasons and usage reasons.

Once you've got your brain moving in a direction, you may well find there's a sudden flow of ideas for you to talk about. Obviously, if something bursts straight into your brain at the start, just go with it. Let it flow.

Interestingly, in the middle of 2013, Google publically abandoned their regular use of impossible-to-answer questions. Their senior VP of People Operations, Laszlo Block, was reported as saying that the use of such questions turned out to be a complete waste and predicted little about candidates that was useful. Instead, they're now asking candidates to explain previous choices they've made in real-world, difficult situations.

Other organisations are still hanging onto their wacky questions, however, so you may still come across them.

> "How many car mechanics are there in London, New York and Paris?"

> "How much would you charge to clean all of the windows in Bristol?

And so on. I'll leave you to Google examples of Google's interview questions.

Also in 2013, Curry's in Cardiff lurched into the news for all of the wrong reasons. They divided candidates into groups and asked each to make up a dance, and then perform it. Some candidates were left feeling humiliated and Curry's admitted that the dance segment of the interview had been a mistake.

Undoubtedly, there is an argument that such a 'test' tells you something about a candidate's personality. However, unless interviewers are specifically trained in such methods of assessment, the consistency and quality of this type of approach will be little better than random.

If creativity and innovative ability really are judged to be of overriding importance, it's quite likely that you'll have a separate interview or test on that alone. You'll then come across a wider range of both open and closed logic-based questions, as well as off the wall ones.

> "If you have two coins totalling 21p, and one of the coins is not a penny, what are the two coins?"

That's a typical logic-based question that may be part of a whole salvo in a time-constrained test paper or interview session.

The only practical way to prepare is to work through endless examples. As soon as you start, you'll notice that questions fall into different types and you'll learn to spot them quickly.

"Why can't people living in Brighton be buried North of Stonehenge?"

Once you spot the pattern type, it's much easier to deal with these questions.

So as not to drive you batty, or distract you from your reading, I'll give you the answers. The coins are a twenty pence coin and a one pence coin. (Read the question again, if you're still wondering.) The people can't be buried North of Stonehenge because they're still alive. (Yep, I hate these questions too.)

You can buy books containing hundreds of examples, although you may find that trawling the web throws up sufficient for you. To get you started, there are some questions provided in Appendix A.

So, after practising all ten types of interview situation above, you must surely be awesome by now? No? OMG – ten press ups, soldier. Now!

Back you go, do it all again and don't stop until you're comfortable with everything they might throw at you.

Now let's step forward in time to the day of your interview.

Attending your interview

Today's the big day, where's that bucket gone?

Actually, the first thing you should do when you open your eyes is start looking forward to the day. You've trained hard, you've done all you can and now you're finally going in. Whether you win, or whether you lose and have to chalk it up to experience, you're one day nearer winning a job.

Let's do everything we can to further shave the odds in your favour and make today the winning day.

Tip of the day – baked beans might not be your wisest choice for breakfast.

You might be nervous. So what? Use the fear to help you stay sharp. Several of your cohort will be cut to pieces later and that'll be mainly because they haven't prepared anywhere near as well as you have. I'm with you every inch of the way today. Your struggle is my struggle. Your pain is my pain. Have faith in your training. Have confidence in yourself. If you don't, who else will?

When you've gathered your wits about you, attended to your basic biological functions, scraped out the parrot cage, equipped yourself with the first coffee of the day and finally got the corpuscles trotting through your brain in an orderly fashion, start to get your head ready.

Remind yourself of your objective today. Is it to win that job? Well, it might be, if this is the final interview. If it isn't, then your objective is to win a place at the next stage in the process. Be clear because the selection process influences the way you calculate and play the odds, as we covered previously.

Your basic strategy will be to:

- show you meet the core requirements;
- demonstrate why you're the candidate with the most potential;
- exhibit the aspects of your character that will make you the best fit.

Remind yourself of the values of the organisation. Think about the qualities you want to display during the day. What qualities would you most like to see in a colleague in that role, if you worked alongside them? Would you like them to be open, honest, supportive, confident, fair and have a good sense of humour? What about their ability to do their job? Would you want them to be level-headed, logical, decisive?

Whatever is likely to be appropriate for the role, those are the behaviours to show today. If you really must be a petulant prima donna with a penchant for divisiveness and a talent for bitchiness, back-stabbing and butt-fucking, by all means go for it – if it's exactly what's needed for that role.

Otherwise, be aware that your behaviour might be categorised as sub-optimal, and your performance level with it.

You might be applying for a role, but today you should aim to play a role.

Let's look at the main areas to think about.

- Dressing appropriately.
- Choosing what to take with you.
- Getting there.
- Controlling your nervousness.
- First impressions.
- Managing the interview.
- Finishing the day.

Dressing correctly shouldn't be a mish to sort out, if you've done some homework beforehand. Even if it's dress-down Friday (heavy sigh) go for smart-casual or a suit. After all, if you feel over-dressed you can always remove your jacket to blend in more. If you turn up dressed in a tee shirt and jeans but find that the interviewer is wearing a suit regardless, you'll feel at a disadvantage, whether you are or not. Conversely, if you're over-dressed, it's not likely to be a mark against you. People know that you're at an interview.

If it's perhaps 'wear something red day', by all means carry a red bag or wear a red tie if you can do so without detracting from your overall appearance. If at all possible you want to look as though you fit right in. Nonetheless, you do need to look clean, smart and business-like. If your only red tie was last used to hoist the engine out of your car, or as a prop in your pole-dancing class, forget it or buy a new one.

For men, ties are a difficult subject these days. Some organisations seem to encourage them, some don't. Do your research but the bottom line is – if in doubt, dress up, not down. Avoid wacky ties. They can be amusing but you risk not being taken seriously.

Men, for God's sake make sure you wash in the morning and apply all of the usual socially-accepted unguents to your personage. If you go in smelling like a char wallah's loin cloth, no amount of pimping is going to save you. Wash your hair, trim any facial hair (real or imagined) and clean your spectacles whilst you're at it.

For women, similar rules apply (although obviously you don't need to be told to wash) and a smart suit and professional look is best.

Avoid showing midriffs, feet and breast cleavage. (Likewise, but for different reasons, men should avoid displaying underpants and / or bum cleavage.) Wear shoes, not sandals. Go for smart and plain every time. Go for a lower hem line. Tone down the make-up. Don't overly accessorise, avoid the bling and lose the fishnets (preferably not in the interview room).

How you smell can be important for both men and women. Reeking of cheap perfume or aftershave can be as off-putting as smelling like the ashtray from a builder's P reg pickup. Try for a fresh, or at least neutral, smell.

That does present a problem for you smokers. There is no way you're going to walk through that door without a last quick fix so stand in the open air when you do so. Preferably, stand in a breeze, blow down-wind and keep the smoke off your clothes. Ideally wear gloves and an overcoat or a more non-absorbent zipped up plastic caggie. A complete rubber suit would be better, but is a tad risqué.

Do not chuck your dog ends in their flower beds, right outside the main entrance.

Take a mint spray with you and use a wet-wipe to get the smoky smell off your fingers and any facial hair you're wearing. (If you think this is extreme, console yourself with the thought that the SAS have to defecate in plastic bags and carry it around for days on end.)

If you're worried about surviving an extended period without ciggies, consider using patches for the day so you don't end up chewing the carpet. If you do, practise first and get the dosage right.

It should go without saying, on no account go in having just hoovered up six lines of marching powder and chugged a wee voddie. If someone gives you 'something for your nerves' a while beforehand, chuck it in the bin and don't look back. The last thing you want to do is to leave the interviewer wondering whether you need a respirator, restraints or a rehab session.

None of us should be judged by our appearance but the simple fact is that we are. If you look smart, you probably are smart. Someone once said that every pound you invest in your appearance will pay you back a thousand fold and never was it so true as on interview day.

If your suit no longer fits, the style is long-dead, or the structure of it has collapsed, then buy another or beg, borrow or steal one. On no account wear a hoodie or a hat, unless it's for religious or medical reasons.

Try to cover any visible tattoos and remove any extraneous metal-work wedged through your face. Gentlemen? I have no idea what to tell you if you're equipped with a massive

Prince Albert and are likely to face a metal detector on the way in. Frankly, you're on your own.

Have a good check in the mirror before you leave home. Remove any hair from dark clothing, make sure shirts and blouses are ironed and clean your shoes, even if they don't need it. Practise smiling in the mirror. Like what you see, remind yourself to enjoy the day and have fun.

Now, what should you remember to take with you? At the very least, I'd suggest you need a summarised copy of your research notes, a copy of your CV / application, the invitation letter, maps, contact names and numbers, your presentation on a USB drive and a conveniently-sized notepad.

Oh, and a list of questions to ask them. On that subject, Appendix A has a bunch of useful questions, just in case the dog ate your others.

Get there in good time. If it's feasible to do so, case the joint and rehearse the journey beforehand. Don't be obsessive about this point but do it if you can, as it can help relieve a lot of stress on the day itself. Time the journey, figure out alternatives, buy all of your tickets in advance.

Plan to arrive an absolute minimum of one hour early, in case your chosen method of transport is randomly disrupted. Do a walk by if possible and find out EXACTLY where the right entrance is, before you park yourself in a nearby Costa for the hour or so you'll have to wait.

One teensy little thing to worry about – what if it all goes wrong?

You're perfectly on time, the train is heading nicely for Victoria and then someone selfishly chucks themselves in front of it. You're pretty sure there'll be a three hour delay whilst they counsel the driver, hunt for body parts, repaint the train and set up an impromptu barbeque. What do you do next?

Make sure you're carrying relevant phone numbers and names with you. Ring up and tell the organisation the problem and ask them what they'd like to do. It's a zillion times better to do that than to just turn up late or not even turn up at all. Be professional about it. Be apologetic but stay factual. There's no need to be nervous or weird – you couldn't possibly have foreseen such a problem.

Do not sob or scream hysterically down the phone. Don't bang on about the blood and guts running down the windows and definitely don't diss the poor sod lying under the train. You never know whether the interviewer is devoutly religious or their partner ended it the same way a couple of years ago.

There is a slim possibility that they won't reschedule and your chance is now blown. Sometimes, especially in the public or third sectors, they'll be planning to make the final decision on who to appoint that day and may have publicised the fact to all and sundry. If so, it's unfortunate, but you probably are screwed.

However, do not yell the c word down the phone as you hang up. They may have another vacancy cropping up next month and feel obligated to give you a better than fair shot at it. They won't do that if they're still in shock at your unprofessional rudeness.

Stay calm. Rest assured, if your lateness is genuine, if they possibly can cut you some slack, they will. If not, I'm sorry but it just wasn't your day. If that's the case, tomorrow's another day. Rise again from the dead, look to the horizon and sniff the air for a scent of blood.

Assuming that everything goes roughly according to plan, use your time drinking coffee to re-read your notes on the organisation. Get clear what you said in your application.

Deliberately think about reducing your nervousness. Consciously relax and de-stress yourself. Play the interview out in your mind, visualise yourself doing well, see the interviewer smiling and nodding. You've done all the hard work, you know exactly how to play it, be confident. Practise smiling but try not to get arrested for being a weirdo in a public place.

A very useful mnemonic to aid de-stressing is ABC.

A stands for 'A meeting'. You're attending a meeting, rather than an interview. Changing the terminology changes the mental associations and may help you to relax. Psychologically, that can shift the balance in your mind and help you to see it as a two-way street.

B is for 'Be an actor'. It can help to reduce nerves if you think of yourself acting a part in a play where you have some lines to deliver and a bit of improv work to do. Perhaps imagine yourself wearing a mask. That way, if you're worried about criticism, it's the character they'll be criticising, not you. Act confident and you'll be confident.

C stands for 'C a benefit'. The bottom line is that you've got a few hours of discomfort to endure and in return there's a very high risk that someone is going to give you tens of thousands of pounds a year, every year for years to come. Isn't that worth some pain? Bring it on.

Additionally, you can be fairly sure you will not be wired up to the mains, gang-raped or water-boarded as part of the proceedings today. Exactly as you walk into that room, some poor sod somewhere on earth will be having a really, really, bad day. By my estimate, on average globally, over seven thousand nine hundred and ninety people will die for every hour you're in that interview. (That figure can obviously rise sharply, if someone with a poor attitude gets enthusiastic with their bag of toys and twitchy with a red button.)

Maybe that interview doesn't seem quite so rough now?

Finally, give yourself some credit. If you've been shortlisted for interview, they already think you're worth considering.

When it's time, put down your coffee, pick up your weapons and cruise on in there. Aim to arrive at the front door relaxed and clear-headed. Smile at the receptionist. Like them. A lot. Clearly, I mean this in an admiring sense, not in a sexual way, so do not tell them that you're not wearing undergarments if such is the case. If they're going to be asked about you, make sure they remember you for the right reasons.

If someone comes to pick you up in reception, don't assume they're the tea boy even if they're wearing a tee-shirt printed with, "I'm the tea boy," and even if they also say the words, "Hello, would you like some tea?"

I still sweat at how close I once came to blowing one of my biggest chances by making that very assumption. My heart is pounding as I type this.

I was in my thirties, chasing a senior job and the guy who met me looked about twelve. His shirt was tired and poorly-ironed and his trousers were so worn the thighs were shiny. Something made me question the assumption I was making so I decided to play safe and talked about the weather, not whether he had any prospects as a tea boy at that place.

We stopped and picked up tea from a machine, before he showed me into an office the size of Kent and then proceeded to kick the shit out of me for an hour. He didn't even break into a sweat. I got the job but I'm certain I wouldn't have, if I hadn't kept my wits about me at the start.

Why did the guy look like a tramp? It turned out he had very young children and one had thrown up over him just as he was about to leave for the day, forcing a quick change. All credit to him, his spanking hand wasn't red.

So next up is first impressions.

Cliché warning. You only ever get one chance to make a first impression. Try not to blow it in the first ten seconds. As professionals, interviewers should not go off first impressions and they certainly shouldn't take a decision to employ (or not) inside that time, but they do. Not every time. Not many times, in fact. But they do.

Actually, I argue that you should already have won it before you even enter the room, but I'm splitting hairs. Do your prep, rehearse, get everything right and you can swing that job.

Every recruitment professional will tell you that they've been trained not to make first impression judgements. They'll bang on endlessly about how they weigh up the whole course of the interview, before reaching a fully measured, truly fair, conclusion.

Solid, but they're either lying or living in denial.

Okay, they don't do this all the time. It doesn't happen with every interview day but every so often it just does and they can't help themselves.

I've experienced this both ways. I'm certain I've won a job that way and I'm sure I've employed people on that basis. It's like love at first sight – you just know when it happens. Okay, both sides need to get through the next hour or so and both sides need not to screw it up but it's job done, if you just play the hand out.

It's not actually so surprising. As I said before, if you've been invited for an interview, you're already well in the frame. Any one of the people on the shortlist that day could be the one to get selected.

So what can you do to make that job yours, in the first ten seconds?

We've covered appearance but posture is at least as important. Head up, shoulders back, positive body language.

Next, with full eye contact divvy up a big beaming, entirely genuine, smile. If it doesn't reach your eyes, you're dead. Just turn around, walk out and get the bus home. If you can't fake sincerity, don't try it, just stay safe.

Really like the interviewer. Beam it across with every fibre of your being. Like their appearance, their office, their demeanour, even their odd socks.

Step forward confidently but not arrogantly. Add a twist of humility, but just a twist.

Make the handshake a goody. Hit it square on and hope you both latch on correctly. Do it without sweaty palms, if you can. Make it firm but not a bone crusher. (If your handshake is limp, ask if they've got a bus timetable handy.) Smile throughout, maintain eye contact and break at the right moment. Don't make it too short but, equally, don't cling on too long.

Follow their lead as they show you to a chair. If they offer you something (like tea, coffee or water) take it and smile.

Sit up straight, face them, be fully attentive and smile.

Okay, if that all goes tits up, what do you do? Let's say the interviewer is just a fat, ugly, repulsive, entirely unreconstructed, misogynistic pig who can't even be arsed to look in your direction, let alone make eye contact. What can you do?

Don't worry about it. You're no worse off than if you hadn't been aware of all this in the first place. It's also quite likely that they'll be a pig to everyone.

Having said that, do keep trying to reach them. The whole time you're with them, smile, like them and beam in the positive vibes. Try again when you sit down and they have to face you. Don't overdo it or they'll ring for security. You have to be a bit subtle but if you manage to break through that exoskeleton at some stage, you're in there with the best chance of anyone.

As the interview moves forward, it's your job to manage it and you can only do that by managing yourself, your behaviour and your responses.

Assuming that the interviewer is a perfectly normal human being, remember to think how much you like them every now and then. If they make a joke, for God's sake laugh, or at least smile or titter, as appropriate.

Take your guide from them. Match their tone and mood and try to (subtly) reflect their body language. If they sit back, you do so too. If they sit up straight, do the same. If they're amused, you're amused. If they're serious, you're serious. If they're angry… well you're screwed at that point. Think of it all as synchronised swimming but don't overplay it, don't make it obvious and don't get rumbled.

How you speak during the interview is obviously as important as how you behave. One disinterested 'dunno', with an accompanying 'I don't care' shrug, will see the tiger don his bib. I'm sure you have more sense than that, but be conscious of the need to pitch your tone and attitude correctly.

Never try to score points off the interviewer and at all costs avoid getting dug into a face-off over, what is in fact, a very minor point. Whether you win or lose a point is less important than how you play the game. The interviewer's job is to challenge you but it's your choice how to respond. Challenging them back is almost never the right thing to do.

"I don't think you're at all suited for this type of work. What do you think?"

185

> "I think you're just another HR lackey, failing to live in the real world and living proof that God did breed a race of spineless human beings."

Clearly, it's all gone wrong at that point and it's you that's at fault for reacting aggressively to a suggested negative.

Why is it you that's at fault? You're a tit.

See? Negativity comes at you all the time. Grow a thicker skin. Learn to recognise negativity, shrug it off and turn it back around.

> "Actually, I think I am suited to this type of work. I have all of the primary requirements and my extra experience would be highly beneficial to the role. My personality type is probably different to most people applying for this post but actually it's an advantage because I'm generally able to come up with more creative solutions. That's backed up by …"

You're directly disagreeing with what's coming at you but not in a confrontational way. You're immediately dodging the bullet and turning it back around by firstly, cementing in stone that you have the right qualifications and experience and secondly, acknowledging that the interviewer is correct. But then thirdly, even better, you're showing that that actually makes you a better choice and you're putting a solid reason behind it – your higher creativity.

Slick, or what? Give yourself a high five.

Once you settle down and get into a flow with the interview, you may well find that digging up answers like that one happens very easily. The trick is to blank your mind and allow your subconscious free rein to roll out your rehearsal work, in a relaxed way.

If the interviewer likes you, the game is a whole lot easier to play because they actually want you to hit those winning shots. They want you to justify the choice they've maybe already subconsciously made. That's why it's always down to you to manage the meeting, even though the interviewer steers it.

What if you get hit by a left-field shot so that your mind freezes and the adrenalin starts to pump like the last fire engine at the Houses of Parliament on Guy Fawkes Night?

Pause, take deep breaths and acknowledge the situation.

> "I'm not quite sure how best to answer that. Could you repeat the question?"

Relax a little, buy yourself time to think and you'll get back in the flow.

If you're very nervous, try sitting on your hands. If you need more time, take a sip of whatever drink you might have been equipped with. Breathe deeply the whole time, to burn off the excess adrenalin faster. It all works.

Importantly, perhaps perversely, don't worry about being perfect. No one is. Don't beat yourself up over an issue or a crashed answer. Leave it behind and move forward again. It's like a guerrilla war. Concentrate on your wins, not your losses. You might come off worst in the odd skirmish but so long as you keep going, you can win in the end.

In managing your interview, always be conscious of looking for an edge with which to shave the odds. If you're the only candidate in the room, then look for opportunities to pitch in with your added value.

If you're in a group situation, work out who is above and who is below the cut line and what you can do to make sure you're on the right side of that line.

In group interviews, the game of 'spot the wanker' can be very useful to help boost your confidence. Just think, "If a wanker like that can make it this far, I can do so much more." You shouldn't attack your peers, but there's nothing wrong with standing at the side of someone in a way that just shows off how much better you are in comparison. That's a throat cut. Score.

You still need to proactively score your own points along the way but you can be sure that the body count has risen by at least one. Often, that's comforting.

Look at who else may not make the cut and why. Make sure you don't display the same faults, but do show the added-value only you can offer.

As you move forward through your meeting(s), remember a couple of the basics. On no account swear and stay away from politics, religion and currently controversial subjects, unless the interviewer specifically raises one of them. In that case, give considered, balanced, non-divisive, responses.

There are a couple of tricky questions that might crop up.

> "Have you got anything else on the go at the moment?"

This might be followed up with enquiries about whether you have other offers on the table, or expect to have, and what types of opportunity you're applying for. It's best to be a little cautious.

> "I've got a small number of opportunities that I'm looking at which are fairly well advanced and that I'm enthusiastic about, but I hope this one here works out," is a great answer, which hopefully chops off the flow of questions.

An alternative, which might not be such a great answer is the following.

> "You betcha. There's two other management trainee posts I'm chasing but I've also applied to be a brain surgeon, although I did want to be an astronaut. There is a great job as a geologist in Madagascar I wouldn't mind and there's a really good one in Tibet, for a project company organising a new yeti-hunt as part of a Channel 4 documentary. That might be a blast and I quite fancy the producer."

You might experience difficulties during the remainder of your interview, if in fact there is a remainder, as people wonder about your range of career choices under consideration. Stay on the straight and narrow and only put across positive information that supports your application.

Another tricky interview question centres around your salary expectations.

> "What sort of salary might be acceptable to you in this post?"

Dangerous territory, indeed.

"As much as I can possibly get for the least effort on my part."

This is, I'm sure, not something that you'd run with but, for the reasons we touched on a lot earlier, if at all humanly possible don't give a specific answer. If you're still being pressed into a corner, remain positive but still try to leave things open.

"Well, I'd hope to be able to justify receiving an offer which sits at, or near the very top end of what is possible for this level of work within your organisation."

That way, you're making it clear that you regard yourself as a high-performing individual and you hope to get recognition for it. Your aspiration is quite likely to mark you out above many others in terms of interview score. If you can stay away from naming a figure, you have less risk of pricing yourself out of the game or underselling yourself. The organisation is still left with the challenge of deciding where to pitch their offer when they make it. You're leaving the door open to negotiate at the time when you're strongest – when you actually have the offer in your hand.

When the dust settles a little, towards the very end of the interview, the stage is momentarily yours alone to both manage and direct. Now is the time for your questions.

You should have in mind, or to hand, your prepared list.

Undoubtedly, you'll already have covered some items during the course of the interview so don't re-visit them – cross them off. You may want to focus on entirely new questions that have occurred to you, during your discussions.

Nonetheless, ask questions that show positive and proactive lines of thinking on your part. Stay away from complaints and negativity. At all costs, you want to leave the meeting with both you and the interviewer on the best high you can muster. If they end up breathing a sigh of relief as you leave, you're dead meat.

It is possible that the interviewer will feel highly positive at the end but you might feel ambivalent about the job, the company or the people.

"The job sounds shit, I'm not taking it."

Don't go there, even if it's the case, for the reasons we looked at before. An offer is an offer and it has value. Even if you don't want it, you might be able to use it as leverage.

If you run out of questions, don't be afraid to explain that you've covered all the other points you wanted to, during the actual interview itself. In any case, don't continue to bang on with endless questions. Your aim is to cover a few key points only. Keep an eye on the interviewer and read the signs. If they clearly want to wind it all up and finish, do so. Don't frustrate them.

As your last (or almost last) question, you could ask if there's anything that raises a concern about your suitability in the interviewer's mind. If you possibly can do that, go for it. It can be an invaluable way to overcome what might otherwise be a nail in your coffin.

"Well, now you mention it, I do still have some concerns about whether you can handle a confrontation successfully."

"Yes, I don't think I handled your question very well earlier. What I can say is that I have had several such experiences before and I did deal with them successfully at the time. Do you mind if I just tell you about one of them?"

You're back on a roll now. There was potentially one dirty great big fat negative sitting over your suitability and now they've told you what it is and you've got the opportunity to reverse it. Brilliant. You'll definitely be stepping out of that room on a high note.

It's possible that it was no big deal in the overall scheme of things and wouldn't have killed you anyway but at least you've been proactive and should get respect for your thoroughness.

When you've handled that, stop and get out of the door. As you leave, use all of the same body language and behaviours that you used on the way in.

If, at that stage, the interviewer is desperately trying to get their tongue down your throat, you've been a little too heavy on the beaming part. My suggestion would be to use it to your advantage but I'm sure not everyone would agree.

Seriously, do adopt a very enthusiastic 'I really enjoyed all this' posture with smiling, eye contact and the same firm handshake.

Very importantly, say thank you. Make it clear that you've enjoyed talking to them, that you like the sound of the job and that you really would like to go through to the next stage. Do that even if you're not sure. As the door closes, see the tiger nod approvingly from the other side.

After the interview

Whew! You're out of the door and on your way back home. Hopefully, if you don't get hit by an anti-climax wall after all your hard work, your heart is uplifted and your feet are skipping so lightly, children watching would be wondering if you're the second coming of Mary Poppins.

Job done, right?

Not quite.

Remember what I said earlier about walls, coffee shops, trains and taxis having ears? Believe it. You don't want to blow it now.

Secondly, as soon as you can, you need to make notes about the interview. If you need to wind down, head back to your earlier café and do it there, whilst it's still fresh in your mind. Otherwise, doing it during the journey back home will suffice. Just don't leave it too long and definitely do it before your mind gets onto other things.

Note down what went well, where you felt you made a hit and what perhaps scored highly for you. Also note where you were weakest. Were there any specific questions that were hard for you to deal with? Did anything actually go badly? If so, in what way and why?

If you could do the whole thing again, what changes would you make in your answers? What lessons can you learn for your next interview? Note everything down. Just scrawl in a non-ordered, stream of consciousness, way.

Also make notes on anything you learned about the organisation, the role and the people interviewing you during the day. Make notes on your peers, if it was a group session. Don't trust things to memory. Capture thoughts now, whilst they're still fresh.

The next day, it's worth dropping a thank-you note via email. Don't be creepy or obsequious. Just a short and genuine thank you for their hospitality and time will do. Add a statement to make it clear that you enjoyed looking at the opportunity and would welcome the chance to work there, if you're successful. It just might make a difference in a marginal-choice situation.

Anything else to do?

Yep. Don't wait for the result.

Crack on with finding another opportunity. Take action this day. Either ride on the crest of the wave from yesterday or, if you feel more negatively about it, use that to motivate yourself to look for something else, armed with the knowledge of how you'll do it better next time. Don't stop. The dead are rising and they're chasing those jobs. Get after them.

Just before you do, what if you do get rejected?

Just accept it, it's their loss.

It's no doubt damned annoying after all that effort. It may even be a complete shock, if you were very confident after the interview, but it's always been a numbers game. You've lost the skirmish but the war is still on. There are other prizes to be had, focus on those.

Sometimes things just do fall against you. If Einstein, Gandhi and Napoleon all turned up for interview, reincarnated in the other candidates, your odds were never that good.

You might have been perfect on the day but someone else's perfect was just a bit better. I once lost a job I was ideal for because someone else rocked up who could speak Mandarin. It wasn't a mandatory requirement, in fact they had zero expectation of finding such a person. I suspect I was the more capable candidate against most of the person specification, but the unexpected bonus swung it for them. It was just my bad luck.

On the other side of that particular coin, it does go to show that if you can calculate out a winning factor for yourself, you may be able to swing the decision in your favour, even if you're by no means the top choice.

So don't beat yourself up. You did the best you could. Next time you'll be in a better position. After all, how many Einsteins can there be? Just make sure that you learn from this last interview and plan to do better next time.

So, how can you do that?

Firstly, look at your post-interview notes. Now you can perhaps see why it was important to capture them quickly? Read them honestly in this new light and take note of where you thought, at the time, that you didn't do so well. Be brutally frank. What would you change for next time?

Secondly, try and get some real feedback, if you can. It's invaluable. Drop an email to the interviewer, the HR department or the recruitment agent (in that order of preference) and make them aware of how important feedback is for your self-development. If you don't get an answer, try ringing them up.

There may genuinely be little or no real feedback to be had.

> "You were great, it's just that someone else pipped you at the post."

> "Can you think what might have swung it one way or the other?" is a good follow up question, if you get the chance.

If you truly were pipped at the post, the interviewer may well feel obligated to give you some help as a consequence. If so, treat it seriously, learn from it.

Many people, if not most, will not ask for feedback, so you'll be separating yourself from the competition and building an edge for next time.

Sometimes organisations won't give feedback anyway for all sorts of spurious reasons. If that's the case, don't worry about it. Use your own notes and your gut instinct and get yourself ready for next time.

Key point summary 5 - Interviews

Key Learning Points

- Be clear about your new objective. It's not necessarily to win that job; it definitely is to win a seat at the next stage of the selection process.
- De-stress by putting things into context. With an invitation, you are already a contender. If everyone else screws up and you don't, the job is yours.
- Everything you do, especially online, is now under potential scrutiny. Think twice before posting comments; job offers can be withdrawn.
- The more you understand about the remaining selection processes and how decisions will be made, the better prepared you can be.
- The four primary assessment criteria will be: your suitability for the role; any relevant experience you've gained; your capacity to adopt responsibility and your potential future value to the organisation.
- Preparation is the key. It can help you win that job before you even set foot in the interview room. It's only with a good understanding of the organisation that you can really identify the correct buttons to push.
- You cannot predict every question or eventuality, but you can learn and practise techniques to successfully 'handle' them.
- Interviewers look to uncover potential by the use of competency-based questions (which look backwards at situations you've experienced and how you dealt with them) and scenario-type questions (which look forwards at how you'd apply previous experience to a new situation).
- Closed questions are used to force specific information from you, open questions offer a blank canvas on which you're invited to paint.
- Personal communication skills are increasingly important. Showing enthusiasm, using positive body language and building a rapport with the interviewer makes a substantial difference to your prospects of selection, even on the telephone.
- Speaking clearly, precisely and appropriately, regardless of your accent, will ensure that your messages hit home and score for you.
- It's better to be a slow starter and then give a concise answer, than it is to start quickly, but ramble through an answer. Think briefly, before you start to speak, because it aids your perceived professionalism.
- People tend to believe what you tell them unless you've lost their trust. Make clear points, with conviction, and you'll hit home.
- If you think that you didn't answer a particular question well, don't dwell on it, as no one is perfect. Concentrate on your wins, not your losses.
- Interviewers are never impressed by geeky, opaque or elitist answers as they're showing your ego more than your talents.
- Never tell people that you're nervous. Interviewers expect you to be whilst other people may never notice, if you don't bring it up.
- In group interviews, The Apprentice is a very bad model around which to build your behavioural patterns for the day. Aim to be a team player, support members of your group and avoid self-serving behaviour.

- If you're required to deliver a prepared presentation, always arrive equipped with a back-up method of delivering it.
- You should aim to leave with both you and the interviewer feeling that the meeting was very worthwhile.

Signposts

- Doubt is useless to you, but fear can be directed and used to improve your focus and motivation.
- You'll need to re-visit your application research and deepen it, before your interview. Use it to develop and rehearse great answers to interview questions and come up with winning questions of your own.
- Larger organisations tend to use assessment days, whereas smaller organisations with limited resources tend to use individual interviews as the primary selection method.
- Telephone and video interviews are now more common as early-stage selection processes, designed to assess whether candidates have the required skillsets.
- Powerful search engines and social media sites mean that key parts of your whole life, history and track record may be almost permanently available to employers who want access to it.
- None of us should be judged by our appearance but the simple fact is that we are. If you look smart, you probably are smart, is how it works.
- In the interview, use eye contact, smile, 'like' the person and show positive body language. Carefully build a relationship; plan to be their best friend.
- During interviews, stay away from politics, religion and controversial subjects, unless the interviewer raises them. Give balanced answers.
- At interview you'll need to show not just that you meet the person specification but that you can potentially add extra value.
- Merely answering a question is insufficient. Learn to identify what a question is looking for and then deliver targeted responses.
- Keep your answers focused on the positive and don't criticise others.
- Answer the question asked, not the question you wish had been asked.
- To make the most impact with an answer, set the context first (where you worked, doing what, in what circumstances).
- As you answer questions, always look for opportunities to show your added value. Even one answer in ten may be sufficient to help.
- Interviewers are risk-averse and will tend to select candidates that conform to their expectations and be wary of unusual candidates.
- Never take criticism personally; use it to improve.
- Strongly disagreeing with the interviewer can be counterproductive but don't be afraid to (politely) stick to your guns, if you can justify doing so.
- In role-play exercises, it's not your acting ability that you'll be marked on, it's the quality of your thinking under pressure and decision-making.
- Inbox-type exercises may test your communication skills as much as they test your ability to analyse and make decisions.

- If you have an offer, you're most definitely first choice and you're briefly in control but stay away from strategies involving threats and blackmail.

Actions

- In the remaining selection processes, at every stage, prepare thoroughly, to show how well you do in fact match the role on offer.
- Identify the three to five 'must haves' required for the role and work out clearly which aspects of your background support each of them.
- Prepare for a possible early-stage telephone or video interview.
- Before the main interviews, if you can find out the names of the interviewers, research them for points of contact with your life. Use any information you uncover to build a rapport.
- Construct a list of 'standard' questions you're likely to face and rehearse your responses until you can respond confidently.
- Use the Spotlight Process to fully internalise your answers, so that you can deliver them naturally, keep a clear head and reduce your nerves.
- Identify the core competences required for the role and develop a range of relevant competency-based and scenario-type questions. Practice answering them using the STAR technique.
- Develop and practise a two to four minute speech, along the lines of a response to the 'tell us about yourself' question, for use if ever you're required to deliver an impromptu personal introduction to a group.
- In rehearsals, regularly record your voice and video your delivery. Learn to like your voice and adapt your performances to improve them.
- To build confidence, read aloud from a book every single day. Develop your vocal range to build power and show emotion.
- Undertake mock interviews, using a friend.
- On the morning of the interview, look in the mirror and smile. Like what you see and remind yourself to enjoy the day. You've created an opportunity for yourself and now is the time to nail it down.
- Allow plenty of time but take relevant contact numbers with you, in case your journey is severely delayed.
- Before you go in, play the interview through in your mind. See yourself doing well. Visualise the interviewer smiling and nodding as you make your key points. Imagine yourself leaving the room, on a high.
- If interviewers can make first-impression judgements, use that to your advantage, rather than theirs, and try to swing things strongly in your favour in those vital first few seconds.
- At all interviews, use eye contact, smile and 'like' the interviewer as mechanisms to build rapport and generate positive feelings toward you.
- Don't dwell on your nerves, focus on the job you're there to do and be confident that your rehearsed answers will help get you into the flow.
- At interviews, give your answer and stop. Hand the floor back to the interviewer, don't ramble on and don't feel obliged to fill silences.

- To avoid using 'um' and 'er', practise thinking before you speak. Structure your answers in your head and then deliver them.
- At assessment centre interviews, it's vitally important that you find out the process and calculate the odds of selection, so that you can decide how to manage your chances and position yourself correctly.
- If you're required to give a formal presentation, use your slide structure and content to act as prompts, for a more natural delivery.
- If you're required to deliver an impromptu speech on a formal topic, use the PREP model (Position, Reason, Examples, Position) to add structure, form ideas and guide your course.
- Always make it clear that you enjoyed the interview, you like the job and you're keen to move forward, even if you're not.
- After every interview, make detailed notes: what went well; what went badly; how would you do things differently, next time?
- The next day, if possible, drop through a note to thank the interviewer for their time and your opportunity. Make it clear that you enjoyed the meeting and that you're very much still interested. Don't creep.
- Don't wait for the result, look for your next opportunity and work on it.
- Carefully read the terms of any offer to make sure they match your expectations and the brief. Decide whether to accept it or negotiate.
- If you turn down an offer, do so professionally – you never know what else you might be offered or what may turn up next year.
- If you didn't win through, try and get feedback on your performance.

Chapter 6 – Negotiations: winning the last battle

"A minute's success pays back the failure of years." Robert Browning.

Bang. Thwack.

No, not the sound of the gun going off and your brains painting the wall. For a change, it's the sound of your letterbox and a job offer hitting the hall floor.

Congratulations. I'm proud of you. I knew you could do it. Maybe you had an email or a phone call before that, giving you the good news? Wonderful. By now, you've no doubt washed the blood away, scraped off the camouflage paint and chugged down a celebratory drink or three. But stand to attention soldier, your war isn't over yet. Look over your shoulder. Your wounded peers are rising, bandaging their wounds and shuffling back into battle position.

The tiger's feasted on the remains of some but hasn't finished the meal. It still has one eye on you and there's a glint in it. Ever so slowly, ever so gently, reach down and pick up your knife again. Think Ripley, preparing for stasis in the Nostromo's escape shuttle when she realises, with absolute terror, that she is not alone. There's one final do or die battle and you're starring in it.

How is all this possible? You've got an offer. The horror of battle is over, isn't it? Isn't it?

Sadly for you, not yet.

Organisations often hedge their bets for as long as possible. They don't know whether you'll accept their offer, so undoubtedly some combatants don't yet know that they're dead people walking. Those people are still out to get you and they may get their chance, if you lose your grip.

When you turn up on your first morning you can give yourself the nod to relax. Only then can you consider yourself victorious against the hordes. Only then will you have been the only one to outrun the tiger.

Until then …

You've got great news and a real offer, but you need to manage your response carefully. It's only once you have that offer letter in your shaking hands that the power momentarily shifts in your favour. Suddenly, you're in charge.

So what's the problem? Turned up, kicked ass, got the job. And?

If you'll be joining a large graduate intake with a major organisation there may not be much else to think, or worry about. You can probably just sign your acceptance, celebrate and then crack on with your career. Well done indeed.

Do, at the very least, read carefully through the terms of your offer letter and make sure you're happy with everything in there. Compare your letter to what was offered in the original advert or brief.

Are they the same, or at least so similar as to make no difference?

Is there anything else to get through? Are they still conducting the reference checks? Might there be a medical? These things are probably just formalities but be aware that you don't yet have the all clear.

Do let your referees know that they'll be contacted. Ease the way by reminding them what you were applying for. Perhaps gently load a few bullets for them, just to make sure they're on message.

If you have a date for a medical or a physical, plan things so that you don't spend the prior three days getting utterly wasted and so that there isn't a wild excess of strange substances trotting around what's left of your veins.

Apart from that, you're in then. Time to celebrate.

If, however, your organisation is smaller, or you're the only joiner after the recruitment exercise, check the fine print a little more closely.

It's not uncommon for an organisation to advertise a salary range of, say, '£20,000 to £25,000, depending upon experience' and you find that you're enthusiastically offered only the 20 k as a starting salary.

If you're a very recent graduate and the position was also open to people with perhaps five plus years experience, then fair enough, one supposes. You have less experience, more to learn, they're taking a bit of a gamble and they'll have to put some training effort in. Afterwards, if they play the game, they'll reward you with pay rises as you make suitable progress. It tends to work out well for both parties. You have a foot on the ladder and an opportunity for career growth you might not otherwise have been able to get.

But if they were only trawling this year's graduates, how would it be possible for someone to have that much more experience to justify the higher amount? The answer is, it wouldn't. It's a cheap trick to entice applicants with the higher amount, but stuff them with the lower amount, when they get through.

I know times are tough but how the hell such fuckwits expect to motivate anyone inside their organisation, I will never understand. Such an approach hardly sets you up to be loyal and committed for the long-haul, does it?

The accompanying offer letter will sometimes offer an almost Orwellian insight into the darker workings of their organisation.

> "Welcome to the team!" Note the frenzied exclamation mark which suggests they're desperate to get you on board before you realise you're being shafted.

> "You're one of the family now." Uh-huh. So getting butt-fucked on the salary qualifies as incest, right?

> "We recognise the true worth of our employees." Yes, but not the value?

And so on. But what can you do about it? If the organisation are still holding other suitable candidates in limbo behind the scenes, then your room for manoeuvre is going to be limited. An outright, "Give me more money or else," just won't cut any ice but rolling over completely can leave you feeling very resentful when you turn up to work.

Having said that, always use your own feelings as a guide. If, despite seeing a bottom of the range offer, you're still deliriously happy, then just go for it. Don't let other people wind you up. Make your own decisions. But if you're just a tad unhappy about anything, read on …

The one advantage that you definitely do have is that you are clearly the number one preferred choice and that certainly counts for something.

Faced with a difference between your expectations and the reality of the offer letter, you have an opportunity to discuss the situation. Just be aware that you'll be walking a tightrope and a great deal now depends on how you approach things. Going in with all guns blazing risks seeing you taken out of the picture, and being quietly disposed of, as your offer gets withdrawn.

However, a polite but logical and well-directed query should elicit a respectful response and a clear indication of what may be possible and what isn't.

> "I understood that the offered salary range was between x and y but my offer is at the bottom of that range. I feel that my skills and experience justify an offer more in the middle of the range because …"

However you put it, stay polite and stay positive.

Note the 'because'. However you go back, you need to put forward at least some justification for the change. In return, you're forcing the organisation to either fully justify their position, or reconsider what they're prepared to offer you. At all costs, avoid direct confrontation. Yes, you're in charge for a change but there are limits.

You can undoubtedly push those limits a little further if you already have an alternative offer on the table. Whether it's better or whether it isn't, it is at least insurance that you can use, but should you tell the employer that you're holding that alternative offer?

Firstly, get very clear in your own mind what you're prepared for, if push comes to shove. Is the low offer still preferable? Even if that's a 'yes', you still have some confidence boosting ammunition to use. Or would either job be okay? If so, then you're definitely in a stronger position to negotiate over the latest one but how wise would being open about your position be?

If you're seen to be just on a blackmail mission, out for what you can get, it's not ultimately going to go well for you, even if you do manage to screw more money out of them. Ideally you need to secure a better offer because they think you're worth it, not because they have no choice. In the former situation, you're increasing your perceived value on the way in and that's better for you in the long haul.

Start by ignoring the other offer up your sleeve. Always go back with one or two good reasons why you're asking for a higher amount. Use the originally advertised range as evidence that it's rational for them to consider it.

If that gets some progress for you, great. If not, you should at least get a justification why not and that might help you understand their position and decide whether it's justified.

Sometimes you'll be asked, "Do you have any other prospects on the go at the moment?" I'll leave you to speculate over quite why that should affect things. If they ask, you can easily answer with a polite, "Yes I do," and see what happens in response. You're not blackmailing, you're stating a fact.

You may get asked what that offer actually is, who it's from or when you have to make a decision by. Bit cheeky, to say the least. Generally, the best approach is to be a little coy about it, if they push past the 'yes I do'.

> "I've got a few days to consider my choices. It's a firm offer in a great place to work, with good long term prospects, although my preference is the position you've offered me."

You're showing that your other choice fills you with enthusiasm, whilst you're making it very clear that outright blackmail isn't on your agenda (even if it really is). It's not what you do, it's how you do it that often gets the best result.

My recommendation is to always run with the truth, or something very close to it if you possibly can, without being too naïve. That way, your confidence will be greater and it will shine through.

If the words above aren't exactly right, find some that convey a good upbeat message about the other offer you're holding, staying well away from threats and blackmail.

If they don't ask if you have other offers, wait and see what they come back to you with, before letting them know that you have a real alternative in place.

That's why you need to be clear in your own mind what you'd be happy to go with, if it comes down to it.

> "Look buster, times are tough. You should be grateful for even this so if you don't want it, there are plenty more fish in the sea so screw you."

If they come back with that sort of arrogant answer, then you know where you stand and can make a decision accordingly.

Once you've made it, stick to it, unless there's a really strong reason to revisit the case again. A couple of quid here and there isn't worth thinking about by that stage. If they were only ever going to respond with more money if they absolutely had to, what does that tell you about their attitude and how much do you really want to work there, knowing that your working life will always be based on an uneasy stand-off?

As I've mentioned before, I would never advocate using a fictitious alternative as leverage as there's just too much scope for a discussion to go badly wrong, unless you really do have that backstop in place.

At the end of the day, if you are very, very unhappy and confident you'll pull something else in soon anyway, don't be afraid to use that as your backstop, if you get a real slap in the face resulting from your polite but firm query.

"Screw you and screw your shitty offer, you cheap-skate bastards."

That's a bit harsh because you never know what else might be available, now or in the future, with that same organisation.

> "To be honest, I'm disappointed. I have several other situations on the go so I'm going to focus on those. Thanks very much for your consideration anyway and

> I'm sorry we couldn't find a compromise. I liked your organisation so I hope things go well with another candidate."

Even if you think they're the worst creeping slime on the planet, something like that has a chance of drawing more out of the bag without burning anyone's bridges. Such a response can be deeply worrying for an employer. They selected you so they know damn well someone else is quite likely to do so. Your argument is therefore a perfectly valid one to run with.

It's the same old story. If you don't care if you lose, you usually win. But you have not to care. Seriously. If you are honestly prepared to play Russian roulette, people will run away screaming and give you anything so they don't have to take part.

The worst position to negotiate from is to make all of those moves but hint that you do care really. The employer then hears, "Please, oh please, oh please, don't withdraw the offer because I will take it really if I have to."

If you actually do care, never use a 'don't care' argument because they'll pull the trigger in your face.

I've written mainly about salary so far. There may be other areas of the package that are at least as important to you, if not more so.

The actual job offered may be different to the one you applied for. Your entry to the pension scheme (which you valued highly) might have been put back a year. Bonuses, employee assistance packages, childcare assistance, training packages, career development and relocation expenses can all have a dramatic difference on your desire, or even ability, to accept a post. Whatever it is, use the same strategy to pick your way through.

Keep remembering that they've invested a great deal in selecting you. Have confidence in that. Just don't push it too far, too hard. Although it's radical, offers can be withdrawn. I've personally benefitted from just such a situation.

Throughout, watch what you post on Twitter, Facebook, LinkedIn, etc. especially whilst you're running a negotiation. If you give the game away, even accidentally, you're finished if anyone's looking.

Staying with an honest, respectful, practical and factual discussion should get your offer thoroughly sorted and your career moving in the right direction.

So, after all that, you're a new person now. Leaner. Sharper. Battle-trained. Look yourself in the eye and believe that the best is yet to come. Are you ready for the next stage of your life?

Square your shoulders, pick up your rifle and advance.

You've got work to do …

Key point summary 6 - Negotiations

Key Learning Points

- You may be able to negotiate some of the terms of the offer, depending upon what was in the original advert or brief.
- Don't push it too hard. Even though you have an offer, some applicants may be kept in the game in case things go wrong with you.
- Threats and blackmail on your part are almost always losing strategies, as is demanding what you want. Avoid confrontation.
- How and why the organisation has varied their offer can tell you a lot about their management style, culture and likely working environment.
- The truth about your feelings, sincerely presented, can often be your most valuable weapon. Conversely, lies can be extremely dangerous.

Signposts

- The fact that you have an offer means that you are most definitely the number one choice and you become briefly in control of the situation.
- Even with an offer, you may not be at the end of the selection process. The reference check is probably still to come but so may be a medical.
- Looking at the offer, use your own feelings as the best guide. If you're happy with it, even if it varies from expectations, go with it.
- If your offer is pitched at the bottom end of the originally suggested range, you'll need to understand whether that can be justified or not.

Actions

- Carefully read through the terms of your offer to make sure they match your expectations and the original brief.
- Do let your referees know they may be contacted. Remind them what job you're after, load a few simple bullets for them.
- If you have a date for a medical or a physical, organise your life so that you don't risk failing it.
- If you choose to negotiate something, offer a justification and make sure not to burn your bridges in the process.
- If you've got more than one offer on the table, choose which one you want and if you have to negotiate, use logical arguments, not threats.
- Consciously refrain from online posting about the status of your application and negotiation, offers can be withdrawn.

Chapter 7 – Work: your new mission …

"The truth is, everybody I've ever met who's successful is a workaholic." ICE-T

"Haven't you done banging on yet," I hear you ask?

"What more can you possibly have to say? I did everything you asked of me. Everything. I got the result, now clear off and leave me alone you sick, torturing bastard."

I will. Soon. It's now time for you to begin stalking your own piece of jungle.

Watch, wait and get ready. The day is already coming when the skills you've just learnt will be needed again. You'll be chasing promotion, or a better job elsewhere, so what I'm about to tell you can help save your life next time too.

I know this is your zero hour, so I'll keep it brief.

First things first. You've only really won that job if you manage to keep it.

Turning up on your first morning with a blinding hangover, wearing clothes you've slept in and demonstrating a flatulence prowess that would earn respect from an adult hippo, is unlikely to get you off on the right foot.

Vomiting in a waste bin part way through your induction is vastly entertaining for your peers but a definite no-no for your prospects of continued employment.

Not turning up on day two, saying you didn't like it, is a bit terminal, as is ranting and raving at your boss for more money after only a week in the post, or sleeping with half of the entire department during your first month.

You may snigger. Sadly, I've seen it all.

Okay, I'm sure you've got more sense than that, so let's jump forward in time.

One day, maybe soon, you're going to be looking for the next step up the career ladder. You'll be applying for promotion or a new job elsewhere.

That means that you have to go through all of this again. (Stop groaning, soldier.) If that's the case, there are things you can do now, that will greatly help your chances of success. These things are almost effortless – honestly.

When it's time to re-do your CV or an application form, most of what you've done up to today's date will be redundant. No one will care anymore, or certainly not very much. They'll only care about how well you've performed in your current role.

Wouldn't it be great if, at that time, you could just pick up a thin A4 pad, flick back through and see at a glance what you've achieved in your present role?

Well, unsurprisingly, you can.

- From today, keep a diary each week. Don't make it a major mish, just a page will do. Make notes under three headings: what did you do this week; what did you achieve; what do you plan to do next week?

That's it, seriously, but it won't half make your life easier later.

- Once a quarter, summarise your successes on a separate page. Keep a note of what they're worth to your organisation.
- Note what you've learned for your working life and career in a 'life, the universe and everything' sense.
- Keep a separate note of new skills you need to develop and existing ones you should extend. Make sure to attack them in the next quarter.

Generally, even on a graduate development scheme, you need to self-manage from now on. By all means get what you can from the scheme, your training, your supervisors and your HR department but what will help you to stand head and shoulders above your peers?

The answer is **perceived capability** backed up by **actual achievement.**

To those ends:

- keep on top of changes and developments in your own field;
- stay abreast of the latest ICT tools that relate to what you do;
- build up your broader experience and plug any holes in your CV;
- develop additional management and leadership skills on the side;
- increase your social capital by maintaining your existing contacts and adding to your networks carefully;
- take every opportunity to improve your public speaking skills.

All of this is clearly a much bigger subject than I can cover here. The above are just a few basic pointers to get you started and to make your life easier next time. Hopefully, if you follow them, they'll accelerate your career by keeping you focused on where you add most value and how much you add.

Here's a few, very final, thoughts for you.

- Don't waste time, they're after you.
- It's the shit that makes you stronger.
- Tomorrow really is another day.

I've enjoyed helping you to find your way through the jungle. Good bye, good luck and thank you for your company.

Keep your knife sharp.

Appendix A – Ammunition locker

"It used to be that 'information is power'. Now it's lying around everywhere so in fact power comes from knowing how to apply that information." Martin Sorrell

It is true that there are 'stock' interview questions that crop up time and time again, so you're well advised to practise those. Perfect preparation really does prevent piss poor performance so, to get you started, you'll find a few helpful questions under these headings.

- 'Standard' questions to prepare for.
- Competency-based questions – (backward looking).
- Scenario-type questions – (forward looking).
- Creativity / lateral-thinking questions.
- Role-play questions.
- Some questions to ask.
- Some questions not to ask.

Do also trawl the web for more questions to play with, but never rely on those alone, aim to generate your own questions, based on your research.

After you've studied the advert, the job specification, the person specification and your application, make sure that you spend time imagining a range of more personalised questions that the interviewer might lob your way.

You've personalised your application to make it unique so it's therefore inevitable that the interviewer will tailor their questions to it.

At the interview, if you don't want that horrendous feeling in the pit of your stomach, caused by the realisation that a carefully lobbed hand grenade has just gone off in your trolleys, put your armoured underwear on and spend some time anticipating what will be coming your way.

Let's get you started.

Basic 'standard' questions to prepare for.

1) Can you tell me a little about yourself?
2) What do you know about our organisation?
3) Why are you applying for this position?
4) What skills will you bring to this role?
5) What experience do you have that will be particularly useful?
6) What challenges do you think you will face in this job?
7) What do you see yourself doing in five years time?
8) What short term goals do you have?
9) What are your major strengths?
10) What are your weaknesses?
11) What achievement are you most proud of?
12) What motivates you to do the best job?
13) What would a friend say about you if they were here?

14) How would a former boss describe you?
15) How did you get on with your co-workers in your last job?
16) Who did you least like working with, or for, and why?
17) Give me three reasons why we should choose you for this role.
18) What do you feel about stress at work?
19) What do you do to cope with the pressure of work?
20) Why are you leaving your existing job?
21) What are you looking for from this job?
22) What salary are you looking for?
23) Would you rather work for money or job satisfaction?
24) What do you do to keep your knowledge and skills up to date?
25) If we offer you this post, would you have any reservations in taking it?

If you can prepare well against that lot, you're a long way towards winning that job.

There are a few tricky questions to pay attention to. For example, if you start offering weaknesses, do they count against you? Aren't you just telling them why you're unsuitable? The other side of the coin is that, if you don't confess to any weakness, are you arrogant in trying to make out that you're perfect?

There's risk both ways. On this and other tricky questions, always avoid the negative as a minimum, then try and focus on the positive.

For example, you could pick a weakness that can be turned to a positive.

> "I know I can get frustrated when things move too slowly. I can get impatient with people but I'm aware of it and I'm learning to manage this better because I know that offering criticism is usually counter-productive."

That answer is a bit on the holier-than-thou side of things but that sort of approach at least demonstrates that you're self-aware, proactive and into self-development.

Asking you about who you least liked working for is another minefield question. If you go off into one about the completely sadistic, baby-eating monster that used to be your manager, are you saying something about them or unconsciously telling the interviewer more about yourself than you should?

Whichever it is, there's a risk of presenting yourself in a negative light so play down the negative, play up the positive.

> "Yes, my manager in my last place was really demanding, perhaps overly so at times. That caused a lot of stress but as I look back on that experience, I feel I learned a lot."

You need to be ready to explain why you thought they were too demanding and outline some of what you learned but hopefully you get the idea about staying with the positive side of things?

Competency-based questions.

It's next to impossible to predict the competency-based questions that are likely to come up because they'll be selected according to the primary competencies judged to be required for the job and tailored accordingly.

Thus, you need to be able to recognise one when it arrives and then construct a comprehensive answer for it, using something like the STAR technique. (STAR – Situation. Task. Action. Result.)

Concentrate on learning how to use the technique. To do that effectively, you need practice, practice and practice so here are a few to be going on with.

1) Tell me about a time when you were personally responsible for implementing something and what the result was.
2) Describe a situation where you had to influence someone or a group.
3) Tell me about an instance where you had to make a tough decision.
4) Tell me about a situation when you had to show initiative.
5) Give me an example of when you had to step up and take the lead.
6) Tell me about a time when you achieved a great result.
7) Describe a situation you experienced where it was vital that you communicated information clearly and concisely.
8) Tell me about a time when you had to work as part of a team.
9) Talk through a situation where you had to develop a solution to a complex problem.
10) Tell me about a time when you had to show initiative in dealing with an unexpected situation.
11) Describe a situation in which you had to force yourself to remain calm.
12) Give an example of a time when you suddenly felt the weight of responsibility on your shoulders.
13) Tell me about a time when you had to deliver bad news. What was the situation and what actions did you take?
14) Describe for me a situation where you were required to gather a large amount of data, to analyse it objectively and to make a decision or a recommendation based on the results.
15) Tell me about a time when you made a suggestion and it was subsequently implemented.
16) Describe a difficult work situation that you experienced.

Whilst those exact questions are unlikely to arise, elements of your answers to them may well come in useful for the ones that do crop up at the actual interview.

In the light of a specific role that you are trying for:

- decide the main competencies required for the role;
- construct half a dozen competency-based questions that you might want to ask the candidate if you were doing the interviewing and then
- try and answer them.

Scenario-type questions

The format of these is roughly the same as competency-based questions, except that they get you to look forwards, not backwards. They cause you to draw on previous experience but project yourself into a fictitious, but plausibly realistic, situation that you might face in your new role.

As a consequence, they can additionally expose details about your character, values and belief systems. It's not uncommon for normally-hidden prejudices to accidently lurch into the light of day, so pay close attention to your answers.

Again, use the STAR technique to get your head quickly around constructing comprehensive answers.

Remember that 'comprehensive' does not entitle you to deliver an endless, rambling, unfocused diatribe, in the vain hope that you'll eventually answer the question, in the same way as shot from a blunderbuss might hit a target.

Keep your answer simple, on topic and as short as you can make it, whilst still covering the STAR ground.

Here are some questions to practise with.

1) You see a potential problem for your department that you're very concerned about. You put it to your boss but he doesn't see it and tells you to stop wasting time and carry on with your other work. How do you handle that situation?

2) There are four of you working together on a critical project and your boss is suddenly rushed to hospital with acute appendicitis. She has a major project meeting in one hour that can't be missed or the project will be delayed. Your peers are reluctant to get involved because it will be a heavy-duty meeting. What do you do in that situation?

3) You and a colleague are working together on a project but your colleague is quite often lazy and sloppy. They are more experienced than you but they take credit for some of your work and lay blame for problems off onto you. You catch some of their errors that could have had serious safety consequences later. What do you do?

4) You've been promoted to supervisor of a small department with three employees reporting to you, previously your peers. You're told that you have to make one of them redundant. How do you handle that?

5) You've been helping your boss by covering up his drinking problem but it has suddenly got much worse. How do you handle that situation?

6) A week ago you arranged to give a presentation to a group of people from some other departments about your findings from an important project you've been assigned. On that occasion no one turned up and the meeting was re-scheduled for today. Your boss will also be attending. What will you do in advance of the meeting?

7) You've been working hard on a project, a deadline is coming up but you doubt that you'll finish in time. What do you do?

8) You're a team leader and are running a meeting in which you invite votes for and against an issue. You usually prefer to lead by building a consensus but the vote is tied. What do you do?

9) It seems clear to you that your boss actually dislikes you. What are you going to do?

10) For the third time, one of your co-workers is chosen for promotion over you. What do you do about that?

A common theme to a lot of these questions is that of a need to proactively take responsibility in some way. Your answers need to show that you're someone with balls, as it's hard to imagine a situation where an employer might prefer a wallflower over an oak tree.

Having said that, if you have fascist tendencies, a world domination complex and a completely unfettered competitive streak, allowing all of these traits to strongly colour your answers may not present you as a balanced team player, in it for the long haul.

Focus on delivering answers which support the values of the organisation (or alleged values) and which support the objectives of the role you're applying for. Again, I would suggest evaluating the selection criteria for the role, identifying the competencies that the employer might require and then constructing your own scenario-type questions against which to test yourself.

Creativity and lateral-thinking questions.

There's even less chance of guessing what might be thrown at you under this category, unless fate deals you a lucky card and you're asked a question you've covered before. Yet again, practising the use of a process to deal with them is the solution. Learn to think on your feet and in non-obvious directions.

In my view, some of these questions are completely insane and can have you chewing the carpet in a surprisingly short period of time. However, practising them, no matter how much you hate them, will make your life so much easier when you have to address such questions for real.

They are split into three main types.

- Brain-teasing riddles.
- Logic puzzles.
- Left-field questions.

Brain-teasing riddles may have only one solution or there may be more than one. Typically, the idea is to account for the unusual set of facts you're given or solve the weird story you're told. Whether you're able to come up with an answer and what sort of answer you offer is thought to indicate something about your creative and lateral-thinking abilities.

The following are some of the classics that have been knocking around for some considerable time and I'm therefore unable to attribute them.

Q1. A man who lives in a tenth-floor flat takes the lift down to the ground floor every morning and then goes to work. When he comes back in the evening on a rainy day, or if there are other people in the lift, he goes to his floor directly. Otherwise, he goes to the seventh floor and walks up three flights of stairs to his flat. Can you explain why?

(And no, it isn't because he keeps his stash hidden away somewhere on the seventh floor.)

Q2. A man approaches the middle of a field and decides he's going to die. He is found lying dead in the centre and next to him there is an unopened package. There are no animals in the field, there are no other people there or nearby and there are no weapons lying about. How did he die?

Q3. A woman had two sons who were born on the same day of the same year at the same hour but they're not twins. How do you explain this?

Q4. A large car-transporter lorry weighs exactly ten tons and starts to cross a four mile long bridge that can only support an absolute maximum of ten tons in weight. Three point one miles across, a blackbird weighing one hundred and fifty three grams lands on the roof of the lorry but the bridge doesn't collapse. Why not?

Q5. You are standing outside a windowless room with a closed door. On the outside wall of the room there are three light switches that each control a respective light bulb inside the room. You can enter and leave only once. How do you work out with total accuracy which switch controls which light bulb?

Q6. Why can't a gay man living in York be buried west of the river Severn?

Q7. A boat ladder hanging over the stern has six rungs, each one foot apart. The bottom rung is one foot above the water. If the tide rises at twelve inches every fifteen minutes how many rungs will be under water in one hour and fifteen minutes?

Q8. A man pushes his car, stops at a hotel and realises he is bankrupt. What's going on?

Q9. A man built himself a square house with triangular windows on every side. Never the less, each window managed to have at least some view to the South. He spotted a bear in the distance. What colour was the bear?

Q10. An ugly troll has a job as a gravedigger and is standing next to a 3m x 2m x 2m hole, looking around for his sandwiches. Where are his sandwiches and, to the nearest cubic centimetre, how much soil does the hole contain?

And so on. You may have seen some of these before and hopefully now you get the style. Try a web search under 'brain teasers' and practise as many more as you can stand, before the will to live leaves you.

If it so happens at the interview that you're asked to answer one of the same questions you've already practised, my suggestion is to conceal that fact. Appear to struggle with your thinking for a short period and then deliver your answer, perhaps a little haltingly. If you get rumbled, explain that you thought you'd heard it before but couldn't really remember the details, so had to work it all out again.

Isn't that a bit sneaky? Yep. But it's a fight so score where you can and take the gift. There won't be many such freebies during the course of your interviews and shame on the interviewer for re-using a tired example.

I suppose you'd like the answers to the above questions?

The man in question one is a dwarf with an umbrella. The unfortunate man in question two was a parachutist with a technical problem. The sons in question three were in fact two of triplets. In question four, the lorry had used up more weight of fuel than the weight of the blackbird. To solve question five, put one switch on for a while, then turn it off and turn on one of the other two, then enter the room. You can see the lit bulb and you can feel for a warm bulb, thereby identifying two of the three switches definitively. The third switch is for the cold light bulb. The man in question six is still alive and therefore can't be buried. In question seven, the boat floats so no rungs will be under water. The man in question eight is playing monopoly. The bear in question nine is white. The hole in question ten has no soil in it, although there is a packet of sandwiches in the bottom.

Heavy sigh.

Wondering why manhole covers are round suddenly seems so much more attractive a question, doesn't it? You could almost be grateful to be asked which animal you'd like to be and why.

Role-play questions

Again, it's impossible to predict the topic of a role-play exercise, in advance of an assessment day, although you can try an educated guess.

- If you're chasing a management trainee position, you might have to meet with a demotivated staff member, try to find out what their problems are and then agree actions which will get them back on track.
- If you're applying for a job in sales or customer service, it's possible that you'll have to meet someone who is a disgruntled customer.
- If you'll be working a lot over the telephone, then you might have to run an exercise over the phone or via Skype.

The trick with all of them is to think your way into the role, stay within the bounds of real-world rationality and make the choices you would tend to make in real life, not false choices which have no foothold in a real situation.

Whatever you're tasked with, it may be virtually impossible to succeed so you'll be judged on how professionally you handle yourself, how rationally you dig yourself out of a hole and how much you protect the interests of your department or organisation.

To give you a flavour, you can run the following role-play exercise with the help of a friend. It steps you forward a couple of years in your career, so the situation may be ahead of your current experience but, although stretching for you, you should still be able to relate to the situation.

The exercise requires no specific knowledge from either of you and tests your creative thinking, interpersonal skills and management potential, in a situation not untypical of that encountered in a supervisory or management position.

Give your helper their brief and a few minutes to digest it thoroughly and prepare, but do not allow them to read your brief before you start.

With your own brief, map out an outline plan of how you're going to handle the meeting and what options and fall-back positions you might have available to you.

Agree a clear signal that you'll make, when you want to close the exercise down.

Stay in character throughout and, as with interview practice, if you get stuck or get a brief attack of the giggles, push on through, just as you would have to in a real situation.

Your helper's brief is as follows –

During this role-play exercise, respond as you would be likely to in a real-life situation. Stay in character and in the role until the end. Do not introduce convenient extra information that is not part of the exercise. For example, "Anyway, I've just won the lottery, so I don't care," is not an option.

So, you're a degree-qualified graphic designer, working for a medium-sized marketing and advertising agency. Your skills are top notch and your ambition is to work on the creative side of the business, designing ad campaigns.

In the meantime, you're employed as an intern and paid minimum wage for 30 hours per week. You're expected to attend every week day, thereby incurring transport costs. It is expected that you will work extra hours (unpaid) and you regularly find yourself still at work at seven o' clock in the evening.

You're barely able to keep a roof over your head and then only through the kindness of a friend, who's let you sleep in a box room for 6 months for only a small amount of money.

Rather than learning how the creative side of the business works, you're actually being used to chase and buy cheap advertising space for the agency's clients. Less than one fifth of your time is spent on design or project work, and you've received zero structured training to date.

In order to eat and clothe yourself, as well as exist, you've been doing small bits of design work on your own account for friends, contacts and small businesses, near to where you live. Whilst this work has been picking up quite well, you're doing it when you get home at night, overnight and during weekends and have become pretty run-down. Without this private work, or a replacement evening job in a bar or McDonald's, you'd be unable to exist.

You think you might like to work for yourself at some distant point in the future but only when you're experienced, as you find chasing the work alien and you worry whether you could find enough to keep yourself busy. You suspect that you probably could, if your agency went bankrupt tomorrow, but it would be a rough ride for a while.

In the immediate term, you really want the security of full-time paid work and to gain some big-industry experience. Your main ambition is to become employed, either with this agency, which is well respected, or with another.

You get on well with your boss. Things have been friendly, and you've been pleased that your boss at least understands your problems, having been there himself / herself.

Your boss has recently been hinting that you may be able to get formally on board shortly. You'll finally be able to work full-time, for a proper salary, in the right department and within the field for which you've trained for five years. It's very clear that the agency has been doing well and dozens of people have been recruited within other disciplines over the last few months.

You're called to a meeting with your boss and you're anticipating either some good news, or at least signs of a good strong light at the end of the tunnel. You expect a small battle over the starting salary, but it's great news at last.

Your brief is as follows –

You're in charge of a small department at a marketing and advertising agency and have called your intern in to see you, for a meeting. They've been very hard-working and done everything that's been asked of them, despite them not being given the type of work or training they expected and are entitled to.

This is something that you've become uncomfortable with due to the extent of your agency's demands on them. Although you were an intern yourself for six months before landing a design job, and later this supervisory job, things were better then, although you didn't get any pay at all, other than travel expenses.

You'd been hoping to give your intern some good news and award them with a full-time post but it's been made clear, that due to the apparent volatility of paid client-work, that time is at least another six months away, if not longer.

Additionally, you've been asked to take on another intern as from next Monday, due to a sudden increase in the workload from a particular project.

The project has been taken on by your boss, at a financial loss to the agency, as part of a plan to win the client's entire account next year. That would guarantee work for everyone in the department, for some time to come.

You've expressed your deep concerns about the short-term abuse of your existing intern but your boss has made it very clear that, not only is that the way it is, but if you don't like it there are other people waiting to step into your job at this very moment.

Further, you're directed to persuade your existing intern that they must give up doing work in their own time. Your boss insists that it's causing exhaustion but you've pointed out that you don't believe it has affected their performance so far.

He / she then instructs you to run with that line regardless and additionally directs you to explain that the intern is effectively working in direct competition to the agency.

You know that this is ludicrous as your agency would never do work for the small scale 'corner-shop clients' that your intern looks after. In addition, you actually believe this work is beneficial because at least your intern is getting some real-world experience, something that your agency is not prepared to give them yet. Never the less, you don't want to lose your own job and prospects.

It's clear that your intern is deliberately being held back and kept as cheap labour. You believe that your boss selfishly wants them to stop their own work, purely to make sure that they're fully alert during the day, in an attempt to cover the risk your boss took on with this extra work. It's clear to you that your boss is just taking advantage of the whole situation, to boost their own reputation and career prospects.

You despise your boss, who you see as a power-hungry maniac, who does more harm to the agency's reputation than good and you suspect that they may not last much longer. However, in the meantime, you have to find a way through for you, your department and your intern. You particularly don't want to lose the latter, as you believe they have a lot to offer the agency. You genuinely believe that there's a way through for them, if only they can put up with it for long enough.

So, at this meeting you've been tasked with: i) breaking the bad news to your intern that full-time work is perhaps six months away; ii) persuading them to stop doing their own outside work and iii) telling them that there's a new intern starting with them on Monday and they need to show them the ropes.

How you play things out is up to you, you're in charge. Good luck.

End the meeting (and the exercise) when you've got some sort of agreement established; you've got no choice but to agree to disagree, or things have become way too heated and there's risk of a fight breaking out between you.

These things can get very intense so afterwards, when you've both calmed down and stepped back into reality, get your friend to help you run through how you did in managing that difficult situation.

- Did you achieve any of your objectives or did you arrive at a different place completely?
- Did you compromise your personal integrity or values?
- As you walk away from the meeting, have you got a workable plan?
- Whose interests does that plan serve?

If your walk-away plan serves everyone's interests (yours, your intern's, your boss's and the organisation's), very well done indeed. If not, would you do anything differently next time?

You can find other exercises if you trawl the web, but select carefully and go for free ones, if you can find them.

Some questions for you to ask at the end of an interview

Below is a small selection of basic questions that you could run with at the end of your interview. Pick and choose a few of the ones that still remain relevant when the interviewer throws it open to you.

- You work here, do you still enjoy it? What's been the most challenging part of working here?
- How would you describe the organisational culture and overall working environment?
- What is the biggest challenge that the organisation will face over the next couple of years or so?
- What do you see as the greatest challenges facing the new post holder and / or what will be my major priorities, if I'm selected?
- How would you see my career developing, if I'm selected for this role?
- What have previous post-holders gone on to do?
- What sort of turnover rate amongst graduate recruits do you normally expect within a twelve month period?
- What are the main reasons why other recruits have left?
- Is there anything from this meeting that would cause you to have reservations about selecting me for the role?

Draw up your own list in the light of your research and the role that is on offer. Try to ask questions which suggest that you've done your homework but don't do so too overtly, for fear of coming across as a slightly inept creep.

Some questions it's usually better not to ask.

At the very least, find a more diplomatic and less suicidal way of asking these questions at the end of an interview, if an issue really is that important to you.

- What does your company do? (It's a bit late for that.)
- Did I get the job? (Did your IQ drop suddenly? You're part way through a selection process and there are other candidates, dummy.)
- What salary and benefits will you offer me? (Normally, stay away from asking salary, package and benefits questions, for fear of weakening your final negotiating position and of appearing to be a grasping bastard.)
- How long will it be before I can take a holiday? (You're sending the wrong signals.)
- Can I work from home sometimes? (Ditto.)
- How many hours will I be expected to work each week? (Is that really of primary importance in the overall scheme of things?)
- What if I don't get on well with my boss? (Whose fault will that be?)
- When can I get promoted? (You may as well ask, "What's my fastest way out of this joint?")
- How often can I be late to work without getting sacked? (Sigh.)
- You don't have random drug testing, do you? (To save yourself a lot of time in life, consider getting the words 'Unemployed Drug User' tattooed on your forehead.)
- Will you monitor my internet usage? (No, because you won't be here.)
- Where do you hang out after work? (Down the local nick, giving evidence against stalkers.)
- Are sexual relations with co-workers allowed? (You're going down fast at this point, and not in a fun way.)
- Do you dispense condoms in the staff toilets? (That's it, you've sunk without trace.)

I've personally been asked most of the above questions at some stage and, with only one exception, they're all shouting, "What's in it for me?" Instead, think what you can give, not what you can get and then ask your questions accordingly.

Generally, ask a couple of relevant questions and then get out of the door. You've already made your mark by that stage, so quit whilst you're ahead.

Good luck and I hope the job works out okay for you. Let me know.

****

ABOUT THE AUTHOR

Jon Gregory helps people to develop their job-search, application and interview skills so that they can follow career paths that will support them for the long haul, in today's volatile working environment.

His working life started as a car valet at the age of sixteen, cleaning the transport wax off brand new Volkswagen cars. He returned to school for his A levels, went on to university, became an engineer and then began to develop his career in management.

He worked successively in project management, operations management and general management before successfully running a market-leading subsidiary for a FTSE 100 public company during his mid-thirties.

To get there, Jon negotiated his way through a lot of tough interviews. Conversely, he also interviewed many candidates for key roles at the places where he worked. He's experienced both sides of the job-search fence and gained invaluable expertise, as a consequence.

He later founded his own business development consultancy and has since worked internationally with dozens of businesses. Fields of work have included: coaching and mentoring; career development; team development; recruitment training and change management, as well as international business development.

Jon has worked on three successful turnarounds, all involving significant re-organisation and people development. His main focus for the last two years has been on helping people to develop their careers in these challenging times. He has a particular interest in helping young people to get the jobs they want and build the careers they choose to aim at.

The creator of numerous guides, reports and websites over the years, this is Jon's first published book. With it, he is aiming to deliver hard-won, in-depth experience to people in a fast and easy-to-absorb way.

The website relating to this book is www.win-that-job.com and Jon would be pleased to receive feedback and queries through the site or via email on jg@win-that-job.com He'll do his best to answer queries individually whenever possible, but will otherwise respond through generalised answers on the site's forum or via his blog.

Follow Jon on Twitter: @letsfirewalk

Assessment centre days.

Agencies

29273093R20124

Made in the USA
Charleston, SC
08 May 2014